From the
Jungle of Belfast

footnotes to history
1904-1972

Denis Ireland

Blackstaff Press Ltd, Belfast

Published by Blackstaff Press Limited, 13 Wellington Place, Belfast BT1 6GB with the assistance of the Arts Council of Northern Ireland.

Softback   SBN 85640 020 3
Hardback SBN 85640 021 1

Printed by Brough, Cox & Dunn Ltd, Belfast.

Contents

	Page
Introduction: A Ghost in the English Mind	7
Scenery Since Bloomsday	9

PART I: A Belfast Proustian Mantelshelf

Flintlock Muskets in the Thatch	13
Academy for Young Gentlemen	14
The Night Willie Yeats Brought the Fairies to Belfast	17
A Sea Jumping with Mackerel	19
Victorian Ice Ballet	21
Gimme That Old-Time (1910) Religion	23
The Victorian Old Ladies Said No	26
A Thunder of Riveting	28
Onward to the Trocadero	30
A Gilt Clock on the Belfast Mantelshelf	35
Curtain-Raisers for Paisley	37

PART II: War

In the Mountains of Inishowen	43
An Encounter with Classical Ghosts	46

PART III: Scenes from War and Peace

A Loud Explosion in Throgmorton Street	59
Two Irish Interiors	61
Fragments After Reading Ulysses	63
Notes Taken on the Eve of War	67
Sketches from War-Time Belfast	69
Yeats's Ghost	73
Oscar Left Again for Paris	77
The Small Fair at Cloghan	79
A Matter of Exports	80

PART IV: A Glare of Burning Tankers

Inishtrahull	85
October Afternoon at Glasnevin	89

PART V: Looking at those United States

Green Dawn from Nova Zembla	95
A Swift Look at Boston	96
Three Slain in Love Nest	99

Chicago Night's Entertainment 101
Through the Hollywood Looking-Glass 104
Reflections in the Californian Night 106
Looking Down at North America 108
A Slight Encounter with Henry Longfellow 110
Shostakovitch Symphony 112
Saturday Evening Post 114
Robert Frost Country 115
Under the Shade-Trees of Saratoga Springs 117
American Myths 119
Fairy Tales of New York 120

PART VI: Europe Revisited
Conversations with Jan Masaryk 127
Twilight of the German Gods 129

PART VII: Island of 18th-Century Ghosts
Last Journey on the Sligo, Leitrim and Northern Counties . . 135
View Day at Mount Panther 138
A Moon Like Green Cheese 140
Requiem for Louis MacNeice 142
Skeletons from an 18th Century Cupboard 144
Goodbye Royal Terrace 152

PART VIII: While the bombs blew up Belfast
Aunt Florrie as Film Star 157
An Irish Fusilier Remembers 158
Postscript for Aristotle of Stagyra 164
My Father Encountered King Edward 165
Hengist-and-Horsa's Other Island 167
Thirteen Dead in Derry 169
Hooded Man Found Shot 170
A Bomb at the Belfast Boat Club 171
Journey into the Protestant Mind 173
Notes Set Down to a Sound of Shots 175

TO MY WIFE
for her part in it
especially for spotting
the fox at Louis MacNeice's grave

'Heureux qui comme Ulysse
a fait un beau voyage'

By the same author:

Autobiography

From the Irish Shore
Statues Round the City Hall

Biography

Patriot Adventurer, a short
life of Wolfe Tone

Political Philosophy

Eamon de Valera Doesn't
See It Through
The Age of Unreason
Six Counties in Search of a Nation etc.

Preface

Several sketches from my *Statues Round the City Hall* (now out of print) are included, slightly modified and under different titles, in the present work. The account of war in Macedonia, 'An Encounter with Classical Ghosts', includes and amplifies passages in my first autobiography, *From the Irish Shore*. Portions of the present work first appeared in the *Irish Times*, *Blackwood's Magazine*, the Belfast *News Letter*, the *Irish Press*, *Hibernia*, and *Threshold*.

I have to thank Diana McLoghlen and Messrs. Chatto & Windus for permission to quote from 'The Last Headlands'; Faber & Faber for the stanzas in 'Requiem for Louis MacNeice'; Jonathan Cape and the executors of Robert Frost's estate for passages from *A Witness Tree* in 'Robert Frost Country'; and Messrs. Macmillan & Company for permission to quote from 'The Host of the Air' by W. B. Yeats.

D.I.

Introduction

A Ghost in the English Mind

When I open the window of my top-floor study here in south Belfast I often hear rifle-fire from the Falls. I also look down on the roof of the house next door where Anthony Powell was billeted in World War Two, a minor Horace exiled to the equivalent of Dalmatia or the Black Sea coast. The goat-mascot of his regiment was also billeted next door—in the shed at the bottom of the garden.

As far as Anthony Powell was concerned, what came of the exile was one of the series of novels called *The Music of Time:* one in which the music was jangled. This one was called *The Valley of the Bones.* It cast very little light on the province to which the novelist had been exiled; none at all on the red-brick Victorian terrace where the exile was endured.

Yet if more than a quarter of a century ago Anthony Powell was sitting there next door making notes for *The Music of Time,* what did he see when he looked out of the window? Possibly, if it was winter and the leaves were off the trees, he saw the outline of the Black Mountain, dark blue or sullen green according to the atmospheric mood of the moment. A dark blue or sullen green Irish mountain, but almost certainly not an Irish mountain as I—as an inhabitant of the island of Ireland—see it. When I think of an Irish mountain, I revert to Slieve Gullion. In my private Irish world Slieve Gullion has always been an historical symbol. Years ago, when I was an Irish senator travelling at intervals from Belfast to Dublin and back again, I watched Slieve Gullion in all its moods from the windows of the train—in those days a big handsome train headed by a handsome blue locomotive. I remembered the wooded flank of Slieve Gullion long after we had roared down from the high plateau of the Meigh (once Irish-speaking) to the wide cattle-rearing central plain of Ireland and the first blue-green vistas of the Irish Sea. I think that, sub-consciously, I carried a mental picture of that wooded flank of Slieve Gullion all the way into the gracious 18th-century interior of Seanad Eireann, past the voluminous bronze statue of Victoria that still, in those days, guarded the entrance to the Irish Parliament.

Once, not so long ago, shots had been fired in anger in those woods— shots still echoing in 1972 under the blue or sullen green of the Black Mountain, Belfast. The shots did not begin in Belfast; they reached Belfast from the background of Irish history, all the way back to the battle of Kinsale. Long before my days in Seanad Eireann, light had been thrown on that subject in a conversation in a Dublin café when a friend—a one-time Gaelic speaker from Connemara—told me what his grandmother said to him about Irish politics, presumably in Irish. 'In Ireland,' said my friend's grandmother, 'the *extreme* party is always right.'

A bitter verdict, but ranging back across the bogs and swamps, through the forests and dark wooded places of Irish history, it has the hard ring of truth. In the light of it we Ulster Protestants should be steering towards an Irish future in which the extreme party will *not* be automatically right; a future in which not only the proper, but the natural, place for militant young Irishmen will be in the official defence forces of Ireland. The forces working to prevent that happening are not all lined up in 'Ulster'; sometimes they lurk behind the scenery of the Irish Republic—both lots seeking to perpetuate the ghost in the English mind, the fear, endemic in England since the days of the Spanish Armada and beyond, that the alien island next door would be a source of danger in time of emergency, a gap in the defences of the North Atlantic.

Now we have reached the point where the island is seen, not so much as alien as foreign, and the more its foreignness is acknowledged, the more it exhibits the normality of an island anxious not only to defend itself, but to establish normal defensive arrangements with its neighbour. That is why a quarter of a century ago I felt a certain sympathy for Anthony Powell, that minor Horace exiled to a red-brick Victorian terrace in south Belfast, looking out at the Belfast mountains in place of the mountains of Dalmatia and those Balkan regions so wildly foreign to the mind of Rome. He was a writer who had now become a centurion; whereas I was an Anglo-Irish soldier who had become an Irish writer. Now I carry that sympathy forward to Anthony Powell's successors, intelligent young Englishmen looking out from barrack windows in Lisburn and heavily-defended mansions in the suburbs of Belfast at the foreignness of the Black Mountain. They are condemned by their imperial heritage to a terrible task, the task of ensuring a breathing space between 800 years of Anglo-Irish history and whatever is to follow.

If what is to follow is more Anglo-Irish compromise, more propping-up of Partition, more rifle-fire on the Falls, more skeletons in the Irish cupboard, more haunting of the English mind by fears for the half-locked entrances to their ocean flank, then the half-locking must continue indefinitely, thereby condemning the British army to simultaneous occupation of the Irish north-east corner, garrisoning of a three-hundred-mile Irish border, and—two seas and several frontiers away—a role in garrisoning western Europe. It seems a lot of military activity for a professedly un-military nation. And the final irony is that here in north-east Ireland those who insist that the Irish portion of this military activity must continue: that—not unconnected with it, the ocean-flank ghost must continue to haunt the English mind—are, in their own curious topsy-turvy vocabulary, known as 'loyalists'. It never seems to occur to them that, whether 'loyally' or not, they could lend a hand to banish the ghost for ever.

Scenery Since Bloomsday

Soon after James Joyce
Staged that confrontation
With Gertie MacDowell's drawers
On Sandymount strand
The morning train from Donaghadee
Carried me with unshining face
To the Presbyterian anarchy
Of Belfast's Academical Institution
Swotting Caesar's *Gallic War*
In the corner of a third-class compartment
While the green-blue North Channel
Sank out of sight in a cutting
And surrounded by cotton-wool steam
Unconscious of foundations collapsing
We plunged under Killaghy road bridge
Passengers on a slow train
To the rising of Romes
Undreamed of while cotton-wool steam
Billowed above Killaghy road bridge
Where farmcarts jolted
With reports like pistol shots
And the whole mechanical future
Lit by green desk-lamps
Foretold by computers
Rushed through at thirty miles an hour
In the form of a green
Belfast and County Down tank-engine
With brass headlamps
Snorting cotton-wool steam
Coupling-rods rising and falling
Like the knees of a hundred-yards sprinter
Striding out for the future
For new computer dictatorships
New popes, new graven images
New Unholy Roman Empires
Waiting behind the Time Curtain
While the green tank-engine with the brass headlamps
Snorted from the salt-smelling station at Donaghadee
To the smoke clouds of Edwardian Belfast
Where in front of the new Portland-stone City Hall
The voluminous statue of Victoria
Sat pendulous-cheeked

Amongst municipal geraniums
And stone-frockcoated Victorian Economic Men
Waiting for new technological Fenians
With gelignite and petrol-bomb conflagrations
To shatter the thousand-windowed warehouses Thackeray noted
Or thin the forests of factory chimneys
Up in red-brick jungles labelled Shankill and Falls
Where to a sound of blast-bombs and Thompson machine-guns
The last red of imperial sunset
Flared behind the Black Mountain.

Flintlock Muskets in the Thatch

I live in a Victorian backwater, a small terrace now surrounded by mountains of Belfast brick, once buried in green parkland. Shadowed by a towering lime-tree—a relic of the parkland—we've got as far as electricity, but electricity disguised, shut in crystal chandeliers and tablelamps that look vaguely Victorian, if not positively Regency. In the small square dining-room with its single low-set window that overlooks a patch of sooty lawn and in spring time the green explosion of the lime-tree, we've hung grand-uncle's portrait over the sideboard. He looks comfortably at home, surrounded by furniture not much altered since the charge of the Light Brigade; fits in perfectly with the ornate cornices, the elegantly-proportioned rooms, the gentle post-Regency curve of the staircase, the plaster archway in the hall that collects dust but maintains its mutely-eloquent protest against life in the twentieth century.

Grand-uncle goes back beyond the archway; his portrait, Hanoverian stock-tie, dangling eyeglass, frilly shirt, elegant gold-knobbed cane and all, was probably painted the year the plasterers were working on that archway in the hall in the middle of the 1860s—1866 to be exact; the year Tolstoy was finishing *War and Peace;* the year after the shot rang out in stage-box Number 7 in Ford's Theatre, Washington, and Lincoln slumped in his red-damask-upholstered rocking-chair never to recover consciousness; the year before the Most Reverend Dr. Moriarty, Lord Bishop of Kerry informed the congregation in Killarney cathedral that Eternity was not long enough, nor Hell hot enough to hold the Fenians and their infernal machines.

Not that any of this, actual or impending, seems to have disturbed grand-uncle; he just sits there over the sideboard, staring out of his shallow blue eyes as if he had never heard of Tolstoy or Lincoln, or indeed, unless he read a piece about him in the *Belfast News-Letter*, of the Most Reverend Dr. Moriarty, Lord Bishop of Kerry. Behind him the artist has painted a modest brown curtain. No trees, no stone urns, no porticos of Georgian mansions, no distant grooms holding horses, or rivers winding in sylvan glades—just a stuffy brown curtain, perhaps in despair at wondering how grand-uncle ever contrived to earn his living, ever emerged from the shadowy courts and back-entries of the Irish linen trade to enthrone himself in that elegant mahogany armchair, with his air of *dolce far niente*, his dangling eyeglass that speaks of nights at the Assembly Rooms, his frilly shirt, his finicking white hands so fatalistically folded on the gold knob of his slender, period-pointing cane.

But I can supply the missing background. Instead of that stuffy curtain there should be white strips of linen bleaching on the green banks of the Lagan; behind that again, Belfast's mountain-dominated factory chimneys (the smoke-canopied forest Thackeray noted in his *Irish Sketch Book*);

13

·with, in the spaces left by grand-uncle's champagne-bottle shoulders, miniature prospects of tumbledown cottages and hand-loom weavers working their treadles in their stockinged feet. Beyond the looming city and its black pall of coal smoke should be wars and massacres and a peasantry dispossessed and starving; the whole leading forward to those white hands and that gold knobbed cane.

But the backdrop is incomplete without the family burying ground. It lies beside the Irish Sea on the shore of the Ards peninsula just above tidemark—broken walls, shattered tombstones, ruined vaults, thick tussocks of sea-grass, clumps of ragwort, remnants of rusty iron railings. Three tall weather-beaten headstones, leaning towards one another like relatives at a fair, survey the wilderness of shattered stone and rusting iron—headstones hollowed out like ancient coins by storm and Irish rain. Moss-grown inscriptions summarise the life stories of the farmers below—summaries acknowledging, beyond the crumbling graveyard wall, the faint blue outline of the Mull of Galloway that sometimes, in the intervals of rain storms, displays its checkerboard of fields. 1720–1786, it says on one of the hollowed out headstones—two centuries in the good farming soil of the Ards; within sound—sometimes in winter within reach—of the Irish Sea; still, if only they could stand up to look and it wasn't for that crumbling graveyard wall, within sight of Galloway, their ancient home that, in shafts of sunlight between rain storms, identifies their bright green fields.

Sometimes by the light of would-be Regency tablelamps I imagine the skeleton farmers in the shadowy corners of our still Victorian dining-room—hear a clink of horses ploughing, the sound of unaccompanied psalms from their meeting-house beside the Irish Sea, a faint clatter of flintlock muskets being hidden in the thatch—all infuriating to grand-uncle with his air of establishment, his unpainted background of mountain-dominated Belfast factories straight out of Thackeray's *Irish Sketch Book*. The flintlock muskets might have been for the battle of Ballynahinch, and grand-uncle, enthroned in his mahogany armchair, with the curtain behind him conveniently shutting out, not only the smoke clouds of his brash new Linenopolis, but embarrassing vistas into the Irish eighteenth century, would never have approved either United Irishmen or muskets hidden in the thatch. Still less, whitewashed meeting-houses down on the rocks by the seashore where the sole disestablished music was the crashing of breakers against the churchyard wall and the tuning-fork-initiated sound of unaccompanied psalms.

Academy for Young Gentlemen

Not long before Bloomsday, the day Leopold Bloom ate that Zola-esque kidney for breakfast and Gerty MacDowell so brazenly exhibited her *Home Chat* drawers on Sandymount strand, I left kindergarten for pre-paratory school. The school was in a small, double-fronted villa covered with grey stucco and almost buried in a leafy suburb of Belfast, a south Belfast Saint-Germain through which, overshadowed by shade-trees, tiny box-like horse-trams crawled, looking at night like illuminated beetles. A brass plate on one of the villa's stucco-covered gateposts announced that the school was run by a Mr. B . . . . ., a stout little man with thick pebbly glasses, devoted—at least in theory—to the task of stuffing young Edwardian gentlemen into his educational sausage-machine at one end, and at the other extracting potential admirals, generals, ambassadors, Indian consular officials (first-class), top-drawer civil servants; or, if supplies were poor, or the machine not working properly, just plain esquires. Some of us never even made the esquire. But we did include one admiral, a sandy-haired cock sparrow given to fighting his shadow. Also a gentleman who achieved fame by leaving behind him an enormous collection of clocks and old china. He was what lawyers might have called an esquire *ab initio*—he had the prospect of a private income and a father with no illusions about the dignity of toil. Only last year I put him in a BBC feature programme, immortalised against the background of his loudly-ticking clocks.

The rest tailed off into raw material for failed medicals, journalists ('the accused's occupation was given as journalist'), plus a smattering of those mysterious persons known as 'agents' who never seem to do a hand's-turn except sit about in cafés drinking morning coffee and afternoon tea, at the same time earning enough money to support surburban villas—even wives and children. A pretty dreary collection except for the admiral and the expert on clocks; not worth a paragraph in the local newspapers. Not a fraudulent company director, not a bogus cinema proprietor in the whole stack, haycock, or stook. Which is curious, for just about the time we short-term prisoners were serving our sentences in Mr. B . . . . .'s stucco-covered penitentiary, James Joyce arrived in Belfast from Trieste in search of empty warehouses and abandoned mission halls—abandoned mission halls with broken windows being just the ticket for the deputation from Trieste. The idea, first replacing the broken glass, was to adapt the dank areas where souls had been saved for the purposes of kinematographic entertainment, the 3d per skull admission fee covering not only flickering screens but tinkly out-of tune pianos anticipating the mighty Wurlitzer. Joyce's fellow missionary from Trieste was always referred to by Joyce's father, that hoary old *farceur* from Cork, as 'the hairy mechanic in the lion-tamer's coat'—which neatly places him, along with tinkly pianos and rainy-flickering screens, right in amongst (American) tomb-rat footnotes of the Joyce industry to-day. But we on-Sundays-bum-freezered young gentlemen from the *faubourg* Malone remained sublimely unconscious of such back-street manoeuvres, blandly unaware of the existence of James, or even Stanilaus, Joyce. And even if we had been aware of them, they wouldn't have been in same race as Hackenschmidt, or Sir Thomas Lipton with his yacht *Shamrock* that never had the luck of the Irish but played a far bigger part in our stucco-covered academy than the author of *Ulysses*. He might—in the intervals of cinema-searching and teaching languages in the Trieste Berlitz—be already banging away at a block-buster of a masterpiece, but we Edwardian young gentlemen from the *faubourg* Malone were unaware of him.

What we *were* aware of was the hole in Mr. X's trousers, I call him Mr. X because, by some miracle, he might still be alive and rivalling Methuselah. Whether Mr. X was aware of the hole we never knew. But there it was, in a vital position, a high light of Mr. B . . . . .'s otherwise monotonous academy, revealing in winter glimpses of pink combinations, in summer archipelagos of hairy skin. Mr. X had, apparently, only one pair of trousers and no wife: to have had more than one pair of trousers and a wife as well would have been tempting providence for what was then known as an usher. Anyhow the hole in his trousers remained, a permanent source of entertainment, a sort of Edward VII music-hall turn.

I also remember the singing lessons. About twice a week we lined up in a long row and literally burst into song, or at any rate into a noise that was liberally interpreted as song, and was, no doubt, charged for as such on our school accounts. A young woman (sister in misfortune to Mr. X except in so far as there were no glimpses of her underclothing) thumped an asthmatic, banjo-imitating upright piano with brass candlesticks that jangled when certain notes were struck, while we theoretical pro-consuls and empire builders roared and squeaked (principally squeaked) a succession of patriotic British ballads. The ballads were nearly always nautical because our revered headmaster Mr. B . . . ., that tubby little man with chronic asthma, fancied himself as a sailor, thick pebbly glasses and all. I remember one about Tom Bowling whose form was of the manliest beauty, who finally went aloft and never came down again. But my favourite (and I suspect, Mr. B . . . . .'s as well) was the one about the jolly sailor boys:

'And we jolly sailor boys were all up aloft,
And the landlubbers lying down below, below, below,
And the landlubbers lying down below.'

We all liked that one, and when it came to the 'below' bits we nearly blew Miss Montgomery off her piano stool. In the language of the classics it would be *dulce et decorum* to record that in the matter of nautical ballads my friend the ginger Admiral shot off with the gun and left the rest of us wallowing in his wake. It would, but unfortunately it takes a lot of intelligent omission to adapt reality for the purposes of art, and the sad truth is that the admiral had a voice like an infuriated bull-frog and didn't know *Alice Where Art Thou* from *God Save the King*— facts I now set down with all the greater assurance because he happens to be dead—having first had his bellyful of nautical ballads translated into terms of enormous battleships and 16-inch guns in the act of sinking the *Bismarck*.

But then nearly all of us jolly sailor boys are either up aloft like Tom Bowling or else fallen overboard—and nothing surprising about that, seeing that we reach right back round the corner to Victoria and jingling hansom cabs. So far back round the corner I sometimes wonder if any of us are still living; so much so that nowadays when I see one of us heaving (and heaving is the word) over the horizon, I immediately clap on all sail in the opposite direction. I do this on the assumption—the very reasonable assumption—that whether he still has all four trotters in the trough or not, he's probably adrift on a sea of ghastly reminiscence and a deadly old bore, eating away at the background of Belfast's provincial scenery like woodworm in a Victorian whatnot.

The Night Willie Yeats Brought the Fairies to Belfast

Back in 1893 Willie Yeats brought a train load of fairies to Belfast. Wide of hat and loose of tie, he arrived at Great Victoria Street and, resisting the call of the lake isle of Innisfree (otherwise known as Rat Island), remained just long enough to give us industrial dwarfs and gnomes of the wee black North a hint of things that did be happening beyond the end of our horse-tram lines, our black regiments of factory chimneys, our smug wee red-brick villas in the red-brick suburbs.

On the platform at Great Victoria Street, backed by clouds of steam from the engine, invisible reinforcements from county Sligo and points west of the Shannon formed up like a pantomime chorus behind the Poet, and— with medieval arguments as to how many angels infinitely compressible could dance upon the point of a needle infinitely sharp translated into the modern Irish of how many presumably Irish-speaking fairies could be crammed into the well of a Belfast jaunting-car—and probably with a few booms from Willie Yeats as well—the procession then set off, in the manner of Duffy's circus doing a preliminary stint down Main Street, over the square-setts and horse-tram lines of Great Victoria Street to the Old Museum building in College Square North, where later that evening the Poet with a capital letter was to address the members of the Belfast Natural History and Philosophical Society on the subject of Fairies, also with a capital letter.

What the Fairies did during the lecture is not recorded. But presumably the gas-lit corridors of the Old Museum Building were fairly pullulating with them—little men in green jerkins and regulation red hats who touched their forelocks and said, 'Yes, yer Honour, he's talkin' about us!' The sad fact remains that it was their last excursion to Belfast—always assuming they had been here before and nobody bombarded them with petrol bombs—for nobody has seen a trace from that day to this, or even heard their little bells tinkling—at least not till they reappeared in glorious Technicolor on the screen of the now vanished Gaumont (then Classic) Cinema in Castle Lane, compèred this time by Walt Disney instead of Willie Yeats. But that was nearly forty years later, with special prices for back stalls and balcony—not to mention coloured cut-outs of leprechauns propped up in what Belfast insisted on calling the 'foy-yer', and not a petrol bomb or a broken window in sight.

Nevertheless, supporters of Willie Yeats versus Technicolor Fairies remained—sad-looking individuals in tweed knickerbockers and lonely Malone Road spinsters in flower-trimmed toques whose sole occupation

17

was pressing flowers or painting bad watercolours till Papa came home from the office. Some were still in circulation when I was old enough to be taken by my mother to exhibitions of paintings in the very room in the Old Museum Building where Willie Yeats once boomed by gaslight. It was a large room on the top floor with a balcony lit by rounded skylights and the paintings crowding its walls—all the unaided work of members or associates of the Ulster Academy—were mostly good hard slaps in the face for Belfast's factory chimneys—whitewashed cottages *ad lib*, in fact till the cows came home; washy green landscapes full of washy green light, as if somebody had pulled down a succession of Hibernian green blinds; bogs with turf stacks in foreground, very popular, and, from the Ulster Academy point of view, the more gloomily Gaelic the better; what are known in Ulster as 'loanens'; and towering blue mountains surmounted by towering white cumulus clouds, a long way after (or was it before?) Paul Henry.

As for the shaggy little men in tweed knickerbockers, who went with the washy green landscapes like wasps with jam, they were—as my mother, straightening her toque and twisting her veil, firmly pointed out—the drones of Belfast, permitted, but only just permitted, to exist as long as they did not carry on their bacchanalian orgies in public, or actually assault the police. From which I gathered that there was not only a connection between Fairies and little men in knickerbockers—there was also lurking in the background a flavour of strong drink.

Whether Willie Yeats fitted into this class of persons, or the bacchanalian orgies, I did not like to ask. As a schoolboy at the Belfast Academical Institution I was, I regret to say, extremely vague about Mr. Yeats—poetry being represented in my mind by *The Burial of Sir John Moore*, together with certain rude, not to say lewd, parodies thereon. Mr. Yeats was associated in my mind and family circle with Dublin and all its works; more accurately, with its lack of them. Dublin was all very well in its way, but except for Guinness's brewery it was deficient in industry. Not only was it full of priests and public-houses, it was also the spiritual home of the shaggy little men in knickerbockers and their intense-looking female companions in tweed cloaks who haunted the top floor of Belfast's Old Museum Building at exhibition time—and it was a pity they didn't all take the first train. Beyond the facts that it was on the Liffey, that it was deficient in industry, that it was addicted to drink, and that it contained Guinness's brewery, there was little to be said about Dublin. As for Willie Yeats and his Fairies, factory chimneys and Fairies were assumed to cancel one another out; if you had one, you couldn't have the other, and we had the factory chimneys.

Such was the state of mind in which I took myself back on a spark-spitting electric tram from the Academical Institution to do my homework. The homework consisted not so much of Caesar's *Gallic War*, nor indeed of the over-rated works of Euclid, as of the more exciting pages of the *Illustrated London News*—pictures of balloon ascents, ironclads, horseless carriages, women cyclists in bloomers, underground railways, dining saloons of Atlantic liners lit by the new electric light, the details

18

(with diagrams) of that new gift of science to man, the Whitehead torpedo —illustrations in a weekly photographic *Inferno* of the rich new world about to shower its blessings on us in the twentieth century. When the cornucopia was finally up-ended and the blessings really started to descend, then (or so we assumed when messing about with test-tubes) we would be right under the shower.

So let west-of-Shannon poets retreat behind their heron-haunted lakes, taking their Fairies with them. And in fact Willie Yeats's bunch began to fade out, scared off by H. G. Wells and women cyclists in bloomers, and never since the night they hung about the corridors of the Old Museum building has anybody in Belfast heard a tinkle. Apparently they took off on the jaunting-car and never came back, except on the screen of the old Gaumont cinema in Castle Lane that is now just an enormous slab of super-market blazing with flourescent lighting. Nowadays, what with pile-drivers, automatic riveters, iron balls knocking things down, not to mention gelignite bombs substituting for iron balls, you wouldn't hear a Technicolor, much less a Willie Yeats, Fairy and it ringing its handbell in your ear; or indeed, when it comes to that Disney crowd from 42nd Street, sounding a klaxon. Fairies, where are ye? As a dimuendo female relative of the Poet remarked to a friend of mine in a third-class compartment of a Belfast suburban train, *'There was always a want about poor Willie!'*

A Sea Jumping with Mackerel

At the quayside Father Donnelly would settle himself in the stern-sheets, one arm laid carelessly along the tiller, his ancient black velour tilted over his eyes, his short thick legs and comfortable paunch threatening to burst his shiny black trousers.

'Haul in that sheet now!' he would say as we slid round the breakwater. Then when the sheet had been hauled in and we were rippling along close to the rocks, he would settle himself for conversation.

'Do ye see that mountain now?'

We all looked obediently at the mountain.

'Yes, Father.'

'Do ye see those trees on it?'

'Yes, Father.'

'Well now, how many trees would ye say are on that mountain?'

'Indeed and we couldn't say, Father. How many would you say yourself?'

'Five thousand.' Father Donnelly's innocent blue eyes would shine with delight at the prodigy. 'Five thousand trees—sorra a tree less.'

To which our invariable reply was:

'Do you tell us that now, Father? They must have been a long time planting them?'

'Indeed an' they were not.' Father Donnelly always defended the tree-planters with heat. 'How many trees do ye think they planted in a workin' day?' And he would regard us triumphantly, like a man about to produce the ace of spades from his hat.

'Indeed and we couldn't say, Father.'

'Four hundred.'

'Four hundred *trees*, Father?'

'Four hundred—sorra a tree less.'

Then when we had been sufficiently crushed with reverence for the art of tree planting, Father Donnelly would tilt his ancient velour still farther over his eyes, order us to haul in, or let out, the sheet an inch or two (just to show us there was an art in sailing as well) and steer for the fishing ground like the competent mariner he was.

Later, off the Fisherman's Leap, with the lines slipping through our fingers as we cruised a hundred yards from the rocks, he would return to the subject of the cave.

'Do ye see that cave now?'

We all looked obediently in the direction of the cliffs.

'Yes, Father'

'Well now, would ye believe it, when they were makin' the aqueduct to the waterworks in the Happy Valley beyond, they found an undergroun' tunnel that led right under the mountain to that cave.'

'Do you tell us that now, Father?' We would gingerly feel the lines, and if nothing happened to be biting, we would continue, in spite of the fact that we had long ago explored the cave for ourselves and found the tunnel to be a myth:

'Do you tell us that, Father? And what would the tunnel be for?'

At this Father Donnelly always looked mysterious and disapproving, as if asked to explain the Seventh Commandment.

'Smugglers. They would carry their kegs o' brandy through there.'

'Where to, Father?'

'Why to wherever the tunnel went, of course.'

'And where was that, Father?'

'Why to the waterworks, as I told ye.'

'But sure the waterworks weren't there then, Father . . .'

But at this, almost as if the Heavenly Father Himself had intervened, one of us would hook a dogfish and in the excitement that followed Father Donnelly would get out of answering the unbelievers.

'Jump on it, Paddy, jump on it!' he would shout, very red in the face as the dogfish threshed and snapped on the floor-boards. Then when the hired man had expertly extracted the hook, had crushed the dogfish's head under his iron-shod heel, and seized it writhing by the tail, had beaten its life out against the side of the boat, and flung it back in the water, Father Donnelly would sink back again in the stern-sheets, the light of retribution in his eye.

'Ye murderin' divil ye!' he would shout, and lean over to shake his fist at the white belly as it disappeared in translucent depths below, 'Ye murderin' divil ye!'—almost as if what we had just witnessed had been the overthrow of the Evil One himself.

Towards evening, on the grey stone quayside, dwarfed by the towering blackness of the Mournes, Father Donnelly would hand us each a string of mackerel and say, as if reciting the doxology:
'There's a fine string o' mackerel for ye. There's nothin' like a fresh mackerel for yer tea!'
Then, looking distinctly horsey in his long black coat and short tight black trousers he would climb into his battered Ford, fish in his pockets for a shilling for Paddy, and wave us all a cheerful farewell.
But if, later in the evening, we encountered him clad in biretta and cassock by the gilded railings of the chapel, it was a different Father Donnelly. At such moments, half deafened by the chapel bell, he took no notice of us, even looked through us with an abstracted blue eye from which all geniality had fled.
'Good evening, Father!' we would say.
And with a vague inclination of the head, indicating that to the sound of the Angelus he had no desire to be reminded of thickly-threshing mackerel, nor indeed of the little Protestants who caught them, Father Donnelly would pass in through the gilded iron gateway towards the gleaming crucifix—like a man who had never cut up bait or shaken his fist at a dog-fish in his life. The sea might be jumping with mackerel, but there were far bigger fish inside, beyond the gilded railings.

Victorian Ice Ballet

The frozen lake, surrounded by wooded parkland, looked like a setting for *Les Patineurs*. Buried in dark woods it lay in the heart of a demesne near Belfast, and the characters appearing on it, the *dramatis personae* of its puppet-show, consisted for the most part of the local nobility and gentry. In strict chronology Queen Victoria was already dead but in fact the scene, with its distant views of the Belfast mountains, its haughty black figures weaving patterns on the ice, was still lit by the afterglow of Victorian sunset.

In those days linen merchants and their progeny scraped in along with the lower ranks of the gentry; hence our family party all happed up in woollen mufflers and gloves. There were, however, subtle distinctions in the manner of arrival. The aristocracy, wrapped in luxurious fur-lined rugs, arrived in shooting-brakes, victorias, ancient landaus, elegant broughams; in one instance, a jingling hansom cab. The rest of us rolled up wrapped in ordinary woollen rugs on hired jaunting-cars. At the gate-lodge I remember a ceremony of initiation, like being challenged by a sentry; a flashing of visiting cards, of invitations written on sumptuous notepaper, to be present on the ice. In those days there was no nonsense about the Common Man. The Common Man's place was back there at his work in the shadow of Belfast's belching factory chimneys, while the nobility, gentry, linen lords, linen merchants, *et hoc genus omne*, together with their sisters, and their cousins, and their aunts, disported themselves on or beside the frozen lake. In fact the gate-lodge keeper, looking extremely superior, like a man holding aloft an invisible flaming sword, shut the gates in the face of the Common Man and made no bones about it. No visiting card, no admission—and back where you belong!

Down by the lake, encircled by swelling green parkland and the purple of the winter woods, the shooting brakes and victorias, even the humble jaunting-cars, were parked as near the ice as they could get. Footmen in top boots, white breeches, long coats with brass buttons, and top hats adorned with cockades carried rugs and hampers. In the background bunched the jarveys, inclined, like most Belfast jarveys, to be sardonic, but slightly subdued by the 'quality', not to mention the footmen.

Hampers were opened, bottles produced, bonfires lit: all that was missing was a brass band playing the Skaters' Waltz, or a Hungarian string orchestra in blue hussar uniforms. Nevertheless, the inevitable couple who disrupt such occasions by skating better than everybody else were already whirling on the ice. *He* wore riding breeches and had skates that turned the rest of us green with envy by curving back over his toecaps; *she* caused a lot of adverse comment and staring through lorgnettes by showing at least two inches of leg below the hem of her long, gracefully-billowing skirt. The general verdict among the lorgnette users in the victorias and landaus was that she was a foreigner—which, of course, explained everything, including the two inches of leg and the fact that she could do the outside-edge backwards.

The rest of us just clattered and stumbled round the ice, getting in the real skaters' way. The instruments (hardly to be classed as skates) on which I clattered were made of wood, with long straight blades inserted underneath. To put them on involved contortions with a gimlet (with which you bored holes in the heels of your boots) and struggles, reminiscent of the infant Hercules strangling the snakes, with complicated ligatures of straps. The snag was that you nearly always forgot the gimlet.

The woods were turning deeper purple in the frosty dusk, the red of bonfires already reflected in the ice, when we turned for home on the hired jaunting-car. There was talk of skating by torchlight, of midnight suppers on the island in the frozen lake. Uproar, no doubt due to bottles in hampers, was already rising from the lake and its surroundings; the whole affair was taking on the abandonment of a crowd scene in a Russian opera; and the young woman showing two inches of leg, now whirling with other partners beside the one in the riding breeches, was enjoying what would have been described in a Paris theatre as a *succes fou*. No place for us, my mother decided; with the addendum for the weaker vessels like myself that, unlike the nobility and gentry, not to mention the raffish elements now appearing unbidden over the demesne wall, we had work, stern Presbyterian work, to do the morning after.

So home, *clip-clop*, down dark tree-shadowed country roads, through the purple of the frosty twilight, to the twinkling gas-lamps of south Belfast and a monumental high tea in a red-brick terrace house—a high tea at which, with bulging silver muffin dishes and silver kettles steaming over flames of methylated spirit as on some kind of Presbyterian altar, the un-Presbyterian motto might have been *Et in Arcadia nos*.

Gimme That Old-Time (1910) Religion

Tiers of gilt organ-pipes tower over the marble-pillared pulpit, like cigars in a Cyclopean pantomime. Stained-glass window (right) shows Prodigal Son returning through a stained glass sunset in rosy apple-pie order with incredibly clean feet.

Above gilt cigars and Prodigal Son, the Edwardian universe stops suddenly with the ornate (distinctly un-Presbyterian) mouldings and cornices of the elaborate ceiling (*circa* 1870). The ceiling drips with lac-quered-brass chandeliers, converted to electricity 1910. Above chandeliers and elaborate ceiling, conjecture and the New Testament. Below, simmer-ing in mahogany box-pews, Belfast shipbuilders, linen merchants (in-cluding my father, thick white hair, gold-rimmed spectacles), mineral water manufacturers, twenty shillings in the pound, against (unknown to my father) back-drop of *Pink 'Un* and enormous chorus girls unfreezing Belfast's Presbyterian Januaries at the Opera House with jackbooted female legs in *Dick Whittington, Mother Goose, Robinson Crusoe* and other moralities (admission stage-door, visiting card and/or gold sovereign) shiny postcards Marie Studholm (all teeth and Edwardian bust), Ellaline Terris (all teeth), *San Toy, The Merry Widow, Our Miss Gibbs* (lodgings, Joy Street, hot stuff), the Lily of Laguna (whoever she might be), 'Lily' Langtry (no doubt at all), the Chocolate-Coloured Coon (see Ulysses) Pear's Soap (he won't be happy till he gets it), Beecham's Pill (worth a guinea a box), the *Illustrated London News*, shiny tableaux of the British Royal Family; Edward VII (like Kings of Israel translated to striped pants), amorous proclivities, bangle-rattling concubines, and all.

That was religion under the Venetian spire of our opulent Presbyterian church, where the illuminati of the Malone road (including my Aunt Lizzie) went round and round, circulating like pantomime choruses in final Entente Cordiale transformation scenes that might have appeared on the programme as *Edouard Sept et les Girls*.

Under that Venetian spire opposite the Botanic Gardens, nobody, including my Aunt Lizzie, could be described as stealing away to Jesus—there were too many legal matters, too many scenes in solicitors' offices, to be got through first. But down in our holiday church in the Ards peninsula where seals listened to the psalms, in our whitewashed meeting-house where the surf beat like a metronome against the churchyard wall, Edwardian plush-and-gilt disappeared in the tide from the Irish Sea and the Solway Firth.

23

Down there, on sea-washed rocks, looking from clear-paned meeting-house windows—when they were not salted by spray—you could see right across the North Channel to the long blue hump, or, in clear weather, the bright green fields, of the Mull of Galloway—including, in exceptionally clear weather, a minute whitewashed tower that was said to be Portpatrick lighthouse.

Sometimes, just below the line of surf, there emerged the square, doggy heads of seals. Beyond them, hugging the coast, stubby little black colliers, spreading luxuriant foliage to the sky and the channel, trailing vast tropical plants of coal smoke from their thin black funnels, sometimes dodging inside the green of the Copeland Islands, thumping their way backwards and forwards across the Irish Sea to maintain the furnaces of Belfast's factories:

'O God, our help in ages past
Our hope for years to come,
Our shelter from the stormy blast,
And our eternal home. . . .'

we sang. Or it might be the 23rd Psalm:

'The Lord's my shepherd, I'll not want,
He makes me down to lie
In pastures green; He leadeth me
The quiet waters by. . . .'

with tuning-forks ready for fear we lost the pitch, while the surf beat like a metronome against the rocks below the churchyard wall. Sometimes, after a long interval, when the *thump, thump* of their engines had already died away, the wash from the thin-funnelled colliers came swishing in amongst the rocks, interrupting the revolving crank-shafts of the psalms.

Down there, with the view through salt-caked windows to the Mull of Galloway, there were no social complications. English discomfort about stratification began with what a Ballymena forerunner of Ian Paisley resoundingly referred to as that bastard offspring of the Church of Rome—in this Ards peninsula instance, the Church of Ireland church that stood just inland, on a hill at the top of a long, tree-shadowed avenue. This, with its smell of mouldering hassocks (hassocks on which we pointedly re-frained from kneeling) was the haunt of individuals from the social-and-personal columns of the *News Letter*—supernumeraries from glossy photographs in the *Tatler* and the *Sketch* showing heaps of dead game surrounded by their only slightly livelier-looking slaughterers: beings so remote from my Belfast world of belching factory chimneys and fraudulent councillors that I scarcely believed they existed. They corresponded in my mind with an Hussar officer encountered at the Dublin Exhibition—one of three Hussar officers in full-dress uniform who, preceded and followed by a wailing of violins, emerged 'all clinkant in gold' from the revolving glass doors of a restaurant, staggered across a strictly-forbidden lawn; attempted, as neatly as their gorgeous accoutrement of sabres, spurs, busbies, *panaches* etc, and what had evidently been a superlative lunch, would permit, to dodge under a row of iron railings. One, forgetting the lofty red plume that surmounted it, promptly lost his busby and uttered in a loud voice a four-letter Saxon word I had heard from farm labourers and ostlers but never from a glittering full-dress Hussar, member of a regiment that would presently produce a Prime Minister of Northern Ireland. This busby-recovering playmate of Lord Brookeborough remained for me a sort of Madame Tussaud figure, an epitome of Anglo-Saxon impudence and insensitivity. I kept mixing him with another Anglo-Saxon specimen, no dashing, if foul-mouthed, Hussar, but a member of the *genus* county family who read the lessons in the church at the top of the tree-shadowed avenue—the Church of Ireland church that, feeling rather daring, in a spirit of you might as well be hanged for a sheep as a lamb, we sometimes attended during summer holidays having, as it were, crossed over Jordan to get there. The sight of the brass lectern in the form of an eagle with outstretched wings, the (to our ears) popish sound of the responses, gave us a feelng of dangerous liberation, like a trip to Paris. On one of these doctrinal excursions, one of these reconnoitring expeditions on the road to Rome, my opposite number to the Hussar appeared, entirely without *panache*—reminding me of a mangy lion I had once seen in Duffy's circus in a field outside the village of Carrowdore—a specimen who proceeded to read the lessons, very badly.

This, my mother informed me in a Presbyterian whisper, was the local lord of the manor. What she really meant was the nearest thing to a local lord of the manor still, unlike the snakes, surviving on this (Donaghadee) side of the North Channel. In fact the poor man was no lord of any kind; he had merely married money; had, in addition, a brother, or some near relative, who had managed to be the British general most completely discredited by the Boer war—(an accomplishment that deserved a graduated insult of the British Empire). Anyhow, there was the general's brother, or maybe it was his cousin, standing up in a faint glow of reflected luminosity at the brass lectern that had taken on the popish form of an eagle, and even if he did read the lessons as if he had a whole bagful of plums in his mouth—even if his false teeth were making a sad mess of his consonants and his pronunciation of Biblical names—he *did* live in the neighbouring 'big house', and glass eye, padded shoulder and all, was the nearest thing to a real live lord our stretch of county Down coast could produce. But he didn't cut much ice with the Old Testament. When he came to names like Habakkuk and Zechariah, he jibbed at them and, with his false teeth as handicap, almost invariably knocked down the top bar; whereas when names like Habakkuk and Zechariah cropped up down in the meeting-house you felt the minister was on back-slapping terms with them; that, along with the Boals, the M'Gimpseys, and Miss Campbell who ran the combined grocery and post office, they lived in the next townland.

Still worse, he made his entry on the hassock-mouldering scene via a wooded drive that led directly to a postern-gate in the churchyard, so to a private entrance; finally appearing in the body of the church like a pantomime character through a trapdoor. Along with the popish eagle, this

25

struck me as unconstitutional, a reflection from the theatrical show of English society unnaturally illuminating our green, rock-studded coast, where for me, if God could be seen moving in His mysterious way, it was in that procession of thin-funnelled colliers trailing vast tropical plants of black coal smoke beyond the green of the Copeland islands, on their way to stoke the furnaces of industrial Belfast where grand-uncle in frilly Victorian shirtfront and Hanoverian stock-tie waited for 20th-century judgement in the shape of the sniper's bullet by day, the petrol-bomb pillar of fire by night. By that time all gilt ornaments, including my Aunt Lizzie, had been removed from Belfast's equivalent to a Proustian mantel-shelf, and to a glare of burning factories we were either retreating from, or advancing towards Beal-feirste, the Gaelic-named ford over the Lagan that, provided they had heard of it in the first place (which was unlikely even though they lived beside it) none of my Edwardian relations on the Malone and University roads—complete with hansom cabs at their Georgian-pillared doorways and Sheffield-plated teapots in their lofty, flat-windowed first-floor drawing-rooms—even knew how to spell.

The Victorian Old Ladies Said No

In the reign of Edward, the year of Our Lord 1907, the year when Belfast's horse-trams, thrillingly electrified, started spitting sparks from wheels and trolleys, I was told Oscar Wilde was 'not nice'. I was told this under the potted palms of our Edwardian drawing-room in a lofty red-brick terrace by one of my maternal aunts. She had a pince-nez that, in moments of relaxation, spun back on a gold chain to a sort of miniature cable-locker on her bosom. Oscar Wilde, said this Ariadne, was just 'not nice'. Bernard Shaw, I gathered, was not particularly 'nice' either—the sort of devilish figure you saw emerging through trapdoors in pantomimes in sheets of red paper flame. Whereupon the pince-nez, like a cable-car on the Matter-horn, after twin adventures on the way, ascended jerkily to the black taffeta tableland of her bosom, and that was that. As far as my aunt was concerned, Dublin could have the pair of them, and good riddance to bad rubbish.

That left Ibsen, and he was out *ab initio*. When they went to the theatre my maternal aunts didn't want to hear a word about divorce, illegitimate children, drains, overcrowding, or the effects of venereal disease. Never having had venereal disease, they didn't want to hear about it. What they wanted—descending from rickety cabs that smelt of damp straw and horse dung, or bunty electric trams stinking of wet shawls and snuff—was a sort of emergency exit from Belfast, a fire-door leading to what our gilt-and-plush Grand Opera House (Music, Drama, Cirque) presented as life in London—head waiters, lords in waterfall ties, monocles (no-one on the Malone Road dared to wear one), young women behind ribbon counters who turned out to be daughters of the aristocracy, impoverished earls, comic butlers, and all the other proper appurtenances of the Victorian stage.

26

As for drama manufactured in our submerged 'other island', the old ladies who circulated around the tea tables of our drawing-rooms had never heard of such an animal; therefore it did not exist. Stretching a point, they might have admitted that plays about the kind of Ireland represented in *Punch* cartoons by beautiful, if cantankerous, Irish colleens were possible, if undesirable. There were, of course, the plays of Dion Boucicault, but by the standard of *Punch* cartoons showing half-witted Irish peasants with clay pipes stuck in the bands of their caubeens, they were hardly subjects for discussion under gas-lit chandeliers in the intervals of listening to the *Indian Love Lyrics* or pronouncements on Marie Corelli. From time to time there were vague rumours of theatrical productions in obscure back-street halls in Dublin; and the name of the irrepressible Willie Yeats cropped up again, this time in connection with a building that had started life as a part-time morgue—being convenient, we supposed, for drownings in the Liffey—a temporary charnel-house later to become famous (under the lacquered-brass gasoliers of our drawing-rooms, notorious) as the Abbey Theatre. But our opinion of Willie Yeats and his morgue was the same as that of the lorgnette-wielding Belfast matron who, informed that a local dramatic society was in the act of staging the *Antigone* of Sophocles, acidly remarked, '*That* will get them nowhere!' In our opinion Willie Yeats would get there even faster, and with that we went back to the discussion of *The Merry Widow*.

But unfortunately for puff-shouldered, wasp-waisted matrons under brass gasoliers, infection spread from the banks of the Liffey, where Willie Yeats's charnel-house was flourishing. At the same time the Ulster Literary Theatre began staging kitchen comedies in Belfast, so that once a year for a short season at the gilt-and-plush Opera House we found ourselves abandoning lords in waterfall ties, comic butlers, young men whose sole occupation was the manipulation of eyeglasses and bank overdrafts, young women behind ribbon counters who turned out to be daughters of the nobilty, and other clockwork figures from the pre-Wodehousian dream. In exchange we got dung, hobnail boots, a clatter of milk pails, talk about hens 'layin' away', china dogs on the mantelshelf, plus highly-coloured pictures of King William crossing the Boyne, complete with mythical white horse.

During this annual *recherche* of the agricultural *temps perdu*, we looked back, rather patronisingly, at what we once had been, recognising, beyond the potted palms and lacquered-brass gasoliers, the prototypes of Uncle William and Aunt Sarah who were still 'down on the farm'. But it was only a flickering recognition, a day out in the (Ulster Literary Theatre) country, a short trip on the steamer to a sort of theatrical Isle of Man; then back to the lords and the comic butlers as if we had never been away. The old ladies were all for the lords and the comic butlers, figures as formalised as those of King William on his mythical white horse—the minor gods, as it were, of our provincial Edwardian society. Sometimes, in self-conscious efforts to educate ourselves, we went earnestly Shakespearian, with a hearty gentleman called Frank Benson taking time off from the hockey field to hang upside-down from palm-trees in *The*

27

Tempest. Beyond *The Tempest*, Maeterlinck's *Blue Bird, et hoc genus omne*, the Victorian old ladies said no. The only way to evade them was via the pantomime—via those brilliant transformation scenes where enormous chorus girls kept coming on in different uniforms, marching in a military, if slightly knock-kneed, fashion that took them nowhere but kept them wheeling in the coloured beams from the limes. Once you were up there marching you were, as Gertrude Stein might have remarked, up there marching; and not all your Scottish Presbyterian ancestors could get you down again—at least not as long as the band kept on playing 'Goodbye Dolly I Must Leave You' or 'Soldiers of the Queen'.

Then, having swept on with the Amazons of the chorus, knock-knees, powdered thighs, wobbly helmets, and all; having relieved Mafeking all over again and taken part in village celebrations complete with villagers, haymakers and comic squire, you were already graduated as frequenter of the Opera House; you could now progress from pantomime to non-pantomine; from dogs dressed up as soldiers executing fellow-dogs by firing squad; from pantomime dames with red noses and striped stockings, down into the 'Baron's Kitchen' past pantomime pies the size of prefabricated houses, on towards the kind of entertainments to which Victorian old ladies said yes. The only trouble was that sitting there as a reformed character in the red-plush stalls, under the gilt elephants on the fronts of the boxes, staring along with other little boys in Eton suits and enormous collars at drip like *Marigold* or Barrie's *Little Minister* was a complete waste of valuable time and but for surrounding cohorts of sisters, cousins, aunts, not a man amongst us but would have risen in his red-plush stall and demanded *Mother Goose* all over again.

A Thunder of Riveting

My father was a mild-mannered man with gold-rimmed spectacles who rarely took time off from the office for anything except funerals. Funerals or shipyards, one or the other; sometimes he took whole mornings off to attend launchings down at the Queen's Island. He appeared at the launchings in the same uniform that served for the funerals—that is, in frockcoat and top hat. The sole difference was that for the launching of anything over about 15,000 tons he wore a strip of white piqué buttoned inside the opening of his waistcoat, as for a festive occasion; which in fact it was.

But perhaps 'festive' is the wrong word. In Presbyterian Belfast a kind of marriage with the sea *may* have taken place down there at the 'Island', on the artificial peninsula at the head of Belfast Lough, but our Belfast version of the Protestant ethic took no account of such fantastic imagery. Down at the shipyards, in that sea of cloth caps and bowlers, a more accurate analogy would have been a harvest festival in a Presbyterian church—a thanksgiving at which slight variations from the psalms were permitted, a sort of Protestant inversion of the Mass at which the pagan rite of breaking a bottle of champagne was regarded as a harmless concession, like rolling eggs at Easter.

The mention of the Mass is opportune, for down at the shipyards, in that cathedral of wooden staging and towering steel gantries, we were giving thanks for a miracle, the miracle of ships built in the north-east corner of an island with hardly any coal or iron of its own; and the congregation gathered in the shadow of the gantries was understandably pleased with itself—particularly that portion supplied with privileged tickets by the high priests, now segregated on a special raised platform or dais of its own, looking forward to seeing itself later, top hats and all, in special editions of the *Evening Telegraph*. Segregated on the dais, ruled off by red ropes from the herd, we did not give thanks we were not as other men, especially as other Irishmen; we simply looked round, especially in the direction of Press photographers, with expressions of beatitude, like the blest ascending in early Christian murals, as the elevator of the twenti-eth century bore us effortlessly upwards towards some scientific millenium, some Polytechnic Jerusalem prophesied by H. G. Wells. And if our smooth, uninterrupted ascent was in the act of separating us from our fellow-coun-trymen, from the turf-burning (in the mythology of *Punch*, highly comic) Gaels of Donegal, Galway, and Mayo, then the turf-burning, and by the standards of *Punch*, backward-looking Gaels of Donegal, Galway, and Mayo, could hardly expect us to throw down our altars and worship something else—at least not as long as the dividends kept rolling in. Let *Punch* cartoons stuff that in their Hibernian-looking *dudeens* and smoke it! Let Dublin go on churning out its literature and its stout; here on the mud-banks of the Lagan we were praising God with a thunder of riveting, anticipating with brass and accordion bands, supplemented by double-column headlines in the *Telegraph*, the ultimate revelation of crystal-chandeliered lounges, *à la carte* restaurants with pink-shaded table-lamps, and sea-going Turkish baths in the new triple-screw *Titanic*.

But while we gathered at the river, complete with top hats and sacrificial garments, the *Titanic* was a blue-print in a mahogany drawer, an outline on a drawing-board, a thunder of water-tight doors bursting and boilers breaking loose to come—and the sole ship name that shines out from my red-carpet memories at the 'Island' is *Baltic*. I remember staring from the privileged platform at that salty, sea-sounding word painted in white lettering on a lofty prow, a vast red-leaded knife-edge that sheered up dizzily over us into the sky. That and the thunderous clangour of riveting from both banks of the river; the prodigious quantities of black soap that (I was told) were used to grease the slipways down which the knife-edge with its sea-sounding name of *Baltic* went sliding towards the water; the roar of cheering and the hooting of ships' sirens in the harbour when the knife-edge turned slowly away from us, slowly, politely, like a duchess backing out of a royal reception, and an enormous ship was floating bouncily on the Lagan, with a frenzy of anchor chains shedding madly from her sides.

That and my father, that quiet man who never left the office except for funerals and launchings, standing beside me on the raised platform, his top hat in his hand, tears running down his face. He had always wanted to go to sea, but his short sight and gold-rimmed spectacles put an end to that. To which I add that he was later to sail to America in the same *Baltic* as a sort of commercial ambassador, taking with him samples of our linen. On his return, again in the *Baltic*, he brought along with orders for the firm a new-fangled American machine for making ice cream, a barrel of shiny red American apples, and a fur-trimmed jacket for my mother.

But that was in the future as the *Baltic* slid bouncily out on to the Lagan and the blast of ships' sirens resounded from the Cave Hill. At that moment, when the sirens shouted to the city and the river, I was heart and soul inside this cathedral of shipyard staging where the miracle had just taken place, this vast nave filled with shattering noise where small boys not much older than myself swung red-hot rivets on the end of tongs as if they were swinging censers. In the dusk of winter afternoons the red-hot rivets flew through the air like fire-flies, so that the shadowy spaces under the gantries where the hulls of unfinished ships, surrounded by their mountains of staging, looked like giant foetuses in the womb, were always twinkling with light. The thunder of riveting was flung across the river, against the quayside sheds and the ranks of cross-Channel steamers with their white-painted upperworks and gaily-painted funnels; the gantries stood like towers against the sunset; red-hot rivets glowed like lamps in the interior of a cathedral where no sooner was one act of creation finshed than another was shatteringly begun—creation only momentarily interrupted when, lifting her stern towards the stars, the *Titanic* slid down with a thunderous roar into the ice-cold Atlantic, abruptly extinguishing the plush-and-gilt Edwardian dream, confining my father firmly to his office—leaving Belfast to face the knavish tricks of the Fenians, and, favourite phantom of its tin-shanty gospel halls, the tortuous manoeuvres of the Pope in Rome.

Onward to the Trocadero

As the youngest son of a linen merchant, my earliest impressions of London were of torrents of hansom cabs and small gaily-painted horse buses making a sound like muted thunder beyond the plate-glass windows of West End stores. That and squadrons of green-windowed cabs in culs-de-sac behind the stores—green-windowed 'growlers' from which emerged loud-voiced, red-faced individuals straight out of the green-backed edition of Dickens with the Cruikshank drawings in our glass-fronted bookcase at home in Belfast.

In the linen departments of the stores, usually behind Dickensian ramparts of blankets and sheets, my father carried on long conversations with walrus-moustached gentlemen in frockcoats, while the Cruikshank drawings from the green-windowed cabs waited deferentially in the background, like courtiers waiting for the Grand Cham of Tartary, and the walruses in the frockcoats ran on happily about their suburban rose gardens, the imbecility of the Government, the insubordination of the Irish, the new horseless carriages that were making a smell on the roads but would never come to anything—anything and everything under the sun except what struck me as the main point of the whole business—namely, were the Grand Chams in the frockcoats about to place colossal orders for our sheets and pillow-cases. But business was kept firmly in the background, like a distant relative in an asylum or the name of some shocking disease, while the Grand Chams in the frockcoats, ignoring the deputations from the green-windowed cabs with oriental unconcern, ran on happily about their rose gardens and their daughters' piano lessons, and my father tried to look as if he had never heard anything so enchanting in his life. These conversations painfully circling round the point took place in what I thought was a strong smell of tom-cats. Eventually I found that the smell came, not from marauding tom-cats, but the ramparts of brand-new blankets behind which the point-evading conversations were carried on.

As well as sheets, pillow-cases, napkins, traycloths, etc. for the linen departments of West End stores, we also made, or contracted to have made, tablecloths and napkins by the thousand for the more resplendent restaurants of J. Lyons & Co., gorgeous palaces where, as if the noise was not deafening enough already, Viennese orchestras and Hungarian string bands in blue hussar uniforms kept adding their contributions to the general commotion. When we sat down to dine under vast glittering chandeliers, surrounded by synthetic marble pillars, waited on by sub-servient German waiters, I, as an unduly logical little boy, was all for lifting a corner of the tablecloth at once, to see if J. Lyons & Co. were doing their stuff, our fleur-de-lys trademark woven in the corner. But my father never took the hint; never even removed from his waistcoat pocket the little magnifying-glass he carried for counting threads to the square inch; though later, out in the entrance lobby, under still more ebullient chandeliers, in the act of negotiating with enormous military gentlemen for cabs, he could invariably inform us if we had been dining off our own table linen. But linen departments smelling of vicarious tom-cats, even gorgeous marble-pillared palaces of J. Lyons & Co. reverberating with Hungarian *czardas* and Viennese waltzs, were only the frontline trenches; the real brass-hat areas, the chateaux where field-boots glittered and red tabs predominated, were located farther back, back in the shadow of St. Paul's.

Our chateau, our combined London headquarters and advanced ammunition dump, consisted of a modest little warehouse buried in a neat, almost secret courtyard in a narrow turning off Cheapside, surrounded by a clachan of Irish linen manufacturers. In the basement, down a steep flight of wooden stairs, an inadequate cold-water basin did duty for washing off the London grime; a water-closet built during the Franco-Prussian war still functioned, a monument to English conservatism of design and solidity of structure. Upstairs, where the jingle of hansom-cabs in Bread Street mingled with the bass-bourdon of horse-buses in Cheapside, was my uncle's euphemistically-labelled 'office'—a small cubbyhole with a roll-top desk littered with dusty papers. Overhead was a cracked skylight that leaked in wet weather. Here under the skylight, hunched over his roll-top desk, my uncle sat at the receipt of custom in the intervals of staring short-sightedly at day-books and ledgers—a small, gold-spectacled spider waiting for West End buyers to come buzzing into his web.

When they did buzz in they usually smelt of cigars—also, publish it not in the *Draper's Record*, of spiritous liquors—having been well primed on the way by my uncle's second-lieutenants, a practice of which my father never approved, though in fact the Bluthner grand that had now replaced the ordinary common-or-garden upright piano under the potted palms of our first-floor terrace drawing-room in Belfast, partly depended on it. I was not supposed to know about all this, and by way of warning, by way of introduction to the facts of life in the linen trade, my father was always telling me about the bad old days—days almost as far back as Dickens' blacking factory—bad old days before Victoria, of pious, glorious, and immortal memory, got herself firmly wedged on the throne—when all the Irish warehouses round Russia Row, had, according to my father, wine cellars as well as storage shelves in their basements. The idea, reversing the traffic arrangements of those complicated Victorian mousetraps in which the immersion came last, was to conduct the buyers first into the wine cellars, later into the private office—so that they arrived at the business end of the arrangement nicely sozzled and slap-happy about the order-book.

All this, like the battle of Waterloo, was over and done with; or so my father kept telling me; though, if my nose was any guide, my uncle's second-lieutenants had their own ways of getting round the absence of wine cellars. The second-lieutenants, glossy, top-hatted individuals, frequently larded their conversation with references to the lounge of the Empire and other Edwardian night-spots I was not supposed to know about, making their expeditions to the West End sound like excursions to the houris, a sort of Edwardian version of Watteau's *Embarquement pour Cythère*, with hansom cabs substituted for barges, feather boas for voluptuous draperies. The point about these glossy, morning-coated assistants was they navigated fearlessly amongst the rocks, shoals, and underground aquariums of the West End stores, finding their way from one set of palatial plate-glass windows to another as expertly as some of us were later to find our way from one barbed-wire entanglement to the next—while all the time my small, choleric, Irish uncle sat well back under the cracked skylight of his cubbyhole, like a medal-plastered general in a chateau, with a map showing the area of operations, from Knightsbridge to the Tottenham Court Road, from Finchley in the far north to Brixton in the south, hung on the wall above his dusty roll-top desk; and the skylight leaking away in wet weather.

Sometimes, like sheepdogs rounding up insubordinate sheep, or tugs nosing liners into dock, the raiders brought back prisoners, linen buyers for incarceration in our temporary pound or mousetrap. I always thought this was extraordinarily courageous of them; going in after West End linen buyers in their glass lairs amongst the bedspreads and the bargain towelling seemed to me as foolhardy as going in after badgers with your bare hands. But then my reactions to linen buyers lurking in their lairs behind barricades of pillow-cases and tom-cat-smelling blankets were, like my reactions to hippopotamuses grunting in their red-brick houses at the Zoo, unsympathetic—especially when, on learning I was just arrived from Ireland, they seemed to expect a wild Irish jig or juvenile song-and-dance act with shillelagh. And apparently the whole *genus* (sub-species Edwardian cockney) got on my choleric Irish uncle's nerves as well, for at regular intervals he would go off like an alarm clock in the direction that, from our side of St. Paul's, was technically known as 'up West'—saturnalia during which he remained incommunicado for anything between forty-eight hours and a week. What went on during the saturnalia was matter for speculation—like looking into a brightly-lit but weed-obscured aquarium, especially when the comings and goings in the aquarium were observed through the telescopes of Presbyterian aunts in Belfast. One persistent rumour was that he had been seen in the lounge of the Empire performing a highly-original ballet—more accurately, a *divertissement*—of his own composition. The *divertissement* consisted in taking running kicks at the stomach of an enormous commissionaire, then retiring and taking another running kick. After each old-style French *coup de pied au corps* (for diagram see early editions of *Larousse Illustré*), he handed the commissionaire a shilling, whereupon the commissionaire saluted, stood back for the next round, and the act started all over again. As an act it was bottom of the bill in Belfast, but a show-stopper in the lounge of the Empire.

Naturally enough, my father, called out to head the search parties, disapproved of terpsichorean exercises in Leicester Square. But then he took the *genus* linen buyer (sub-species Edwardian cockney) only in small doses, managing them in a conciliatory Irish fashion of his own, transporting them in jingling hansoms to roaring underground grottos like the grillroom of the Trocadero, where, to a background of Viennese waltzes or Hungarian *czardas*, shooting their only too detachable cuffs, damning the Government for incompetent rascals, denouncing all foreigners as anarchists, lamenting the rise, or it might be, the fall of prices and the general wreckage of the times, they ran on happily as the unacknowledged legislators of Edwardian England and a sort of Gilbert and Sullivan libretto stood on its head—while all the time my father, selecting as his tipple a glass of water, or, at the most, a small bottle of cider, was steadily administering the Liebfraumilch and at the same time, on the evidence of his own and neighbouring tables, working out when Messrs. J. Lyons & Co. would be likely to want more tablecloths and napkins. What I didn't realise, thrilling to Viennese waltzes and Hungarian zynballum, anticipating the dessert and enormous dollops of pink ice cream, was the pathos behind the unacknowledged legislators. Elevated by wine, music, and the sound of their own voices, the Grand Chams might be having a field day, a holiday from bargain basements, from ramparts of tom-cat-scented blankets; but life *du côté de chez* Kipps could nevertheless be brutal and short; beyond the wax ladies in the windows (discreet, if busty, and undressed only with the blinds down), the hinterland of the 'white goods and drapery' was red in tooth and claw; for all their privilege of lording it over red-faced courtiers from green-windowed cabs, the *grands seigneurs* of the linen departments were in reality very small beer, labouring like Sisyphus to keep their 'figures' climbing up and up; for the moment their 'figures' started to come down, or even stopped going up, they were liable to find themselves not only on the carpet, but outside on the pavement with only a slightly shiny (possibly second-hand) frockcoat as uniform against a wintry world and the bill for their daughters' piano lessons as near being paid as their suburban rose gardens to bearing bloom in January.

This was in the golden reign of Edward, when snowstorms of lingerie imitated Walter Sickert paintings in the display windows of West End stores, and the Great War was still invisible through the glass lanterns of hansom cabs. Meanwhile, if only vicariously, there were wine and music and the gorgeous palaces of J. Lyons & Co., even if the pillars were synthetic. Meanwhile there was the Bluthner grand to be maintained in the state to which it was accustomed; also my school books and my Eton suit for Sundays. Soon, all too soon, it was time to leave imitation marble pillars and German waiters, to abandon this *Strand Magazine* London, this thundering metropolis that was quite certain it was the centre of the world, as witness the red spaces on the map—time to set sail via the Liverpool boat train from flotillas of horse-buses and hansom cabs, the smell of horse dung just beginning to be flavoured by petrol, from red-jacketed bootblacks, khaki-smocked street-cleaners miraculously dodging torrents of horse-buses and hansom cabs, mysterious Robert Louis Stevenson cigar-divans where frockcoated dandies lit cigars at tiny gas-jets, toothy photographs of Marie Studholm and Ellaline Terris, pantomimes at Drury Lane that knocked the Belfast Opera House sideways with harle-quinades in which clowns, complete with strings of sausages and red-hot pokers, invariably triumphed over comic policemen who always lost their helmets; long, jingling processions to Euston through the dusk of autumn or winter evenings, with the lamps of cabs and hansoms strung out like the lights of ships at sea; street-lamps like parterres of daffodils; and beyond the Doric columns of Euston, scenes of smoke and confusion like a Frith painting at the Royal Academy.

Then dinner on the train as we roared through the night, past the glare of smelting-furnaces towards red-and-green-lit buoys on the Mersey, the Liver building with its lofty lighted clock, the clatter of the elevated railway, lighted ferry-steamers that made us feel half-way to New York. Then the melancholy of ships' sirens, the departure of the Edwardian, roast-beef-stuffed emigrants for the West, the joggle of sea, even on the calmest nights, off the Isle of Man, the triumphant passage up Belfast Lough, green hills of Down one side, blue-green mountains of Antrim the other—back to the Protestant thunder of the shipyards, and the winking of red-hot rivets; back to the mountain-dominated, smoke-canopied city with its forests of church spires and factory chimneys, and the bold cylinder of its gas-works;

34

back to the clatter of power-looms weaving tablecloths for crystal-chandeliered Trocaderos in red-brick weaving-sheds in the shadow of the Black Mountain; to the *clack-bang* of hand-looms sunk in the green rusticity of county Armagh—deep green pools of rusticity from which, armed with shillelaghs, dressed like Irish comedians in an English music-hall, we might at any moment emerge in a riotous up, down, hands across, an' leppin' to the wall, and hadn't we the gaiety at the *Punch* cartoonists' ball. The wogs begin at Belfast as well as Calais, and when shall we Irish, crawling out from our tombstones of legend, escape from this ghastly Hibernia we have created by gazing at our reflections in an English mirror?

A Gilt Clock on the Belfast Mantelshelf

The gilt clock was Aunt Lizzie; the mantelshelf, the *faubourg* Malone, a state of mind in south Belfast supported in its hey-day by investments in 'the funds', in Messrs. Dunville's distillery, and, God help us, in the Great Southern Railway of Ireland. Gilt-edged was the word for it in those days and Aunt Lizzie was gilt-edged till she glittered, a star in the *faubourg's* firmament, shining from a red-brick Victorian mansion on the banks of the Lagan that, translated from its background of distilleries and red-brick linen warehouses, corresponded to a chateau on the banks of the Loire.

Not that Aunt Lizzie was all that gilt-edged to begin with; she simply had the sense to marry into the whiskey business and never looked back afterwards. She kept the whiskey business safely shut away in a dark little book-lined study at the back of her chateau overlooking the Loire—I beg your pardon, overlooking the Lagan—where it smoked the best Havana cigars, drank (presumably its own) whiskey, and never, according to tradition in our family, interfered with Aunt Lizzie in the slightest beyond signing on the dotted line.

I begin with Aunt Lizzie (*arma virumque cano*) the way you begin with fabulous creatures in the corners of maps—the map in this instance of the *faubourg* Malone and the lower Lagan valley as unrolled in the golden reign of Edward. Not that Aunt Lizzie was any dragon; she was the kindliest creature in the world, and no reason to be anything else—smelling in winter of warm furs; at all seasons of port, plum cake, and violet scent. Nevertheless, driving to town with Aunt Lizzie was like driving to town with Catherine the Great; you were not only protected in cold weather by exuberant layers of fur rugs, you were encapsulated in 'the funds', ennobled by the divine right of whiskey dividends—let the serfs by the roadside shiver their acknowledgements. Even the lower Lagan valley, smoke clouds and all, looked different from Aunt Lizzie's landau. All those factory chimneys belching away under the Black Mountain were just a vulgar painted background as far as Aunt Lizzie was concerned; in behind them was a dark forest where the princess put in a furry paw, yanked out a husband-director, then retired again, wrapped in fur, to

35

Belfast's outer belt of woodland, to the long green vistas of the Castle-reagh hills, and everybody lived happily ever afterwards as if some magician had put a spell on them, with consols doing nicely and fairy prince Edward VII on the throne.

Talk about *la belle et la bête*. Not that, except for occasional shopping expeditions to Lindsay's or Robinson & Cleaver's (complete with fairy-tale coachman, top hat, cockade, and all, on the box seat), Aunt Lizzie made many descents to the dark forest of Belfast; her business was in the *faubourg* supported by the forest; enchanted woodland, and no black smokestacks for her. She had regular snowstorms of visiting cards (first and third Thursdays) to distribute right down the Malone Road, cards from an elaborate silver card-case chained to her fur-wrapped person with a silver chain. To get into this card-scattering act you rolled, violet-scented, right down into the Boulevard Saint-Germain of Edwardian Belfast, right in amongst the mansions of the linen manufacturers and the coal kings, almost as far as the slightly superfluous Queen's College and the ghastly little Victorian clock-tower-cum-*pissoir* at the entrance to the Botanic Gardens.

Here, where mansions gave place to high red-brick terraces, was the tell-tale heart of the faubourg, a sort of local market place where the inhabitants could be seen coming round again like a stage army or a pantomime chorus gathering for the final scene. There was old Mr. G. who put on an act of driving down-town in a hansom to his office, with, perched on his knee, an important-looking attaché-case, much as a British Chancellor of the Exchequer might convey his despatch-box to the House. There was nothing in the attaché-case except a roll of toilet paper and the *Belfast News Letter*. There was also nothing in old Mr. G's office except a desk to put your feet on, and, beyond a frosted-glass door marked PRIVATE, a water-closet. Having attended to his morning functions, old Mr. G. then put his feet on his stage-property desk and dealt with the *News Letter*. This took the rest of the morning, front page, back page, advertisements, and all. Having read the *News-Letter*, deaths, births, marriages, stock exchange, legal notices, bankruptcies, above all death columns, it was then time for lunch, time to lock up the office, time to drive home up the Malone Road in the hansom. Appearances had been saved, pressure on the domestic water-closet, or closets, relieved; lower orders, policemen, horse-tram drivers, crossing-sweepers, office cleaners, etc., kept in their places.

Old Mr. G. and my Aunt Lizzie were, in fact, a pair of highly individual ornaments on the Belfast Edwardian mantelshelf. There were, of course, minor decorations in between, There was old Mr. B. who said all this perturbation about love and marriage was a waste of time and energy. You just walked into the drawing-room and picked the first woman you saw. He had acted on the principle himself, and it worked, to the extent of twelve editions. But the outstanding figures were Aunt Lizzie and old Mr. G.—Aunt Lizzie scattering cards, first and third Thursdays, old Mr. G. with no need to lift a finger, stoutly maintaining his role of Edwardian magnate, jingling up and down the Malone Road with the regularity of a

Greenwich time-signal (switched off Saturdays and Sundays), tolling out his own particular version of *Land of Hope and Glory* on his lavatory chain behind the frosted-glass door marked PRIVATE.

Yet by some magic of her own, some radiance unextinguished by fur coats and violet scent, Aunt Lizzie stood out amongst the Edwardian bric-a-brac like a magnificently florid gilt clock. Having said that, I add a confession that she wasn't really my aunt at all, except by adoption—a fact wih legal consequences. When the whiskey business stopped smoking its cigars and drinking (presumably its own) whiskey in that dark little book-lined study where nobody read the books at the back of Aunt Lizzie's chateau overlooking the Loire—I beg your pardon, Lagan— stopped, that is, for ever—Aunt Lizzie, in the kindness of her heart, tried on *her* deathbed to arrange that some of the whiskey money would trickle through to us down in the comparative underworld of the red-brick terraces almost opposite the now vanished clock-tower-cum-*pissoir* at the entrance to the Botanic Gardens. That was her intention, but it was defeated—nullified by legal finesse, by backstairs manoeuvres that shook the *faubourg* to its foundations, even faintly reverberate in some of its tree-lined parks and avenues to this day.

My father, a teetotaller except for the odd glass of white wine, or, under the same kind of misapprehension that set down the French as a sober nation, the odd bottle of cider, was philosophical. He said the whiskey money would never have done us any good. Slightly altering the language of army orderly-rooms, I have read over and do *not* corroborate the above statement. The whiskey money would have done us a lot of good. After all, it did Aunt Lizzie a lot of good; shaking down the golden berries never gave her ache or pain. Indeed if I had some of them today I would be raising a glass with very little water in it to her memory, in the sure, the almost certain, hope that she is at this moment enlivening some celestial suburb of the *haute bourgeoisie* the way she once enlivened, some would have said, scandalised the *faubourg* Malone. *La belle*, with her *bête* safely behind her, was a goer to the last.

Curtain-Raisers for Paisley

I

One Edwardian Sunday morning the veil of Belfast Presbyterian com-placency was rent in twain. I watched the operation from a red-cushioned box-pew in the gallery of our opulent tabernacle opposite the Botanic Gardens. The gallery looked down on a towering row of gilt organ-pipes (like monstrous cigars in a pantomime) and an elaborate marble-pillared pulpit like a Gothic advertisement for Young's *Night Thoughts*. The preacher, the Rev. David . . . . ., D.D., an eloquent Scotsman, was *in medias res*, emitting a steady stream of Biblical comment. If he had paused for a moment, I would have roused myself in the red-cushioned box-pew like a ship's captain rousing himself in his bunk the instant the engines stop at sea. But though the piston-strokes from the *Night Thoughts* pulpit were maintained without a pause; though theological crank-shafts were revolving with a steady *thump, thump, thump*, immersing themselves at every revolution in the lubricants of the Old and New Testaments, there was obviously a bearing heating somewhere. Sniffing the burning oil, I roused myself in the bunk.

I found my mother fidgeting, violently adjusting veil and Edwardian toque; saw my father scarlet-faced in the choir below, overwhelmed by the gilt organ-pipes. Obviously a spanner had been dropped, landing right down in the engine-room. Years later I discovered that the preacher, like Aristotle before him, had strayed over from ethics into politics. But all I knew at the time was that during the Sunday dinner that followed the sermon with the inevitability of joint following soup, my father, still scarlet in the face, brandishing a carving-knife he had been sharpening with unnecessary zeal, remarked of the preacher, as of some animal in a zoo, 'The man's nothing better than a Little Englander!' Whereupon the discussion over our Sunday roast suddenly went up in flames, ending as a sort of Presbyterian rough house, a north-eastern version of the dinner table discussion of Parnell in Joyce's *A Portrait of the Artist as a Young Man*.

Looking back now, I see the reason for the flames—the fact that the pronouncement from the *Night Thoughts* pulpit—whatever kind of heresy was involved—came before, but only just before, the Ark of the Ulster Covenant. Apparently the Rev. David . . . . ., D.D., surrounded by red-cushioned box-pews and luxuriant stained-glass windows (one showing the Prodigal Son with remarkably clean feet), was still harping on about the Boer war, still trailing his Scottish Liberal coat, when everybody thought the redecoration of the manse had put paid to the whole business. The frockcoats down in the red-cushioned front stalls below the *Night Thoughts* pulpit were fed up to the back teeth with post mortems on the Boer war; what they wanted, justified by bloodthirsty texts from the Old Testament and trumpet voluntaries from Rudyard Kipling, was a panegyric on imperialist expansion; and the slightest suggestion that imperialist expansion might, like the redecoration of the manse, some day have to be paid for was, to say the least of it, unpopular; the main lesson for the day being the *Investors' Chronicle*. I can still see the preacher, his handsome face aglow with conviction as he thumped the red cushion on which the Bible rested. My conviction was that some Sunday he would thump so hard that cushion, Bible, and all—possibly sable-gowned, scarlet-hooded preacher as well—would descend in a miraculous shower on the flowery hat of the leading soprano in the choir below—and might I be there to see!

But no sable-gowned, scarlet-hooded figure ever descended on that flowery hat; nothing except, metaphorically speaking, the preacher's reputation. His eloquence on the subject of the Boer war and the fallibility of empires merely greased the slipway of his own decline and fall, the paths of Scottish Liberalism leading, in Edwardian and post-Edwardian Belfast, if not directly to the grave, then by a process of isolation to a sort of Presbyterian Siberia. From the day my father started sharpening his

38

already sharp carving-knife, the skids were under him; he became a prophet without honour, a John the Baptist crying in a wilderness of Harland & Wolff (plus, in those days, Workman & Clark) launching-slips, prosperously-belching factory chimneys, and brand-new red-brick villas in the suburbs.

The frockcoated burghers in the red-cushioned stalls below the *Night Thoughts* pulpit saw to that—the stipend-subscribing linen merchants, the sustentation-fund-supporting shipbuilders, the stained-glass-window-presenting mineral water manufacturers. If I had been old enough to know what it was all about that far-off Sunday, I would have known that ritual murder was being committed; that a cauldron was being stirred, from which, half a century later, sinister black-robed figures (what the French call *corbeaux*) would emerge to darken the 'Ulster' scene. All unaware, I was there when the rooks took off from the Venetian spire of our ornate tabernacle opposite the Botanic Gardens. Now the sky is black with them; the streets loud with explosions nobody dreamed of the day my father, still scarlet in the face, brandished that razor-sharp carving-knife, and, with a posse of Presbyterian sisters-in-law waiting at the foot of the guillotine for the Rev. David's head, the flames shot up from our all-too-prophetic Sunday roast. And the tragedy was that nobody half so eloquent, or a quarter so liberal, ever adorned that marble-pillared, *Night Thoughts* monstrosity of a pulpit again.

II

The day the rooks took off from our Venetian spire was a footnote to 'Ulster' history. The next was a small red-faced blimp called Crawford. When I first encountered him he had retired to cultivate his garden—a garden so flourishing you had to hack your way to the front door. Inside, shut away amongst the cobwebs of his suburban Tchaikovsky palace, was the Colonel—red-faced Colonel Crawford recovering from the fact that war, when it came, wasn't war as foreseen from the *Fanny* or the *Clyde Valley*, but an irrelevant first act of Armageddon in France and Flanders, and not a word about 'Ulster' except in so far as the *Clyde Valley* and its load of secondhand rifles entered the calculations of the German General Staff.

Three weeks after the bitch goddess of History started what was for him the wrong war, I was in his tree-darkened study looking for his signature. What he was witnessing was my suitability for a commission in the Irish Fusiliers—August, 1914. Three months after that car-headlight-illuminated landing of guns at Larne harbour. He signed, but he didn't like the look of me. He probably realised I hadn't been illuminated by the car headlights. Still worse, that I hadn't signed the Covenant, in blood or anything else.

And by *Oh! What a Lovely War* standards, how right he was. Outside his study window the jungle had still to proliferate: Kipling, with his trumpet voluntaries, was still the one true prophet; the red spaces were

39

still on the map; the guns from the *Clyde Valley* comparatively unrusted. I have always thanked God that my gold-spectacled father was never called upon to fire one of the Colonel's guns. He may have called him Fred and lunched with him at the Belfast Reform Club, but firing his guns was another matter. Some were stacked in our Belfast suburban attic next to a dressmaker's bust and a discarded sun-helmet from the Boer war. If my father had been called upon to fire them, his spectacles would have slipped down his nose, and ten to one he would have shot the man next to him. Either that or one of Fred's blunderbusses would have blown his spectacles sideways.

No, better leave the Colonel and my father to their untidy military manoeuvres, their sloppily-sloped arms. War was coming all right, but it wasn't their war. In the end we paid the reckoning; we marched up the long, straight, tree-lined roads that led to gun-muttering horizons; we watched the star-shells nightly reconstructing a sort of ghostly Piccadilly Circus; we were collected in the equivalent to Samuel Beckett dust-bins; we pushed up those crops of later-to-be-exploited poppies in machine-gun-dominated Flanders cornfields.

What occurs to this survivor from the cornfields is to wonder whether Colonel Fred and my gold-spectacled father were watching from the next world the night the *Clyde Valley* so glibly popped up again on television as floating pulpit for Paisley. The blue hills of Antrim were calling him home, so he hogged the historical limelight and addressed them (O God our help in ages past!) through a loudhailer, looking like an enormous flapping *corbeau* escaped from that cauldron the frockcoated Presbyterian burghers (including my father) were stirring the day that, with a horrid threshing of black wings, the rooks took off from the Venetian spire of our freshly-gilded tabernacle in the snoblands of south Belfast; the next steps down that road being pillars of fire in Divis Street, the reformation of Belfast's watermains by gelignite; finally, the startling emergence (armed with loudhailer) of a 'black-mouthed Luther from the preachin' north' from the historic, in fact the sacred, waters of the North Channel outside Larne harbour.

Who says History isn't a bitch?

In the Mountains of Inishowen

I

GRANDFATHER PREACHED IN IRISH

A winter night in Derry. Huddled in my Irish Fusiliers greatcoat I was walking round the walls. Flush with the parapet was a lighted window, obscured by curtains, with the blind pulled down to make certain. From behind blind and curtains came a voice speaking in Irish, a high insistent voice, interrupted by bursts of frenzied applause.

No place for newly-joined second-lieutenants in British greatcoats. I stood back from the window, moved into darkness. With me moved my maternal grandfather, invisible, but present in the frosty night. I never heard him discussed in the family, not with Carsonite rifles in the attic. If he figured at all, he figured as a sort of disreputable relative from the Australian outback, never to be mentioned in polite Belfast society.

Actually he was a Presbyterian minister, and somewhere about the middle of last century he preached from the pulpit of a small Presbyterian church in county Louth—in English one Sunday, in Irish the next. No wonder we kept quiet about him on the Malone Road. At the height of Carsonite 'Ulsteria' grandfathers who preached in Irish were pushed in behind the historical background, and kept there. Yet without my knowing much about him, he was there the night I stood by the lighted window on Derry's walls; there when, in a mood of black infantry man's despair, I wrote a sketch about another 'lighted window', this time a hatch for serving drinks. I was sitting, in mufti, in the snug of a combined public-house and grocery store in the shadow of Inishowen mountains, drinking stout and at the same time watching, through the hatch, a beautiful girl at the grocery counter:

> 'Unconscious of her beauty, she stood directly under a paraffin lamp, her shawl flung back, laughing and joking with the storekeeper, a prim pince-nezed young woman from Derry—the pair of them oblivious of male attention, surrounded by stacks of groceries.'

I called this sketch 'A Free Woman', stressing the paradox that freedom sprang from a life spent in obedience:

> 'Day in, day out, she obeyed a rule of living, was free because it never occurred to her she was bound. Her life was marked out for her; already, sitting there in the snug, I could follow it in imagination to the time when, an old woman, white-haired and stooped, worn out with child-bearing and rearing and mending, she would sit by the fire, gazing at her life, and know without bitterness it was ended.
> 'Then when the priest had come and given her absolution for the

43

sins she had never committed, she would close her eyes and slip away from the cares and burdens of this world—from children, husband, cattle—inscrutably feminine and unknowable to the last. Something like that would be her life story, though at the moment it would have been beyond me to declare just what had fired my imagination.'

The next sketch went back to 1915, to the mountains of Inishowen and an old man I met on a mountain road. I called it, 'After Kinsale':

'Battered hat, tattered trousers, and all, he had the air of a Spanish aristocrat. Behind him, stuck like swallows' nests against the scar-faced backdrop of the Urris hills, lurked a clachan, a collection of tumbledown cottages with whitewash stained and discoloured and thatch sagging drunkenly.

'A fine mornin'.' He stood by the roadside, detached, quizzical, a lord at the gates of his demesne. Beyond Trawbreaga bay, inlet of the dark blue Atlantic, black clouds of rooks wheeled and manoeuvred in clear spring sunlight over the rookeries at Malin town. In the valley below, beside the twisting road to Clonmany, a tumult of seagulls followed a plough drawn by a stumbling horse in a patch of field rescued from surrounding bogland. The black stony field looked from the mountain road like a miniature square on a chess board.

'A grand morning.'

Conversation came to a halt. The old man eyed my Irish Fusiliers uniform, my shining brass buttons stamped with the French eagle.

'That's a fine uniform ye have there!' He surveyed me sardonically from head to foot, swaying slightly on his stick. 'Tell me,' he said as if asking the time by the town clock, 'how's this war o' yours gettin' on?'

'Not so well,' I said. 'Not so well at the moment.'

A sardonic twinkle, rising as it were from the depths of a mountain pool, illuminated his battered, drowned exterior. If the Lord of Hosts saw fit to chastise the English with scorpions, the old man found no reason to object. Far below, framed in a gap in the mountains, a line of trawlers was strung across the stormy entrance waters of Lough Swilly, mine-sweeping.

'Do ye tell me that now?' He stared with rheumy satisfaction at the spot far out on the blue Atlantic where only last autumn the battleship *Audacious* sank, her bilges shattered by a German mine. It was as if he were saying, 'Lord, now lettest Thou thy servant depart in peace!'

The beautiful girl and the old man made a pair. The girl, doing her Saturday night shopping in the store, was a symbol of security, the product of an enduring religion, the flowering of an ancient culture. Behind her Europe lay in ruins; out here, two seas away, framed for the moment in the hatch-way from the bar, lit by the paraffin-lamp, something was preserved. As for the old man in the Urris hills, beside him stood the ghost of my maternal grandfather, the man who used his gift of tongues to preach in Irish, thereby excommunicating himself from our Belfast tabernacle with

44

the stained-glass windows. In the light of the stained glass windows, both the girl under the paraffin-lamp and the old man on the mountain road stood in outer darkness, sentenced to the burning fiery furnaces of the 'Ulster' Protestant mind.

II
PHILOSOPHER IN TURF CART

'A fine day!' He stopped his high red cart that made reports like pistol shots. 'A gran' day for the walkin'!' He relit his pipe, watching me at the same time shrewdly from the corner of his eye.

'A grand day.'

The bog stretched black and silent around us. Far below, Lough Swilly shone deep blue in a gap in the mountains

'Aye, an' a gran' day for the thinkin'!'

'What makes you say that?'

'Sure I knew ye comin' along the road. There's a thinkin' man, I said.' He bent down from the cart, peered more intensely. 'Ye have the face of a thinkin' man.'

'Have I now?'

'Ye have.'

He spat with emphasis into the road.

'Well, and what am I to do about it?'

'What *would* ye do about it?' he remarked, rather crossly. 'Isn't that the way ye are?'

He stared for a moment across the bog.

'Tis lonesome up here,' he said suddenly, as if thick black curtains had descended all round us.

Then, bending again from the cart, he peered more intently, and said: 'Ah was a thinkin' man meself once't.'

'Were you now?'

'Ah was.'

'And are you not now?'

'Ah am *not*.' He let the reins hang slackly for a moment, peering inwards into the depths of his being.

'Ah'll tell ye the gran' cure for it,' he said at last, a hint of despondency in his voice.

'A grand cure for what?'

'A gran' cure for the thinkin'.'

'And what's that?'

'Marriage.' He gave the reins a chuck. The horse merely shook itself and subsided again in a philosophic trance.

'Marriage?' I said. 'I'll take your word for it. You're a married man, aren't you?'

'Ah am *that*.' He hit the horse over the hindquarters with the loose end of the reins. 'Ah am *that*.'

The cart started with a jerk.

'Well, good day to ye!'
'Good day!'
I settled down to more thinking, more contemplation of dark blue Fanad mountains beyond Lough Swilly. But with loud reports the turf cart stopped again.
'Ah seen ye below in the camp,' he yelled back.
'Below in the camp' meant the Irish Fusiliers camp in Clonmany. I was identified, signed up in the visitors' book. We let it ride. The cart started with another jerk, more reports like pistol shots. I sat by the roadside, watching, until cart, philosopher, introspective horse, and all, had dwindled to a red speck against the blackness of the bog. Up here in high bogland where columns of smoke meant poteen stills and the I.R.A. kept a watchful eye on all activities, including bank lodgments, in the valleys below, it was better to stick, like my new friend in the turf cart, to strictly non-political matters like birth, death, marriage, and the loneliness of the human soul.

An Encounter with Classical Ghosts

A chateau near Amiens. November twilight. Outside, in the park, the first snow of winter. From the east, a subdued muttering of guns. I sit with mud-stained companions in what was once a gilded salon, at a table made of packing-cases, drinking whiskey out of a tin mug.

Overhead, fruit of ages, vast crystalline chandeliers, cracked but still magnificent. The chandeliers jangle brokenly as guns mutter in the east.

The light is from guttering candle-ends stuck in the necks of empty whiskey bottles. In the background a tinny gramophone grinds out last year's song-hit from the Palace Theatre, London:

> 'I'm Gilbert the Filbert
> The Knut with a K
> The pride of Piccadilly
> The blasé roué:
> O Hades, the ladies
> All leave their wooden huts
> For Gilbert the Filbert
> The kernel of the Knuts.'

To-morrow to fresh woods. To-morrow sore heads, secret movement orders, chaos of departure, frost-bitten rails of Amiens junction.

Lights of Paris seen from a darkened troop train on the *ceinture* railway. *Hommes* 40, *chevaux* 8, dilapidated smoking-carriages for the officers.

Over there, under that faint red reflection in the sky, beyond those red-and-green-carpeted shunting yards, a gentleman called Proust, looking in his photograph like a small Persian prince, is about to lock himself in a cork-lined room. All the best people having disappeared from all the best restaurants, nothing remains but to lock himself in his prison house and write a masterpiece.

Piccolo squeaks from locomotives—sounds that later prostrate American doughboys. Exeunt lights of Paris. Curtain, end of chapter. We clatter southwards, *hommes* 40, *chevaux* 8, dilapidated smoking-carriages. End of a European tradition—bodies, military units, *Kannonenfutter*, candle-ends stuck on luggage racks illuminating endless games of *vingt et un*. Destination, squared-off sections on yet unissued maps.

Spires of Marseilles, jacket-illustration for Zola novel. Dockside arc-lamps. Whistles, general profanity. Immaculate gentlemen in red tabs set it down in typescript by light of green-shaded lamps. Now by light of flares and dockside arc-lamps we untangle it. Which go first, mules or limbers?

Following night's dusk. Gulf of Lions. Short, steep, crashing green seas through which escorting destroyers go madly plunging and bucking, smothering themselves in spray.

Mediterranean holiday. Dark blue island to starboard. Ibiza. No more destroyers plunging and bucking. Travel-poster sea. At midnight ghostly cracklings from masthead aerials: *sotto voce* observations about submarines.

The first Greek land. Island of Cythera—Watteau's *Embarquement pour Cythère*. But then Watteau never saw Cythera on a December evening from the crowded deck of a 17,000-ton transport. Those amorous draperies in the Louvre would have been sadly disarranged by the wind now blowing from the Balkans.

Still the first land. (*Larousse Illustré* says that on Cythera *Venus avait un temple magnifique*, which conceals a loud French fanfaronade of trumpets for *l'amour*.)

No temples. Night amongst the Cyclades. The violet shadow to port is Euboea. 'Violet-crowned' Athens in the darkness beyond.

Scattered lights. Talk on boat-deck of Gallipoli. Skyros ahead. Padre in smokeroom says Rupert Brooke's grave is in an olive grove, surrounded by marble ruins. His last encounter with classical ghosts, a backdrop of genius.

Mudros. Ghosts classical and Irish. Like the Grand Fleet at Lough Swilly. Inlet packed with transports, repair ships, hospital ships, destroyers. Throb of gunfire from Gallipoli. North-west, the violet cone of Athos. To the east, Imbros, Cape Helles, the invisible Hellespont. From the Hellespont, in thick winter murk, the curious double thud of French 75's, sounding as if they were firing on the plains of Troy. Units of the Persian fleet must have anchored here on the way to Salamis.

Lemnos creased with dirty snow.

From our anchorage in the gulf Salonika looks like an illustration on a box of dates. White domes, minarets. Ashore, a smell of murder. *Passé* electric trams on the waterfront. Winter climate cold. Bitter winds from the Vardar valley and the snow-topped mountains of Serbia. Amusements bawdily sad. A Turkish-smelling mattress of corruption stifles the city. Small Greek boys anxious to sell their sisters. Astonishingly virtuous Lancashire dancing girls in tawdry little music-halls and *boites de nuit*. Judging by the pimps hanging about the Tour Blanche, St. Paul's acid epistles were right on the bull's-eye.

Beyond the gulf, the snowy peak of Olympus. Gods winking up there in the snow dazzle, a pantomime chorus from *Lemprière* bawdily amused at us Christians.

Monastir road, leading to sweet Fanny Adams, like a scene in a faded western. Light snow falling. Desolate mountain background, muddle in the commissariat, best Crimean tradition. Bombed by Austrian aeroplanes. Austrian music-hall joke. In clear Aegean sunlight between snow flurries you swear you could put a rifle bullet plumb through the black crosses on their wings. Pilot leans over, waves fur-gloved hand. *Auf wiedersehn.* Bombs about the size of cricket balls. Total result, profane eruption of Cameron Highlanders from snow-powdered tents.

The fur-gloved aeronauts turn back over the mountains. Back to their ramshackle empire, their not-so-blue Danube. We resume our search for a missing tin of plum-and-apple jam.

On the Hortiach plateau. *In hibernis*, in holes covered with corrugated iron. Not a man sick, not a cold in the head. With one companion I climb the mountain labelled on our maps as Kotos. The snow-patched landscape falls away to the Aegean. A large hawk or buzzard circles overhead; otherwise nothing moves—a blank space since St. Paul followed the Via Egnatia; since the fall of the Turkish empire; further back, since Xerxes, cutting his canal through Athos to circumvent omens and storms, moved his fleet against Athens. Kotos feels as if it has opted permanently out of war.* Even Salonika, that hotbed of military intrigue, with its ironical Place de la Liberté, its bawdy music-halls, its rattling trams, its sad Turkish mosques converted to warehouses, its smelly, twisting streets, its perpetual military gossip in Flocca's café—Salonika, with its green-blue gulf, its ironical view of snow-capped Olympus, is sunk below the edge of the plateau.

Near the summit of Kotos, a series of small circular ponds, frozen to the depth of a foot. A small figure stands by one of the ponds, an ice-cutter holding some sort of rudimentary saw. The little figure watches us plodding through the snow with malign distrust. In Macedonia the fewer people you meet, the better: men in uniform—Turkish, Greek, Bulgarian, or any other kind—worst of all. Soldiers in Macedonia mean villages ransacked and burnt, crops destroyed, women with their bellies ripped open by

*South of here, mountain lions attacked and ate the horses and mules of Xerxes' land expedition.

bayonets. No wonder the little ice-cutter watches us like a mouse watching a cat from a mouse-hole.

Eventually, when no shots are fired, he goes back, the seat of his trousers sagging, to sawing ice-blocks from his pond. If only these successors to the Turks will go away and leave him in peace—leave him to cut his ice and earn his miserable drachmae by transporting it, with painful loss by leakage, on the back of his starving mule all the way down Kotos, over the edge of the plateau, down to the great metropolitan city of Salonika, where it will end in the drinks of gentlemen with highly-polished field-boots on the comic-opera Place de la Liberté. The *effendi* in the polished boots must have his ice; the ice-cutter his shack, his ancient mule, his ice-ponds on Kotos, his painful trickle of drachmae, his semi-starvation. After all, it is better than having your throat cut, your wife spitted with bayonets against a wall. It is all written in the Book and in the hard clear light of Aegean winter it is difficult to imagine it being written any other way.

Spring, sudden Balkan spring. Bull-frogs boom, irises bloom in the marshes. The snowy peak of Olympus glitters beyond the green-blue gulf. Along the Salonika water front, dislocating the comic-opera trams, a Serbian regiment comes marching, new British-pattern hobnail boots striking sparks from the *pavé*—stocky, deep-chested men, some with wound stripes from two previous Balkan wars. A fiery little colonel marches ahead, behind him rank after rank of the toughest fighting men in Europe. They were forced, still fighting, out of Serbia, retreated, fighting, through the Balkan winter and the snowy mountain passes of Albania; re-formed and re-armed in Corfu. Now, newly landed, they come back for more, singing as they come. They are unbeatable; the sound of their singing—the buried clatter of Kossovo resounding on the quays of Salonika—like the sudden fighting uprush of the Balkan spring.

The via Egnatia. Once highroad from Rome to Byzantium. As a dysentery patient just out of hospital, I travel on a large, cantankerous mule, navigating in the opposite direction to St. Paul when he arrived by way of Amphipolis and Appolonia to rebuke the Thessalonians—probably for pimping and trying to sell their fourteen-year-old sisters. At night we sleep where we fall. In the ruins of Appolonia I wake with something crawling inside my shirt. I shake my shirt and out falls a vole. No sign of St. Paul, no word of the gospel—the Turks have obliterated all that. Also no sign of the mountain lions that attacked Xerxes' transport mules.

The third night—after a glimpse of moonlight on Lake Bolbe—we come down through rocky defiles to the sea, to Stavros (Stagyra), the gulf of Rendina, to sounding Aegean breakers breaking, like glass splintering, on classical beaches. After the ruins of Appolonia, the vole, the ghostly wastes of the Via Egnatia, the sight of the sea is like a long drink of cold water. *Thalatta! Thalatta!*

Rumours with the ration-cart about rebellion in Ireland, a naval battle in the North Sea. All Greek to us. At night we sleep to the sound of tinkling Aegean breakers. Landscape out of Thucydides. Green breakers, steeply-shelving Aegean beaches. The *Atlas of Ancient and Classical Geography* we used at school in Cambridge showed three-pronged Chalcidice sticking down like a trident into the Aegean, as if on purpose to entangle Xerxes.

The gulf we are skirting (beyond which we heard the guns at Gallipoli) was labelled Strymonicus Sinus.

Camp near the site of Amphipolis, in the sandy gorge where the Struma, the Strymon of the ancients, finally meanders to the sea. On the farther bank Thucydides failed to relieve the siege of Amphipolis; was banished for twenty years. Hence his voluminous *History of the Peloponnesian War*. Amphipolis, on the eastern bank of the Strymon, has disappeared from the light, but every time we dig in our bivouac on the western bank for the necessary purpose of latrines, we turn up spadefuls of history, including clusters of small, battered coins. One coin shows a head, presumably of an emperor; on the reverse a figure on horseback; another, a beautifully-executed quadriga; a third, a heavily-embossed portrait of a busty young woman, empress or goddess.

From the gorge at the mouth of the Struma and the site of Amphipolis a sandy track leads north-westwards to Lake Tahinos (Prasias Lacus), a shallow, reedy extension of the river, breeding ground for mosquitoes; according to Thucydides, a death-trap for military operations. Here, on rising ground overlooking the lake, we build our summer quarters—a straw-thatched hut open at the sides to catch the breeze, and, scattered about the hillside so as to be invisible from the air, rough erections of boughs, twigs, rushes, waterproof sheets, and the lids of biscuit boxes.

Here we watch through field-glasses for signs of a Bulgarian advance into the plain beyond the lake. Other duties: turning over heaps of assorted rags that once served as beds in deserted villages along the lake shore. In this occupation we collect more fleas and lice than information, and the odd scraps of printed and written matter we find in closets and mattresses, below beds, behind images and ikons, and in other classical hiding places, turn out, on translation by our Armenian interpreter, to be nothing more incriminating than marriage licences, grocers' bills, almanacs, *et hoc genus omne*. If there are spies waiting for the Bulgarians to descend from the Rhodopes, we never discover them.

Except for flocks of pigeons, some villages feel like temporary graveyards, with the departed still watching; we even find an abandoned grocer's shop, still stocked with goods, with a well-fed cat glaring at us from the dark corner of a shelf. Cats, an occasional mongrel dog, rarely the owners of the cats or dogs. In some ghost villages only a few old women remain; a few children peep from doorways, unnaturally listless, with the abdomen protruding in an extraordinary manner over the region of the spleen. A sallow-faced child lurking in a doorway looks as if she is pregnant. Malaria is the villain of the piece, not the Turks or the Bulgarians or the *comitadjis* of any faction. The people of this valley have been dying off for generations;

most of the villages it is our duty to examine will be abandoned in any event, wars or no wars, Bulgarian advance or no Bulgarian advance.

I set out across the bridge at the mouth of the Struma, eastward bound on a battered motor-bicycle. My job is to carry despatches to the British consul at Kavalla. I am now in the no-man's-land between two armies; if the Bulgarian advance has been rapid, I am likely, short of something worse, to spend the rest of the war in a Bulgarian prison. Meanwhile the battered Douglas hums like a sewing-machine and I have time to survey the landscape. The mountain mass to the north-east is Mount Pangeus, where Thucydides, the *genius loci*, held the right to work gold mines. Somewhere to the north-east, behind the mountains, is the site of Philippi.

In the market place at Pravista, half-way to Kavalla, I encounter the Greek army. A mob of Greek soldiers is milling aimlessly in the market place, simmering on the verge of revolt, and my arrival amongst them on a motor-bicycle triggers off a kind of crowd scene from Euripides. A solid phalanx of odoriferous Greek soldiery forms round this strangely-mounted messenger from the gods; everybody flings his arms about and shouts; some point backwards the way I have come; others point northwards towards Philippi and Drama and draw their hands across their throats; everybody shouts at once, naturally enough in Greek. I simply repeat the word Kavalla in what I imagine is a Greek accent and point dramatically towards the east.

This crowd scene goes on without anybody getting anywhere. Finally, at the point where in the Greek theatre there would be a sound of trumpets and a clash of arms, I simply start up the engine, charge into the thick of the chorus with a roar from the exhaust, accelerate out of the town in what I take to be the direction of Kavalla, and leave the Greek army to fight it out behind me.

Kavalla was once Neapolis, the port where St. Paul landed from Samothrace on his way to Philippi—once famous for its citadel and Roman aqueduct. With the Roman aqueduct still bringing part of its water supply from Mount Pangeus, it is now a jumble of white buildings strung round the shores of two bays or inlets, a site for tobacco factories.

By the time I set out to find the consulate it is nearly dark. I walk in the middle of the street, one hand on my Colt automatic, the other on my satchel of despatches. In an alley-way between blank white walls, possibly of tobacco factories, I meet a mysterious figure and ask my way in French. The mysterious figure replies in Balkan-American, 'Straight on, Johnny, and first turn on your right.' He is a tobacco worker just back from Chicago. We have an amiable conversation about conditions in the tobacco trade, and I set out again feeling less like a character in a novel by William le Queux.

At the consulate the courtyard door is grudgingly opened by a little man in a black suit who looks like a Bulgarian deserter. He takes me to the

51

consul, apparently an Oxford undergraduate masquerading as a consul. The consul accepts my despatches, signs a receipt. The code word, 'Lobster', is solemnly reconstructed in block letters and solemnly burned. The consul then locks the despatches, unread, in his safe. 'Bumph, my dear boy, pure bumph,' he says, slamming the door. 'All these military types have the wind up!'

Disillusion, followed by dinner at a candle-lit table, beside an open window. Real china plate; much *mastic*. The little man in the black suit (in sober reality a deserter from the Bulgarian army) serves bowls of soup to sop up the *mastic*. Below the open window the surface of the harbour is dotted with the masthead lights of ships—transports packed with Greek troops. The troops sing Greek melodies, strangely harmonised, to an accompaniment of zithers. The consul says they form part of a mutinous division centered on Kavalla under General Z.; that they have decided to return to Thessaly and the girls they left behind them; that they have bribed the captains and crews of the rusty old tramps and coal boats in which they are now embarked; that, packed like herrings in a barrel, they will soon, like Odysseus, be island-dodging back towards home and beauty—with nobody fool enough to stop them; that, in short, as far as the ..... division is concerned, a typical Greek schism is under way in the harbour below, waiting for a head of steam. I tell him about the pandemonium in the market place at Pravista. He says this was part of the mutinous unrest in General Z.'s division; one faction wanting to go home, the other to stay and face the Bulgarians.

I then ask him if Madame W., at whose inn I propose to spend the night, is in fact a German spy. He says she 'goes through the motions', but that I have been stuffed with legends; apart from sentiments about the Fatherland, she is a very decent old soul, a perfectly hopeless spy; consequently, a magnificent channel for relaying false information to Berlin. He then piles Pelion on Ossa by taking me to the window and showing me a path that leads precipitously downwards to the harbour, where he keeps a motor-boat loaded with petrol and provisions. If the Bulgarians appear at the courtyard door—maybe at any moment now—he and his Bulgarian butler-cum-valet simply hop out of the window, descend the path to the harbour, and set off for the island of Thasos. Thasos lies across a narrow channel from Kavalla. From the consul's account it sounds, after several glasses of *mastic*, like the island valley of Avilion 'where falls not hail, or rain, or any snow, nor ever wind blows loudly.' Beyond that, harking back to my schoolroom *Atlas of Ancient and Classical Geography*, I remember, as through the bottom of a *mastic* glass darkly, that it was once famous for gold mines. Anyhow it now figures in the consul's mind as a pleasant retreat in time of war; Thasos *mastic*, he says, is the best *mastic* in the whole Aegean.

About midnight return, as steadily as possible, to the inn, politely known as an hotel, where General Z., a shabby little man in a drab uniform, is still at table. Through open windows comes the uproar of his troops in the harbour. At sight of me, General Z. bows coldly, looking like a commercial traveller who has had a bad day; evidently the job of commanding

52

a Greek division in these parts is bad enough without third parties butting in, even if they are only oil-stained, two-star lieutenants.

Madame W., a large stout woman with a bosom on which tea trays could repose in comfort, then takes me to her private balcony overlooking the harbour at the rear of the hotel, where we sit on iron chairs, drink coffee, and discuss the war in a mixture of French and (on my part) bad German, while the moon shines romantically on the water and Madame W. kills mosquitoes with lightning claps of her large, capable hands. Madame W.'s main points are (a) that the British army must be in a bad way if I, at my tender age, am already a full lieutenant, *schon Oberleutnant;* and (b) what do we mean by allying ourselves with those barbarians the Russians, *diese russische Barbaren*? Madame W. once lived in East Prussia and knows all about Russians; is in fact prepared to write a book about them. All this time masthead lights twinkle in the harbour below, where General Z.'s disorderly troops are still plucking zithers, packed like herrings in their rusty little coal boats, serenading their prospect of return to mainland Greece, their exit from the complications piling up in Thrace.

About 1 a.m. I get to my room, wedge the door with a chair, put my Colt automatic under the German-style pillow, fall exhausted on the bed. In the morning, Madame W.'s daughter, a Wagnerian young woman bursting with *inneres Gefühl* and already exhibiting symptoms of a moustache, gets up specially early to make my breakfast, undercharges me for my night's lodging, sees to it that the petrol tank of the Douglas is refilled free, gratis, and for nothing. Apparently I have been an honoured guest, and we all part with florid protestations about 'seeing again'; Madame W., protected by an inadequate peignoir, waving from her bedroom window.

Again the Douglas hums like a sewing-machine; the Bulgarians remain discreetly hidden behind Thucydides' mountains; the market place at Pravista is empty of Greek soldiery; and I cross the bridge at the mouth of the Struma like a tourist returning from a short holiday in Thrace. At brigade headquarters in a deserted monastery overlooking the Struma gorge I hand over the receipt for the despatches, plus the empty satchel, and am told to return to my unit. I have just enough sense not to repeat what the consul said about 'military types' as he slammed the door of his safe. At the same time I do nothing to disturb brigade headquarters' firm conviction that Madame W. is a dangerous German spy.

The camp overlooking the lake. At tea time in the straw-thatched mess hut we see white plumes rising from the clumps of elms beyond the water, as the afternoon train from Drama to Salonika slides like a mechanical snake across the tree-dotted plain. This gives us the idea of a shopping expedition to Seres. We cross the lake in a motor-boat and catch the train at a wayside station.

Seres, with its white domes and minarets, turns out to be a sort of Turkish backdrop; part still in ruins from the 1912–13 Balkan wars. In the bazaars, like a character in a Balkan thriller, we meet our friend MacC., a large hefty Scotsman, last seen in the bars and music-halls of Salonika.

MacC., wearing a Balkan sombrero, and looking more like a secret agent than a secret agent ought to look, exhorts us with much profanity to clear out of Seres at once. According to him, a Bulgarian patrol, under German officers, is already in the outer suburbs, followed by Bulgarian light artillery moving up to the lake front. We retreat, as unobtrusively as possible from the bazaars to the railway station.

At the railway station we stand about, waiting for the next train to Drama (and, presumably, Constantinople), ready to dodge into the station lavatory, imagining the insides of Bulgarian prisons, probably worse than the lavatory, which is presumably Turkish-style. Fortunately the train for Drama comes in almost on time, and we are able to use our (first-class) tickets. But MacC. was right, at any rate about the artillery; no sooner are we back on our side of the lake (the motor-boat having been hidden in the reeds), than there is a *flash-bang* from the clumps of elms on the farther shore, and shrapnel bursts, ineffectively, over marsh and stunted forest down by the water's edge.

The end of shopping expeditions to Seres.

Trains still run on the farther shore. Bulgarian artillery or no Bulgarian artillery, it is still possible to switch agents backwards and forwards from one end of the line to the other: British agents to Constantinople to find out what the Turks intend; Turkish and Bulgarian agents to Athens to ferret out the intentions of the French with their Napoleonic-sounding *l'Armée de l'Orient.**

In the evening we sit in our straw-thatched fox-hole, drinking whiskey, swatting mosquitoes, playing the gramophone, looking out across the lake and the valley to the steep wall of the Rhodope mountains in Bulgaria. In the nostalgic moment of the evening light, when the violet-tinted Rhodopes loom like a backcloth from *The Chocolate Soldier*, the favourite record is the 'Hindu Song' from *Sadko*—the right music for this meeting place of Europe and Asia, for the malarial marshes down by the lake, the stunted forest ,the domes and minarets of Seres, the violet wall of the Rhodopes.

Up there to the north-east, somewhere behind the mountains, the lights of Budapest and Vienna will just be flickering on—there are cafés, restaurants, theatres, opera houses, bookshops, symphony orchestras, women. Nevertheless, our company commander is philosophic. He gets *Land and Water* by post—when it isn't sunk on the way—follows Hilaire Belloc's war maps, black arrows and all. His point is that by sitting here staring at Lake Tahinos and the Rhodopes we have escaped the slaughter at Gallipoli and the Somme.

Action at the Angista river, north-east of Tahinos. A group of men in dark uniforms stand in a patch of maize on high ground beyond the river We examine them through field-glasses; they examine us in return. MacC.

*That is, if *l'Armée de l'Orient* ever had any intention beyond keeping General Sarrail out of France. For ironic sidelights from Athens, see Sir Compton Mackenzie's *Greek Memories*, more specifically *The Three Couriers*.

54

was right about the German officers; amongst the dark-uniformed group stands a taller figure in field-grey.

The conference in the maize field breaks up; Bulgarian infantry stream down the hillside, closing fan-wise on the bridge, their curiously-shaped caps with downward-pointing visors visible above the standing corn. We move forward to give covering fire; a lieutenant of yeomanry, stripped to shirt and breeches, dashes in at close range, runs out onto the bridge under fire, empties a petrol tin, throws down a lighted match, and runs for his life, dodging like a rabbit.

The bridge roars up in flames; we open rapid fire on the maize field beyond; the mountain guns bark, pumping out shrapnel shells that burst with sounds like tearing calico over the smoke-and flame-erupting bridge and the standing corn. Lines of Bulgarian caps appear at intervals, moving above the standing corn like targets at a fun fair. The air cracks and stings, as if full of hornets.

Whistles blow from the high ground behind us, signals to retire. I discover, when the excitement is over, that I have been hit on the elbow, either by a ricochet or a stone kicked up by a bullet. We turn for home, with one man slightly wounded; smoke from the bridge behind us. The Bulgarians, wary of the mountain guns, stay hidden in maize fields beyond the Angista. But all the way back to the bridge at the mouth of the Struma we are pursued by a comic-opera chorus of *comitadjis* who stream parallel with us, just out of range, along the heights of Perim Dagh, pausing every now and then to fire volleys from ancient, comic-opera rifles—all without the slightest effect except noise, waste of ammunition, and warlike echoes from rocky gorges on the mountainside.

The gunners, having used most of *their* ammunition, don't even bother to give them a spray of shrapnel in return, and no doubt they all go home to their wives and children, well-satisfied with their afternoon's entertainment—*l'après-midi d'un comitadji* and possibly their first outing since the Balkan wars of 1912–13.

Note: the Turkish-named Perim Dagh on which they were letting off their *feux de joie* was the same, history-echoing mountain where Thucydides had his gold mines.

Storks. Down in the stunted forest by the lake shore we encounter an old man, Turkish, Greek, or, as so often happens in Macedonia, a nameless mixture. How he got there, where he comes from, nobody knows. He is just suddenly *there*, materialising from the stunted trees, old, withered, no longer interested in wars or rumours of wars—not even in the *flash-bang* of Bulgarian artillery; too old to be interested in anything except the growth of crops, the wild fowl on the lake, the migration of storks.

He points across the lake. Over there, he tells us through our interpreter, is the golden bowl of Macedonia; over there, especially in the neighbourhood of Seres, everything, including maize and tobacco, springs up by magic—like the magic beans in *Jack and the Beanstalk*. Likewise the lake teems with wildfowl. Then he comes to the storks. To-morrow the storks will arrive from the north. He points across Tahinos and waves his arm northwards, in the direction of Hungary, Rumania, Russia, the Black Sea delta of the Danube. How does he know they will come to-morrow? Because they have always come to-morrow. And what happens when they come? Much gesticulation, violent pantomime, gestures imitating storks in flight. Apparently they rest overnight round the lake. Then, the following day, they set out again, flying in massed formation, first over the Bosphorus, then south to Africa.

And it all happens as the old man says. Next day storks arrive in regiments from the north—the air is white with them—thousands of fairy-tale ghosts, circling, settling on tree-tops—drifting like a snowstorm round the lake. Next morning they rise, circling slowly. Then at a certain height, as if at a secret signal, they all turn together and head for the Helles-pont. Apparently they have been arriving at this rendezvous at Lake Tahinos for thousands of years, drifting south from the Danube countries, possibly before the coins we dug up at Amphipolis were minted, or Xerxes set out for Salamis.

Thirst like a ship's furnace. Beyond a tree-shaded hospital tent, a sound of breakers. I am carried on a stretcher across a sandy beach, hoisted to the deck of a lighter. The lighter bobs like a cork in the breakers. Prospects for mortuary, right and left, each with its sun-helmet tilted over its eyes. Close inshore, a hospital ship, dazzlingly white, rides the dark blue waters of the gulf like a sea-gull.

A white-painted cabin. Visions of waterfalls descending through wooded Inishowen glens from steep green Inishowen mountains, eliminating sandy wastes where they carried corpses from Amphipolis. Engines beat. Violet cone of Athos framed in porthole. Enter white-coated figure with potion in glass. Violet cone of Athos moves across porthole, vanishes. Thirst like ship's furnace. Visions of waterfalls, wooded glens, slate-green loughs.

Night. . . .

A Loud Explosion in Throgmorton Street

The restaurant was underground, at the back of the Bank of England.
A steep flight of stairs led down to a sort of underground aquarium,
garishly lighted, with revolving glass doors. We always entered in the
same order: my uncle first, small, choleric, with a bristly white walrus
moustache stained and frizzled by cigarette smoke, benign blue eyes behind
gold-rimmed spectacles, a blue suit, sudden fits of violent rage, the kindest
heart in the world, and a pantomime backdrop of Victorian scenery. Once
through the revolving glass door in the main aquarium, where a frieze of
plaster goddesses (early J. Lyons & Co) gazed down through a sea of
tobacco smoke, a babel of Throgmorton Street speculation and a clatter of
cutlery, on the mingled top hats and shining bald heads of the worshippers
of Mammon, we swam forward more purposively, with confident fin
strokes. We were looking for Alice, a shrimp of a Cockney waitress.

'Any seats to-day, Alice?' my uncle would roar at her when at last we
had located her flashing to and fro in an outlying cave or grotto of the
aquarium. He sounded like a small kindly sea-lion demanding a herring.

And Alice, who adored my uncle (they were two of a kind, the small and
the valiant), in the act of wiping spotless knives and forks on her spotless
apron and taking orders from top-hatted or bald-headed denizens of the
grotto for, say, a *vol-au-vent de Toulouse*, a lobster salad, and three pints of
bitter would reply after a lightning survey of her apparently sub-aqueous
dominion:

'Yessir, there's two gentlemen just a-going.'

Whereupon, whether the gentlemen knew they were just a-going or not,
they were evicted by bills slapped beside their coffee cups. Whereupon they
disappeared, top hats, bald pates, Eversharp pencils and all, through the
revolving glass door to play with their Rio Tintos and their Argentine
railway trains all afternoon, safely out of Alice's way; having, according to
the custom of the grotto, first secreted shillings, even—if markets were
'buoyant'—florins under cups and saucers. They knew, we knew, everybody knew that the more beneficent the silver collection Alice could
compress into one crowded hour of Throgmorton Street gastronomic
life, the better for what were generally understood to be her somewhat
complicated domestic arrangements.

Then, once seated in the underwater grotto, safe from the ebb and flow
of the main aquarium, the ritual began. Would it be two tenderloin
steaks (one medium, one slightly underdone), two portions of fried potatoes,
one portion of spinach, a braised onion, two bottles of Guinness, an
ordinary roll, and a crescent roll? Or would my uncle, abandoning
England's green and pleasant land (as interpreted by J. Lyons & Co),
plunge head-first over the ramparts of the New Jerusalem and take a little
fish? Alice, moistening her pencil with the tip of her tongue, was all for

the fish; her unspoken verdict being that my uncle ate too heartily for a man of his age and was in danger of apoplexy. And usually Alice had her way, chalking up to herself credit for at least some of the few occasions on which my uncle took advice from anybody.

So the ritual continued. We descended to the tank, searched for and found Alice in her grotto. All this time my uncle—barking like a sea-lion behind whose turn the management had let down the wrong scenery—was convinced that the Empire was hell-bent for ruin, lurching downhill with the brakes off and a bunch of congenital idiots in the front seat; the word Empire in this connection denoting spaces coloured bright red on the map, not his theatre of former terpsichorean triumphs in Leicester Square. The imperial nadir, the all-time low, came with the Irish Treaty of December 1921. My uncle's views were simple—shoot the lot: just a series of short, sharp explosions, and, hey presto, the Irish question would be wiped off the blackboard. Encompassed by English stockbrokers with striped trousers and glittering Eversharp pencils, he would fluff out his tobacco-stained white moustache and, by way of demonstration, bang the table—eliminating by table-banging gunfire not only the entire Irish nation, but Lloyd George, Birkenhead, Churchill and Company, together with a list of lesser devils from the inferno of his imagination; all looking very like themselves in the pages of *Punch*, all condemned to outer darkness, all consigned to the flames of his Victorian political hell. He was, he said, Irish himself; nevertheless, he would 'shoot the lot'; whereupon he banged so explosively that the English stockbrokers imprisoned with us in the grotto, started looking for their hats.

'Traitors, sir,' he roared, 'nothing but a pack of traitors!'

At which point, in spite of frantic signals from Alice, I swung down off my trapeze, and joined in the act.

'Traitors to whom?' I shouted, and banged just as loudly as he had, so firmly that Guinness frothed over on the tablecloth; the tablecloth, not the Guinness, of our own manufacture. This produced a sensation. The stockbrokers stopped looking for their hats and gazed longingly towards the revolving glass door. Any minute now there would be cracked skulls and police whistles; that is, unless Fleet Street had been cooking the books.

'Traitors to their King and country, sir!' roared my uncle, going up again like an explosion in a quarry.

'What king and what country?' I roared back. 'Did ye ever,' I demanded, remembering something seen in a newspaper, 'did ye ever hear of the rights of democracies and small nations?'

'Blatherskites,' roared my uncle, gold-rimmed spectacles glittering, walrus moustache bristling, prepared to defend the Empire to the last gold bar in its vaults across Throgmorton Street.

After that, in a momentary lull, while both sides were bringing up more ammunition, and the upsurge of Guinness had subsided, one of the imprisoned stockbrokers, a particularly glossy specimen, intervened.

'What about Land Purchase?' he said, his top hat in position, ready for instant flight. The idea was to create diversion before the belligerent Irish started heaving glass and cutlery. But it got nowhere. My uncle, vaguely aware of batteries firing from unexpected positions, turned on the stockbroker.

'Shoot the lot, sir!' he roared, blue eyes blazing behind gold-rimmed spectacles. This was a private war and the English had better keep out. Indeed, so concentrated was he on the English front, that he ignored my somewhat irrelevant interjection from the rear: 'Did ye ever see a gun go off in your life?'

'Blatherskites!' roared my uncle in a sort of *nunc dimittis*, a final shrapnel-burst designed to flatten the lot, English stockbrokers and Irish nephews alike.

And that was that. Having fired his last ritual salvo, my uncle rose with great dignity, sweeping spoons and forks off the table in the process. I helped him on with his overcoat, and, leaving the English to clear up the battlefield behind us, we swept affably out through the main aquarium, past the ranks of Tuscany and the astonished worshippers of Mammon. Looking back from the revolving glass door into the apparently underwater *caves du Vatican*, before I helped my uncle up the staircase towards the Vatican itself, that is (genuflections all round) towards the Bank of England, the last thing I saw was Alice shaking her head at me in reproof. Her prognosis was, no doubt, an apoplectic fit. But she needn't have worried. My uncle, taking his Victorian scenery with him, fluffing out his tobacco-stained white moustache, bearing his rolled umbrella like a Guards' officer on parade, started out past the back of the Bank towards Cheapside and his skylight-illuminated cubbyhole as if halibut, plaice, lobster salad, even delicious platefuls of whitebait garnished with lemon, were the last things he had in mind. And avoiding it as a no-man's-land bursting with booby-traps and trip-wire mine-fields, we never mentioned the Irish Treaty again.

Two Irish Interiors

I

THE LAMP OF VIRGIL

The Irish dusk falls, dimming the miraculous blues of the Bog of Allen; the tint of distant Slieve Bloom deepens to purple; illuminated by the headlights the roads suddenly switch to corridors of vivid green. Away beyond the boggy plain the last flare of sunset fades over the Atlantic. A right-angled turn between gate posts, past a blind, crouching gate-lodge; the headlights eat up a narrow, winding drive to where a white-painted gate shuts off the inner gardens from the cattle up to their bellies in the lush grass of the paddock. A final crunching of gravel and we pull up before a square Georgian mansion with a magnificient pillared portico, a jewel of a springing fanlight over its hall-door.

A bell jangles in the basement, searching empty kitchens, larders, wine cellars. With a rattle of bolts the host unlocks the massive outer door, fortification for another siege of Derry. Then sherry and biscuits in a square, book-lined study off a white-painted hall, a room so lofty that the light from the single oil-lamp is lost in the shadows of the richly-corniced ceiling. Our host shows us the vast drawing-room; strikes matches to exhibit a gem of an Adam fireplace. His riding breeches are shabby, his tweed jacket leather-patched at the elbows, but every syllable of his deep, vital voice resurrects echoes from Berkeley and Swift; overtones from the Irish eighteenth century; murmurs from the fountains of Greece and Rome.

A grandfather clock strikes ten from a turn in the winding Georgian staircase and we are off into the night. A shaft of lamplight shines from the study into the yew-protected peace of the inner gardens, lights up the white gate where, under a yellow summer moon, the cattle stand up to their bellies in the lush grass of the paddock. It is the lamp of Virgil, the light of golden Italian summers, still shining through the turmoil of two thousand years—reflected from a lamp-lit Irish study where, against a background of Radio Eireann *ceilidhe* music from the kitchen, dog-eared editions of the Latin poets still proclaim the grandeur that was Rome, wafting it, along with a reek of turf smoke, to the cattle in the paddock and the Irish summer night.

II

LIKE A PAGE FROM *War and Peace*

Lough Neagh flung itself in white-capped breakers, apparently surrounding the promontory on which the house was built. A weed-grown path led by the water's edge, past deserted kitchen gardens, past colonnades of sagging glasshouses, to a gravelled sweep before the front-door. A man whom I took to be a steward was standing on the steps, surveying riotous flower-beds and leaf-strewn lawns.

I asked for his master. In London. They were all in London. The steward unlocked the front-door. A vast crystalline chandelier, shrouded in linen, dominated the hall. At intervals in the white-painted, winding staircase were recesses filled with valuable china. The steward caught me eyeing the chandelier. It hung there like a stalactite, glittering through the chinks in its shroud.

'That chandelier came from Portugal, sir.'

'Indeed.'

'Yes, sir. The Duke of Wellington, sir.'

He flung open a door leading from the hall. 'And this is the drawing-room, sir.'

A portrait by Reynolds hung over the white marble mantelpiece opposite the great bow window with its distant views of water and trees. The inland sea of Lough Neagh, apparently surrounding the house, filled the room with subdued roaring.

'Did he sit here much?'

'He did, sir, before his son was killed in the war.'

'Was that his only son?'

'Yes, sir.'

'What regiment?'

'The Irish Guards, sir—same as his father. This is his picture.'

From the drawer of a Sheraton writing-table he produced a miniature, obviously painted from a photograph. It showed a vacuous, blue-eyed young man with a wisp of corn-coloured moustache, tightly buttoned in a scarlet tunic and clasping an enormous bearskin.

'Where was he killed?'

'Givenchy, sir.'

'Were you there when it happened?'

'Yes, sir. I was his servant.'

He replaced the miniature in the drawer and led the way from the room. We tramped religiously up and down empty, echoing staircases, through empty, echoing rooms, along empty white-painted passages. It was like being back-stage in a theatre when the play was ended.

Back in the hall, he stood to attention under the shrouded chandelier.

'Would you like to see the stables, sir?'

'Not to-day.' More belated scenes from Somerville and Ross—rats scurrying where ancient dog-carts had been shifted to make room for vintage Daimlers.

Beyond the pillars of the portico, dusk was falling. A blackbird, sheltered from the wind, raised a tentative chuckle from the laurels. In the background the roaring of the lough had risen in volume.

'Well, good-bye, steward!'

'Good-bye, sir. Come again.'

'Some day.'

Some day if the house was still standing. Behind it, half-hidden by a plantation of beeches, rose the exquisite clock-tower of the stables; withered leaves detached themselves; floated serenely, as if they had all the time in the world, past the clock-face. In the background, submerged in its orchestra-pit, the lough roared incessantly, rumbling and grumbling like a distant artillery duel in Flanders. Under the stormy Antrim sky, with the young Guardsman in the scarlet tunic locked in the drawer of the Sheraton writing-table—immobilised in that vast, empty drawing-room with the white marble mantelpiece, the portrait by Reynolds, and the shallow Georgian bow-window with its wide views of water and trees—it was like a page from *War and Peace*, translated and set on the shore of an Irish lough, under a threatening Irish sky.

Fragments After Reading Ulysses

I

A GOOD BOOZE-UP AT JAMMET'S

That evening the Wicklow hills stood up like a steep blue barrier from the sea. Erin, green gem of silver sea. Breathes there a man? Suburban stations —boat train from Dun Laoghaire (Kingstown). Martello towers, snot-green sea. More flickering suburban stations. Booterstown, nasty mouthful for Gaels. Banquet halls deserted. (Black-faced poster of Mr. Eugene Stratton, music-hall voice singing, 'Does yer mother know ye're out?'). Snot-green. *Thalatta! Thalatta!* Our great sweet mother the snot-green (silver?) sea. Between us and Europe, *Deo gratias.* Also, thanks be (Protestant) God, the snot-green (silver) English Channel.

Back of stand at Lansdowne Road. Foreign games. Gasometers, Homeric wine-vats, with, floating against untidy Irish sky, gigantic Dublin sea-gulls, raucous, ready at drop of hat with shattering Dublin comment. Snot green, more snot than green. Invades Ringsend, laps round wine-vat gasometers. Grinding points, station. Golden sunlight smirches dirt yellow.

O Irish summer eve!

Westland Row, station and thoroughfare. Oscar Wilde first saw light. No plaque, raucous sea-gulls. Dublin, still dear, not quite so dirty. Lincoln Place, now thank we all our Mahaffys. Rational iron railings, green lawns (battle of Rorke's Drift nearly lost on), melancholy Georgian splendour—level golden sunlight from behind encircling mountains. Silence, everybody dead. Like Troy. Archaeologists still uncovering site, American voices reading check-lists. Leopold Bloom still eating kidney for breakfast (check), Gerty MacDowell (check) still exhibiting *Home Chat* drawers on Sandymount strand (check).

Remembering Sion. (Check). *Clip-clop* of jaunting-cars, are ye there Blazes Boylan, are ye there? Miss Douce (bronze by gold) still fingering cool porcelain of priapic beer-pull. Bars—bars with mahogany counters bottles reflected in mirrors between mirrors, adenoidal Dublin voices dismissing present, any present, as bad joke. *Old Mary Ann, she didn't give a damn.* Fabulous taverns (*sunt lacrimae*), throaty tenors raised (illegally) in Italian arias, marble counters swimming with porter, barrels of Galway oysters, red-plush alcoves (bronze by gold) devoted to malt rather than *la femme* or *l'amour*, clattering of viceregal cavalry steely-ringing, re-echoing from mournful red of flat-faced Georgian house fronts, see pages of *Ulysses.* A man's city, a sea-gull's city. O great mother the scrotum-tightening sea. *O genius loci* in whose shadow tomb-rat typewriters tap!

'A large Jameson, please!' City of drink and dreams, conversation and disillusionment. Privileged interior *chez* Jammet. White tablecloths, bottles. Academic backdrop, green lawns, Mahaffy-Wilde iron railings. As if by arrangement Mahaffy-Wilde cabs drift past. Expect wheels go backwards, but maybe that's in films, not against Trinity railings. Or have cabs something to do with Berkeley—merely *ideas* of cabs? Anyhow, nothing changed since Thackeray's *Irish Sketch Book:* same old waiters, same atmosphere of Queen Victoria ascending throne. Enchantment hangs upon the scene, drips heavily through the air like honey—gilds M. Jammet's Second Empire *decor*, marble pillars and all. Dressed crab, sole Colbert, Montrachet. Should be music by Offenbach, chorus of arthritic waiters in black ties, early Victorian dress suits.

'A large Hennessy's Three Star.' Darkness, lamps on semi-republican lamp standards leap into radiance. *Old Mary Anne she didn't give a damn.* Scrannel sounds of Dalkey trams whining round corner into Nassau street, *pianissimo, rallentando, fortissimo*—signature tune of Edwardian Dublin. Any mention in Good Book? Must look up Sylvia Beach authorised version, gospel according *transition. Ut implerentur scripturae.* Incidentally, did your man ever dine in Jammet's? American tomb-rats forward to rattle tomb-rat typewriters.

Hennessy till cows come home. Alternatively, till Berkeleyan cabs disappear. Shade of despised and rejected Bloom behind pillar, primed with Davy Byrne's burgundy (by the glass). Swim out back entrance to Grafton Street. Plate glass jewellers, statues of Goldsmith and Burke, black Protestant front of Trinity, O'Connell (*ci-devant* Carlisle) bridge over which in famous *Irish Times* misprint Her Majesty pissed slowly. Hibernian metropolis, heart of. Citizens discuss tragedy. 'Dey found him in de batroom wid his troat cut.' Sad. Basement thumping of *Irish Times* and *Independent*. Prominent citizen. Words GOLD FLAKE wriggle, upside down, in Liffey. Remember contact Bertie Smyllie Palace bar. Senatorial pillars Bank of Ireland illuminated street lamps. Lights to lighten our darkness.

Liffey, by the odorous waters of. The harp that once. Twice, counting Zurich, Paris. O'Connell street glittering Broadway—Word made electric. Disapproval Gaelic League—'small body mourners following the Erse.' Stuffed shirts stuffing steaks behind plate-glass. Descendants of royal Irish kings my royal Irish arse. Young women with plastic rain-coats, eye shadow. Whoors. No place Daedalus. Turn aside, brood Bachelor's Walk. Glasnevin. Black plumes, marble angels, stage-property round tower. Wolf hounds next. Not till my country takes its place. WITH UNFEIGN-ED REGRET ANNOUNCE DISSOLUTION PROMINENT DUBLIN BURGESS. Thump. Poor Paddy Dignam. Thump. Maybe (thump) he knows better now. Black plumes, marble angels, rats sliding under glass-covers. Last round, gentlemen, plee-as. American tomb-rats, please copy. GOLD FLAKE adrift in Liffey. Hennessy fades. WITH UNFEIGNED REGRET ANNOUNCE DISSOLUTION DRESSED CRAB SOLE COLBERT MONTRACHET. En route glass-topped artificial flowers on Black Mountain. Belfast *News-Letter*, American tomb-rats, please copy. No hand-grenades or Molotov cocktails by request!

II

JAMES JOYCE AT THE BELFAST OPERA HOUSE

Mammoth Turkish bath, Great Victoria Street. Proscenium curtains part. Seats slam. Veil of temple illuminated Sacred scriptures—bar parlours, bookies, shiny motor-cars. House lights up. Rococo tank fitted with red-plush stalls for drowning occupants. Gilt elephants, rococo gilt fronts of boxes, fat-bottomed goddesses on ceiling. 'Not tonight, Josephine!' Haze of tobacco smoke. Blue-remembered from last week. Orchestra swims out from grotto under stage, saws piece off *Merry Wives of Windsor*, scuttles back to grotto.

Curtain rises jerkily. Reveals Belfast sceneshifters' idea of bedroom in English country house. No use showing bedroom in Irish country house. Nothing doing except sleep. English have word for it. Religious silence. In bedroom, against background of twin beds by (see programme) well-known furnishing firm in Royal Avenue, gentleman in red dressing-gown informs lady in blue dressing-gown (presumably wife) that Jewish gentleman down corridor just had thousand pounds pinched from under pillow while having bath.

Sensation in stalls. Here beginneth first lesson. Having shaken moth-balls out of blue suits, crammed down early high teas, value for money. Better than Agatha Christie. Twin beds, English accents, dressing-gowns, spot of larceny. Night out for Belfast suburbs. Only wants fornication and adultery, holy writ of English leg-papers made flesh in glare of footlights, gospel according *Tatler-Sketch*. Now thank we all our Anglo-Saxon (Unionist) gods!

Smoke from Anglo-Saxon altars. Twin beds to West End Club—club pronounced in Anglo-Saxon, with genuflections and capital 'C'. Scarlet major-generals, prep-school vocabularies, lords with eyeglasses, waterfall ties. Tinkling of English mass bells. Reverent hush ascends to blowsy classical goddesses on ceiling, by-passing gilt elephants on front of boxes. *Favete linguis.* Pray silence for representatives of Moss Bros. From mumblings of lords, major-generals we gather dashing young officer (bugle calls, faint sounds of military band) who occupied room next to Jewish gentleman in country house also member of (genuflections) Club. Bad show. Probably swiped thousand-pound lolly. Scarlet major-generals, lords, fumble simultaneously with eyeglasses and English language. Pretty rotten. After all, you can't (or rather, seeing this is the West End, 'carn't') have a fella in Club who . . .

Quite. All prostrate towards Royal Enclosure at Ascot. Lords mono-syllabic to point of blowing up. Interval. Proscenium curtains swish. House lights reveal Belfast Grand Opera House (Music, Drama, Cirque) as Victorian period piece under water, many waters, with effect of rococo Turkish bath or aquarium. Wavering in tank, full fathom five, goddesses on ceiling; Unionist blue suits in stalls; elephants on gilded front of boxes (sunken treasure); Councillor X in front row of dress (blue suit) circle. Replete with racing results from *Belfast Telegraph* (6th edition), orchestra regurgitates from grotto under stage to saw chunks off *Chu-Chin-Chow*. Rush for licensed grotto off main tank. Sodden ten-shilling notes on counter. Uproar. Did ye hear the one about? Oh to be in London W. Harlots cry from street to street. French lessons in every stationer's window.

Adjust minds before rejoining ladies (ladies is word), waiting, chocolates suspended, in red-plush stalls. Curtain rises on apartment of dashing young officer (clash of small arms, military band) in Mayfair. Lantern slides from Holy Land: good tidings of great joy for Unionist blue suits. Unfortunately dashing young officer (clash of small arms, military band) is struggling along with hardly racehorse to name, witness towering velvet curtains, spindly gilt chairs, enormous crystal chandelier left over from

66

last week, hoisted by Opera House scene-shifters in intervals of reading *Belfast Telegraph* (6th edition) and dreaming about French lessons as advertised in London.

In light of chandelier, dashing young officer's wife, looking like advertisement from *Country Life*, all tweeds, pearls, and prominent teeth, informs similar advertisement from *Lady*, tweeds, costume jewellery, still more prominent teeth, that she has just tried telephone him but (sensation) he *isn't at Tattersall's and he isn't at* (genuflections) *the Club*. Question: what would fella be up to if he wasn't at Tattersall's and he wasn't at (genuflections) the Club? Obviously no good. If no pheasants (*hibernice, peasants*) and things shoot at, odds on shoots self in study furnished with sporting prints, Debrett, bound volumes of *Field*. Whereupon inspector of police, bowler hat in hand, enormous boots at attention under Buckingham Palace chandelier, sound like frustrated squib. Talk about Ibsen. Red curtains swish. Orchestra surfaces for synoptic version God Save King. O Queen Mary save us. As long as *Sketch-Tatler* lords tinkle eyeglasses in Opera House, all well in Belfast suburbs, bar Falls. O fire curtain descend between us and 1960. O Apollo standing on one leg at entrance holding up electric light. O shade of William III. O glimpse of Paradise. O Galsworthy's Kensington through bottom of Bush Liqueur glass darkly. O King Edward intervene for us!

Notes Taken on the Eve of War

I

An hotel lounge. Four old ladies knit in time to wireless music, like priestesses in a temple. Outside the windows, forest, then the snot-green of Carlingford Lough. Beyond the green lough, dim blue mountains.

When the music stops, the clock will strike, the wand will wave; like victims of a magician's act on the music-halls, the old ladies will turn into faded photographs from Victorian albums, withered flowers pressed between the pages of Lord Tennyson's *Maud*, melodies whispered to Chinese-lantern-lit conservatories by Victorian violins. But as long as the wireless-set ladles out extracts from *The Geisha* (or is it *San Toy*?), then the scenery of today remains, stretching back for the old ladies beyond their flashing-needles into the day-before-yesterday—back beyond August 1914 when the lights went out in Europe and waltz-time had to stop; back beyond Edward VII and the Gaiety girls to long draughty corridors lined with ghastly marble statues of Victorian statesmen; back to tartan-curtained boudoirs at Balmoral and the strictly-edited memoirs of the Good Queen.

Meanwhile the magician waits in the wings. As long as wireless goes on distributing cream-cakes of Victorian sentiment, sugar-plums like Tosti's *Goodbye* and the *Indian Love Lyrics*, so long the supernumerary old ladies, still industriously knitting, remain unconscious of sunken ice; unconscious the stage-set of the present is about to plunge, as the *Titanic* plunged, down into ice-cold darkness, carrying with it the arts, crafts, sentiments of a world that was.

Then the thing happens. The wireless slithers to a stop: old ladies halt knitting needles by numbers. Nobody moves or speaks. Beyond the windows, the snot-green, mirror-like lough, the green-reflected mountainsides steeped in golden sunlight, the spinach-slabs of forestry, the rock bastions of Mourne, loom more unreal than ever, like a stage-set in *Swan Lake*, waiting for the entrance of the evil magician unfolding stagey black-out wings. Silence. An interval before the clock strikes. Then with preliminary whirrings of weights and chains, an unctuous voice from London announces that the Munich conference has ended in agreement, that life in the Bavarian Alps is once more *couleur de rose*.

La vie en rose resumes on the forested shores of Carlingford Lough. Teacups tinkle. Old ladies knit as if switched on again. It had all been a false alarm; the wand was never waved; the clock, instead of striking, merely stuttered; the evil magician, folding stagey black wings, disappeared behind Bavarian mountains. Like mice re-emerging from the wainscoting, all slip back into safe suburban slots—back to tea-time tinklings from *The Geisha;* back to smut from the circulating libraries; back to English leg-papers made flesh at the Belfast Opera House; clockwork adultery simulated beneath the gilt fronts of empty, lorgnette-presuming stage-boxes.

For a moment, threatening the clockwork, back-numbering even smutty novels and *Gone With the Wind*, the grinning skeleton of reality in Europe beckoned at the door of our provincial Irish woodshed. Then drops and lotions from the B.B.C. faded the frosty spectacle beyond the hotel windows where in the golden haze of a glorious September afternoon, against the forested background of dark-blue Carlingford mountains, there had glimmered for a moment, like icebergs on a summer sea, the ghosts of the new Ice Age in Europe, the skeleton horsemen of the now-postponed Apocalypse, the ghastly arc-lit abattoirs of the Third Reich, the greasily-smoking shimneys of Auschwitz, and all the horrors still to come.

II

Beneath the looming bulk of Notre Dame. A small restaurant sunk in a tree-shaded *place* on the *Île de la Cité*. Stirred by faint breezes from the Seine, the black beard of the Anatole France character at the table on the pavement outside undulates like seaweed in an inlet of the ocean. Inside, behind firmly-shut plate-glass windows, not a breath; the face of the dark, five-o'clock shadow young Frenchman the other side of our wine-stained marble-top table is covered with a thin layer of sweat. And no wonder; he is simultaneously in love and eating; proper occupations for the French.

Every now and then, in intervals of sweat-wiping, he lays down his fork, pokes with his finger tips at the shoulder muscles of the young woman beside him with a gesture like that of a poulterer testing the plumpness of an expensive chicken; gazes ardent adoration into shallow blue eyes. She is *petite*, blonde, with an elaborate high-piled coiffure; has every appearance of impenetrable stupidity; wears high-heeled boots that lace over her

68

plump calves; is in fact the spitting image of plump-calved young women who rode flaming bicycles in trick turns on Edwardian music-halls. But even in 1939, with Hitler raving beyond the Rhine, she is his Melisande, his Heloise, if you like, his Helen of Troy. Hers is the face that launched the *Île de France*, the *Normandie*, the battle cruiser *Strasbourg*, all rolled into one. In spite of uproar in Bavarian cellars, in spite of lofty thunder clouds beyond the Vosges, the well-known human race is still renewing itself with love, food, wine, hope for the future, just as it must have done two thousand years ago upon the plains of Troy.

Outside the window, the tall, thin, distinguished character from an Anatole France novel speaks to the plain, dumpy little woman at his table. Perhaps he asked her to pass the mustard; if this *were* an Anatole France novel, I would say his wife. Lights spring up in the windows of the tall, shuttered houses beyond the *place*—shuttered facades still brooding over 1870 and the siege of Paris. The green twilight under the shade trees that Harpignies might have painted deepens into night. Some one switches on the lights in the restaurant; the din of conversation, the clatter of crockery, rise in a deafening crescendo. The dark young Frenchman and his blonde *bicycliste* make no attempt to deal with the uproar. They simply hold hands under the table and gaze at one another like characters in Flaubert's *Salammbô*, alone in the Sahara—bed, or more fittingly, a couch, scenery for the next act. The middle-aged Frenchwoman with the moustache puts more Vichy water in her wine. The young Englishman beyond her again reads his Tauchnitz with exasperated concentration—this noisy, eating, drinking, love-making world is getting on his languid nerves. In addition, he has quarelled with his equally languid, suede-shoed friend at the same table, and the pair of them are now regarding one another with malign distaste, like two cats shut in a basket and getting ready to fight.

The twilight deepens under the shade trees. More lights spring up in the shuttered houses brooding over 1870. Inside the restaurant, like passengers in a liner forgetting the hungry ocean in the commotion of the lounge, we plunge about in the present—fascinated by the uproar, the clatter of crockery, the popping of corks, reassured by our vociferous reflections in fly-blown mirrors—while all the time remote from the uproar, from the dark young Frenchman testing the plumpness of his expensive chicken, the black-moustached Frenchwoman putting Vichy water in her wine, the bored young Englishman reading his Tauchnitz—away beyond the roof-tops of Paris, the dark, wooded heights of the Vosges, the grape-bloom valley of the Rhine, the evil magician has already waved his wand, and German tanks are massing on the Polish frontier.

Sketches from War-Time Belfast

I

Belfast docks, summer morning. Pillars of smoke from the shipyards, like pillars from war-time Troy. A dockside crane, its framework wrenched and twisted, lies overturned, its jib pointing derisively to the green, dawn-lit hills of Down. A ship, its upperworks pitted by bomb splinters, leans drunkenly against a quay, unnaturally embracing this outpost in the Atlantic, this island of saints and scholars.

No sound from red-brick factories under the Black Mountain; no ships' sirens re-echoing from the sullen Cave Hill; no squat red tramcars sliding over the Queen's Bridge festooned with shipyard workers—just the mockery of sea-gulls screaming round the shipyard gantries, wheeling over tell-tale oil patches in the ship channel—wheeling, screaming as they may still be wheeling and screaming long after the oil patches have cleared from the channel, green grass has smothered the launching-slips, and man accompanied by his mechanical monsters has vanished from the scene.

II

Gramophone concert in a restaurant lit by shaded table-lamps. Beyond black-out curtains, processions of blue-lit tramcars in High Street, crammed with passengers like mutton stacked in blue-lit refrigerators.

Overture to *The Barber of Seville*. Conducted by Toscannini. Songs by Grieg, sung by Kirsten Flagstad—ice floes in the blue waters of a fiord. Then, against an uproar of fire-engines in High Street, the crystal clarity of Mozart, conjuring up crystal-lustred salons in Vienna; not even the bombers flying high over the fire-sprinkled city can obliterate the sound tracks from the backs of our minds. Bonn, Salzburg, Vienna: if only a stack of records remains, we can re-draw the map of Europe, the world before the Nazis.

Mozart is followed by sparkling cascades from a Chopin fantasy. Now, banishing black-out curtains and shaded tablelamps, we are in dark green forest, turrets of medieval castles rising above tree-tops—the flame of romanticism still burning in the heart of Europe. We soar inwards from our outpost in the Atlantic, from twisted steelwork, burnt-out factories, to dark green forests of Poland—it is as if someone had suddenly switched on a glittering chandelier, as if by the light of it some incredibly beautiful ballet, some piece of sugar-plum deliciousness like *Swan Lake* or *Les Sylphides*, with snow-white ballerinas and conventional fir-trees in the background, is performing itself against the darkness of the brain—bringing the same sense of wonder, of heightened human dignity, Nijinski used to bring when he suddenly leapt, soared, and seemed to hang suspended in *The Spectre of the Rose*.

Last, as late night final, with blue-lit tramcars still transporting frozen mutton, Bach's Toccata and Fugue in D Minor, orchestral version by Stowkowski, with the musicians raining out long rounded bars of violin and cello tone—honey stored against the winter of civilisation. So much honey that the darkened restaurant suddenly shines with the lighted windows of ruined castles on the Rhine; the dying Goethe calls for still more light; lilac blooms again in Heidelberg *wie einst im Mai*; the lamps of pre-1914 Germany are switched on, twinkling along the Rhine and the

Neckar; and drowned by the trumpets of that last crashing crescendo, the clamour of fire-engines in High Street, the trams transporting citizens like frozen meat in an abattoir, the monotonous throbbing of internal combustion engines beyond fire-reflecting Irish clouds, all fade and diminish like the phantasmagoria of a madman's dream.

III

Beyond plate-glass windows, grey rain-washed waters of Belfast Lough, green rain-washed mountains of Antrim. Somebody switches on the gilt chandelier, substituting mechanical glitter for Irish literary twilight. The glitter is reflected in rows of whiskey bottles on the Sheraton sideboard, Irish regiments lined up in front, backed by equally aristocratic relations from remote Highland glens; a clear amber-coloured gathering of the clans, flanked by black files of Guinness.

Drinks circulate; the literati respond *fortissimo*; journalistic crumbs are trodden into the deep, royal-blue carpet. The westering sun, struggling with black rain clouds, first lights up the green hills of Antrim, then the clear amber bottles on the sideboard. Nobody notices that the room is full of sunlight; nobody switches out the gilt chandelier burning war-time electricity at nobody knows how much an hour. From the drawing-room across the hall come the crystal notes of a piano and the sound of a rich young tenor voice singing *Santa Lucia*; whereupon literary conversation vanishes down the drain, banished by a warm, radiant bath of Neapolitan melody, rain-washed sunlight, gilt chandeliers, whiskey, opulent melancholy.

Nevertheless, somebody switches out the chandelier. Beyond the lough, framed by the dining-room windows, the brilliant green hills of Antrim shine still more brilliantly green; suitable Irish backdrop for the rich young tenor voice with nostalgic echoes of MacCormack. The amber level of the regiment on the sideboard sinks steadily lower. *Santa Lucia* and Neapolitan sunlight give way to melancholy and grey, untidy Irish skies as the pianist across the hall plays the opening chords of *My Lagan Love*. Everybody sings. Politics, concealed behind doors and curtains, enter hand in hand with melancholy, producing, when the final notes of *My Lagan Love* have faded, new historical tableaux. Drowned in Guinness, sunk in black gulfs of melancholy, exhorted by the pianist across the hall, we join in singing *The Three Flowers*:

> For Emmet, Tone, and Dwyer I'll keep,
> As I do love them all;
> And I'll keep them fresh beside my breast
> Though all the world should fall . . .

Beyond the windows, over wooded headlands and rain-lashed mountains, the eternal drama of the Irish sky, light struggling with darkness, is re-enacted, witnessed by British warships crowding Belfast Lough. But now light is winning. Black clouds vanish; the sodden August afternoon suddenly switches to gold; rain-washed sunshine brightens the line of surf along the Antrim shore, shoots out to touch the green squares of fields on the lower slopes of Antrim mountains to deeper emerald. A towering white plume of exhaust from a railway engine strides at lazy intervals through the green squares, halts at Carrickfergus—then climbs towards the sky in a glittering cenotaph, short-lived memorial to 1690, celebrating for one ghostly moment in its shunting-yards the spot where William III, of pious, glorious, and immortal memory first set foot on the green sod of Erin. Belfast, with its canopy of coal smoke, its thick forest of factory chimneys, its fretwork of shipyard gantries, its towering, silver-painted gasworks cylinder beloved by John Betjeman, lies hidden behind wooded head-lands—the town where Tone once broke his glass thumping an Irish toast —the city that, stuck with its Edwardian Acropolis of a City Hall, its ghastly tribal gods of Victorian Economic Men standing with enormous stone feet planted on plinths above beds of municipal geraniums, no longer remembers him except for an odd green placard on an entry wall. The war-time pianist strums; the literati respond:

> For Emmet, Tone, and Dwyer I'll keep,
> As I do love them all;
> And I'll keep them fresh beside my breast
> Though all the world should fall . . .

Nobody hears the stutter of buzz-bombs over London, the *tok-tok* of machine-guns in Polish forests, the roar of tanks or the screaming of dive-bombers from the sands of Africa. And still the song goes on in the drenched green island:

> For Emmet, Tone, and Dwyer I'll keep,
> As I do love them all;
> And I'll keep them fresh beside my breast
> Though all the world should fall . . .

the process of falling still lowering the level of the bottles on the sideboard. More journalistic crumbs are trodden into the deep royal-blue carpet. The gilt chandelier is switched on again; literary twilight falls over the green hills of Antrim. From the drawing-room come the staccato notes of the Bechstein grand, a chorus of voices raised thickly in unison. This time they are singing *The Bold Fenian Men*. Beyond the entrance waters of Belfast Lough, with Ailsa Craig just a faint shadow on the horizon, lines of British corvettes and mine-sweepers sentinel the Irish Sea—all withdrawn to a respectful distance from the plate-glass windows of Belfast's stockbroker-belt:

> 'Where falls not hail, or rain, or any snow,
> Nor ever wind blows loudly; but it lies
> Deep-meadowed, happy, fair with orchard-lawns
> And bowery hollows crowned with summer sea . . .'

to which might be added 'crowned with 5%' instead of summer sea.

Yeats's Ghost

Sometime during the reign of my Aunt Lizzie as a floridly-gilt clock on the south Belfast mantelshelf, a large stout man was obliterating my view of *What Every Woman Knows* in a London theatre. The large stout man was G. K. Chesterton, number one in my collection of literary lions. Number two was George Moore, also in a London theatre. Instead of being large and stout, he was small and helpless-looking. So helpless-looking that I never batted an eyelid when, later in life, I read his confession to Somebody-or-Other (was it Yeats?) that he always had difficulty in keeping his pants up—for pants read underpants. The Somebody-or-Other explained to Mr. Moore that the little tapes at the top of his pants were for putting his braces through—a stratagem that had never occurred to the author of *Hail and Farewell*. From that point onwards conversations in Ebury Street were, presumably, less liable to awkward interruption. But on this intimate subject I defer to the professors, and especially the American professors, who pontificate at great length (usually three volumes) on Anglo-Irish literature in general and George Moore (see underclothes) in particular.

The affair of the underpants (involving a glass of milk in the Dublin suburbs) was either *fin de siècle* or early 1900s, just before G. K. Chesterton, as well as obscuring my view of the stage, shook the seats all round him when he laughed; also before that ghostly little apparition labelled George Moore appeared in the front stalls, dressed up like a trussed chicken, with, as some one unkindly remarked, a complexion like cold pork, and pathetic blue eyes.

Then Bernard Shaw, London perambulator. I associate him with lamentable processions of wounded and mutilated ex-service men jerking along the gutters, playing musical instruments, holding out battered hats for pennies. The European scenery had collapsed with a crash; the corpse of feudalism was rotting in the London streets. At such moments the sight of Mr. Shaw, consciously erect, over six feet high, immaculately dressed in an Edwardian fashion of his own, was like a glimpse of snowcapped Olympus across the blue-green Thermic Gulf—coldly glittering but refreshing. He always gave the impression (unlike my cornet-playing, banjo-strumming companions in the gutter) of knowing exactly where he was going. No ambiguity about Mr. Shaw. At least not until my last strange encounter with him, this time in Piccadilly. But that was nearly twenty years later, on the eve of World War Two.

The first encounters, usually in Regent Street, went on for a period of years. During that time I lived in the narrow street leading down from the Strand to the Embankment where Samuel Pepys once lived, with its iron gate framing what was once the Watergate overlooking Embankment Gardens where bands played in summer time. Shaw lived round the corner in Adelphi Terrace, presumably unconscious of alcoholic, barrel-scented vaults below—a literary lion almost in my backyard.

Later, coloured lights outside a Dublin cinema showing *Pygmalion* billed him as 'Local Boy Makes Good.' But in my London day he was *the* literary figure, making suitable entrances from Adelphi Terrace. Also down my street lurked Sir James Barrie. Every morning my landlady would dish up my bacon and eggs, then, twitching the curtain, remark on the presence, or absence, of a face at a back window in a tall narrow building in John Street. The back window in the tall narrow building was supposed, at least by my landlady, to be the window of Sir James Barrie's study, and the face at it (shades of the Theatre Royal, Belfast!) was assumed to be the face of the author of *Mary Rose*—a face that, performing within its own copyright, obscured by London fog, was either an illusion or not there when it seemed to be. Sometimes, descending from my two rooms and bath to hard cold London pavements supposedly streaked with gold, I met the owner of the face in John Street or the Strand. He was, I thought, the saddest little man I'd ever seen.

After that, a twenty-year time gap. From James Barrie's disappearing acts in the Adelphi to bomb-shattered streets and houses exhibiting their interiors from roof to cellar, like anatomical specimens in a museum. More specifically to a war-time luncheon at the Savoy attended by Mr. Priestley and other literary chandeliers from a darkening world. I suppose some literary pearls must have bounced from those beer-and-wine-glass littered tables to luxurious Savoy carpets. If so, they disappeared. All I remember is a boring little man who kept crashing against literary façades with a presumably epoch-making stock exchange tip. 'Do you want to make £60,000?', like a cracked record on a gramophone. Mr. Priestley spiked *his* guns. 'No thanks,' he said, 'I've got £60,000.' Whereupon, in the manner of old *Punch* captions, collapse of party with tip, and the rest of us got back to our more or less literary muttons. This at the back of the cages where the literary lions were being fed. Not that it was necessary to do much feeding: most were perfectly capable of feeding themselves—not to mention whole menageries of divorced wives, female camp followers, women's magazine predators, all fitted out with leopard-skin coats, amber cigarette-holders, arty jewellery, and other paraphernalia peculiar to literary vivandières of the period; for photographic illustrations see back numbers of the *Tatler* and the *Sketch*.

But nobody was feeding my next lion, with stock exchange tips or anything else. He was in trouble at feeding time; about to be trampled in the rush. It was H. G. Wells, encountered by accident at a tea party given by the English Speaking Union; a party at which so many people were speaking English at once, and so loudly, that it was next door to impossible to make yourself understood.

The English-speakers had collected in a herd round a help-yourself tea buffet, instituting a sort of Anglo-Saxon dogfight, and there in the middle of the dogfight, making very heavy weather of the business of getting himself a cup of tea, stood the more or less English-speaking Mr. Wells, looking like an orphan of the P. E. N. Club storm. As I was more of a size and weight for these encounters, I plunged into the scrum like the prop-forward I once was, and emerged, not only with a cup of tea, but with a

74

slice of cake wedged in its saucer. I silently handed them to Mr. Wells, and went back into the scrum for more.

Like American footballers gathered for private consultation in the midst of pandemonium, Mr. Wells and I then formed ourselves into a private English Speaking Union of our own. As a former medical student I should have noted whether Mr. Wells, as a diabetic, ate his slice of cake, or just chased it round his saucer as a status symbol. In fact I don't remember what he did with the cake, probably for the reason that only a few weeks earlier Mr. Wells, breathing fire and slaughter in the correspondence columns of the *New English Weekly*, had been demanding my head upon a charger, and all that now stood between us and another shattering explosion was the fact that in our tea-and-cake-facilitated introduction no names had been mentioned. I knew Mr. Wells as Mr. Wells; Mr. Wells knew me, not as the apprentice toreador who kept planting banderillas in his rump in the *New English Weekly*, but simply as a fortunate accident, an ex-prop-forward who kept plunging in the scrum for tea, performing miracles in the dog fight round the English Speaking holy-of-holies.

The original *casus belli* was an article I wrote for the *New English Weekly* severely criticising a broadcast by Mr. Wells on his favourite subject of the World State. A. R. Orage, the editor, no more enamoured of Wellsian World States, sometimes referred in his editorials to 'Mr. Wells and his floor-games;' and he probably accepted my article as a fire-lighter for conflagrations to follow. At the sight of it, Mr. Wells would probably charge into the correspondence columns like a bull at a gate, and *hey presto* we would be back in the brilliant days of the *New Age*, back in the golden era when Shaw, Wells, and Arnold Bennett turned somersaults every week just for the fun of it, and the fireworks went up free, gratis, and for nothing.

Which was exactly what happened, up to a point. Mr. Wells charged into the ring, roaring, but when, instead of being impressed, I turned on him, he promptly charged out again and was never heard from again in that particular contest. In fact he disappeared as completely as the Cheshire cat, leaving behind him, not so much a grin as a few derogatory inferences. This just at the moment when, with Orage promising me all the space I wanted, I was getting wound up to flatten him with haymaker in the solar plexus—such was the prelude to the business of tea and cake from the English Speaking Union. The champion had ratted at the first sign of an honest-to-God slugging match, and now, as the new white hope of the *New English Weekly*, the unknown challenger from beyond the Irish Sea, all I saw standing beside me holding a teacup was not the mountain of intellectual muscle I had, in my innocence, expected, but a muddled little Anglo-Saxon, a pert, jovial little cockney with a bow tie that had got itself jauntily crooked—a refugee both from concealed man-traps in the correspondence columns of the *New English Weekly* and the dog fight round the English-speaking buffet—a helpless little person who if I didn't feed him tea and cake would starve, and if I didn't use my seventeen-and-a-half stone to stem the rush of English speakers would be trampled in the scrum —leaving me to register the great H. G. Wells, not as he appeared in the days of my Malone Road youth as a bold bad socialist, a subverter of morals with novels like *Ann Veronica*, but as an attractively boyish little man who, bow tie crooked, stood balancing a teacup, talking sixteen to the dozen in the high, squeaky cockney voice I first heard on the radio about this, that, and the other—the kind of talk that goes on at tea parties when nobody has the faintest notion what is being said or why—in this particular instance thanks be to God!

Indeed our private English Speaking Union went like wedding bells, and I, for one, was glad to let them clatter *ad lib*—to compound for a quiet life and let the great H. G. Wells entertain his simple, all too simple, Polytechnic notions of world politics to his heart's content—meanwhile scrounging as much tea and cake from the English Speaking Union as the dog fight round its buffet would allow. By this time I was getting a little tired of literary lions roaring, and so, I think, was Mr. Wells.

The next lion, as it says in Shakespeare, in another part of the forest. It was George Bernard Shaw padding down Piccadilly on a sunny morning of May 1939, five months after the death of William Butler Yeats—a time and an interval with a bearing on what followed. I was passing through London on my way to Paris and had arranged to meet a young woman at Piccadilly Circus, at Swan & Edgar's corner to be exact.

And there, against a surrealist background of waxen young women displaying bathing dresses, came my last encounter with Mr. Shaw. I was standing with my back against Messrs. Swan & Edgar's plate-glass, with the bright May sunlight shining on my shock of white hair, not to mention my horn-rimmed spectacles; and there, advancing down Piccadilly, was Mr. Shaw—very erect, beard now snow-white, tweed suit still buttoned high in Edwardian fashion. Just like old times, I thought—just like the roaring twenties when I was a demobilised officer selling linen to London stores and Mr. Shaw was always heaving into sight to remind me there were other things beside sample ranges, walrus-moustached buyers, calculations of commission *à la* Kipps, and keeping in with Mr. X of Harrod's.

But it was no longer the roaring twenties and worse tyrants than Mr. X were on the prowl. It was the sinister thirties, with poison in the air, thunder clouds over Europe, and Mr. Shaw behaving in a thoroughly un-Shavian manner—hesitating in his stride, staring straight towards me with a stricken expression—like an old lady who had just seen a ghost. My immediate reaction was to look behind me at Swan & Edgar's plate-glass windows. Strange, I thought, he can't be looking at me—whatever frightened him must be behind. But there was nothing behind except waxen young women in bathing dresses—surely Bernard Shaw wouldn't be frightened of them after those much-publicised assertions that he was once a supercharged, red-bearded devil with women. Arnold Bennett, with his Balzacian curiosity about big business, about the Grands Magasins du Louvre and the Galeries Lafayette, might have set down those waxen figures in his journal as *choses vues*, but not, I thought, George Bernard Shaw.

Then Mr. Shaw, recovering himself, went his way; the shadow that, like something dipped in solution, had darkened the sunlight of Piccadilly, evaporated. I stood there, puzzled, staring after the Olympian figure with the snow-white beard and the resolutely Edwardian suit—a figure that for an astonishing moment or two had lost its poise, had suddenly looked like a thoroughly frightened old man. Strange, I thought—Bernard Shaw, of all people, behaving like an old lady at a tea party who had just seen something sinister in the tea-leaves. Then the woman I was waiting for arrived, and for the moment I forgot the whole strange business.

I went, with war darkening the horizon, to Paris. I returned to Ireland. War not so much broke out as gradually unfroze. Then one night in the following winter I was in the Abbey Theatre, Dublin. I forget the title of the play; all I remember is that I had booked a seat in the third row of the stalls; that I was late for the opening curtain; that the lights were already dimmed, the famous gong had boomed three times, and I had to grope my way in in the dark.

The play, whatever it was, began. But I don't remember much about it, for I couldn't get attending to it. The audience behind me was restive; there was movement, rustling, subdued conversation. I kept looking round to see what was wrong; but the rustling and the sibilant conversation only got worse. The Abbey audience, not for the first time in its history, was in a state of 'chassis.'

At the interval the lights went up in the auditorium—the dim religious lights of the old Abbey—and I went out for a cup of coffee. In the foyer, Denis Johnston, who had been standing, all six feet four of him, at the back of the stalls, came up and said:

'Did you notice a lot of commotion during that act?'

'Yes,' I said, 'I did. What was it all about?'

'It was all about you,' said Johnston. 'You were causing it.'

'*Me*?' I said, in my best literary manner. 'What have *I* done?'

'It's not what you've *done*,' said Johnston. 'It's the way you look. It's that big white head of yours and those horn-rimmed spectacles. *They thought you were Yeats's ghost!*'

And with that the spotlight shot back to that sunlit scene in Piccadilly and the un-Shavian behaviour of Mr. Shaw. Apparently there had been something in the tea-leaves after all!

Oscar Left Again for Paris

The foyer is a revue of Anglo-Irish Ireland, horse Protestants and all. Hoydens from remote Georgian mansions, looking as if they had rushed in from the hunting field, earls, mountebanks, literary playboys from the Palace bar, dramatists who had a play on at the Abbey for a week, hungry-looking authors who would be the better for a steak and a pint, even respectable bookmakers and publicans about to squirm through the fence—all cawing like rooks in a rookery, with an effect of Bloomsbury translated so far west that nobody would bat an eyelid if some of the authors in need of a shave, or the sprigs of nobility gone native in leather-patched sports jackets were suddenly to produce six-shooters and start shooting-up the chandeliers.

Suddenly, as if somebody had pulled the chain, the foyer empties. Book-makers, publicans, female horse Protestants with wild hair-dos, sprigs of nobility in jaded corduroy trousers, surge in noisily for short sessions of assassination in the stalls. The play is *The Importance of Being Earnest*, and judging by the acid slopping round, it had better be good. We hitch up our sports trousers and wait for the fireworks to begin. A trio of refined young women play refined music in a sort of altar niche, struggling with the up-roar of the natives, the clatter of Dublin alligators snapping reputations.* The house-lights go down, the proscenium curtain up, displaying a brightly-lit inner curtain embellished with Wildean drawings. Art, as Goethe remarked, is Art because it is not Nature. Momentary hush. Assassination resumed. The refined young women in the altar niche finally wilt under the barrage, slither into silence. Inner curtain rises on apartment of Algernon Moncrieff. Goethe presumably delighted: Alger-non, in addition to smoking (according to Lady Bracknell, an occupation in itself), wolfs cucumber sandwiches, at the same time pouring cascades of wisecracks over the head of his singularly espicopal-looking butler. Algernon terrific; the very glass and fashion of all the Algernons that ever coruscated in the foyers and drawing-rooms of London S.W. alternatively the Haymarket theatre; not to mention the stagey floodlit mind of young Mr. Wilde, late of Merrion Square.

Not so Lady Bracknell; nor, when we come to them, those images of suppressed desire, the Rev. Canon Chasuble and his icily-tinkling but nevertheless inflammable Miss Prism. Algernon seems to have swum the Irish Sea in the reverse direction to his creator; nevertheless, the sea has its revenge. Real vintage Lady Bracknells, Rev. Canon Chasubles, and their attendant Miss Prisms are evidently the song the sirens sang in Dublin and its environs, even on the sea coasts of Monkstown and Killiney. Lady Bracknell never gets nearer Belgravia than the Butt bridge and the lower reaches of the Liffey, Guinness barges and all; Miss Prism's situation was advertised in the Irish not the London *Times*; and the Rev. Canon Chasuble calls up more images of Our Lady of Lourdes than of the vicarage garden. Algernon alone transports us from the Rotunda and the ghostly neighbourhood of the Parnell statue; down past Amiens Street, out over the snot-green sea—toothy, eyeglass-shining, sandwich-snatching, lying, spouting epigrams, behaving in the fashion a brilliant young Irish-man decided English society ought to behave, if only the Lord had granted it Irish clarity and ruthlessness.

For a moment, with the help of the monocled Algernon and a sweet young Irish actress bravely, but not very successfully, pretending to be a 'nice gel', the Guinness barges and the snot-green sea almost disappear; young Mr. Wilde, late of Merrion Square, almost works the oracle—is on the verge of translating Belgravia to the north end of O'Connell Street,

*Cyril Connolly remarked of Dublin's literary pub, the Palace, that it had 'the friendly warmth of an alligator-tank'.

back to the neighbourhood of the Parnell memorial. But the new Dublin defeats him; *The Importance of Being Earnest*, damaged in transit across the Irish Sea, its bouquet ruined by salt water, eventually vanishes in a sort of Irish limbo, 'swamped an' dhrownded' in a black mixture of Guinness and champagne, with the Guinness 'too bloody Irish' for the champagne.

The curtain falls. We rise for Shaw's 'music-hall tintinnabulation' of *The Soldiers' Song*; aristocratic hoydens on their way to decaying Georgian mansions, and sprigs of nobility with dates in improvised flats in Fitzwilliam street, make a wild rush for the exits, again giving the impression that, if only they had time, they would 'shoot up' the chandeliers on the way. Behind them, like a square in a country town suddenly bereft of men and cattle, with only mud and dung to show where life had been, the barn-like interior of the Gate is left to the shades—with the exception of the shade of Oscar Fingal O'Flahertie Wills Wilde, which, if present in the first place, almost certainly went out at the end of Act One. What it thought of green pillar boxes, or, when it got there, the horrible rash of new bell-pushes round the once stately doorways of Merrion Square, is another matter; probably it set off instanter, muttering epigrams ('You will, dear boy, you will!') back to the comfortable nineteenth-century aphorisms of Père-Lachaise. Anything to be away from the alligator-tank on the Liffey!

The Small Fair at Cloghan

Two seas and a barrier of blue mountains from the stench of concentration camps, Cloghan is all taken up with its cattle fair. Tremendous stir in its whitewashed main street; roaring business in its public-houses; dung spattered up and down its roadways; geese marching in Prussian formation; trick-o-the-loop men shouting their heads off; two sad-faced Indians selling gaudy handkerchiefs (probably manufactured in Manchester) from a rickety trestle-table propped against the whitewashed gable-end of Donnelly's long-suffering general store.

Up on the fair ground, a green hillside loud with protestant cattle, a bargain is in process of being driven. The seller, a small black-avised man with ragged tufts of hair projecting from under his cap, a stub of blackened pipe inserted permanently in an upside-down position and never lighted, holds two calves on the end of a piece of rope as if in half a mind to take them home again. Set over against him, like a china dog on the far end of a mantel shelf, is the buyer—large, truculent, with his cap on the back of his head, bursting with meaningless good humour. Now and then a third party, god-like, isolated on snowy peaks of neutrality, announces in a voice that drowns barking sheepdogs, quacking ducks, hissing geese, protestant cattle, and the clamour of the cheap jacks in the main street below:

'*Come on now; Johnny Devlin's a dacent mon!*'

But still the contest goes on—a sort of public entertainment, free, gratis, and for nothing, while Johnny Devlin, having his hand slapped and returned to him, puts it thoughtfully back in his pocket not too certain whether it still belongs to him, undisturbed by the clamour of cattle, the uproar of sheep dogs snarling, ducks quacking, geese cackling, the stentorian chorus of cheap jacks rising from the whitewashed mainstreet.

And down in the whitewashed mainstreet, where Civic Guards peep indulgently from the windows of the barracks, I am guilty of a social error. In one of the numerous public-houses, where a dark tide of porter is already rising though it is scarcely past mid-day, I remark to the barmaid that it seems to be a busy fair, and she, pausing in the act of scooping the froth from a pint, replies with a pitying look, as at one barely in his right mind:

'Tis only the small fair; ye should be here on the proper fair day!'

Whereupon, first finishing my pint, I go my way. But proper fair day or no proper fair day, the uproar follows me up the long road to Lough Finn, long after I've lost sight of Cloghan and its whitewashed mainstreet that looks out across the green valley and the rich bottom lands to where the Blue Stack mountains maintain their rich blue remoteness from the foul-smoking chimneys of Auschwitz, the glare of tankers erupting in the Atlantic, the stutter of buzz-bombs over London, and all the tumult of the western world.

A Matter of Exports

Mr. Doherty's general-store-cum-public-house-cum-post-office comes to its operative conclusion at the back with a small bar and a zinc-covered counter. Here, like an elephant lurking in a jungle of tin cans, brushes, boots, and sides of bacon, I found Mr. Doherty himself, all eighteen stone of him. He was in the act of replacing a bottle of real yellow Irish whiskey on a shelf with the air of a high priest restoring some priceless relic to its niche in a cathedral.

'Mr. Doherty,' I said, 'is it true that poteen's still flourishing in these parts?'

'Is it that firewater?' said Mr. Doherty, scandalised, like a bishop confronted with heresy. 'Do ye know how it's made?'

'Well,' I said, 'I've heard stories.'

'Stories is it?' said Mr. Doherty. 'If ye had a been here twenty years ago, ye'd a heard more than stories. All them mountains,' said Mr. Doherty, flinging an eloquent arm towards a window through which it was impossible to see for dust and dead bluebottles, 'all them mountains,' said Mr. Doherty, eloquently, but mixing his metaphors, 'was fairly leppin' with stills.'

'Do ye tell me that?' I said.

'I do,' said Mr. Doherty.

'And what did they do with it all?' I said.

'What they didn't drink themselves,' said Mr. Doherty, 'was exported to Glasgow in butter boxes.'

80

'Is that a fact?' I said.

'It is,' said Mr. Doherty.

'All the same,' I said, 'I *did* hear of American soldiers getting a brave drop in Derry.'

'Mebbe they did, mebbe they did,' said Mr. Doherty with finality, as if the whole thing was over and done with, like the battle of Clontarf, 'mebbe they did. But if they did *so*,' said Mr. Doherty, calling to his aid the expert knowledge of a man who sold wireless batteries, 'if they did *so*, God help them, they might as well a been drinkin' sulphuric acid.'

The mention of sulphuric acid reminded me. 'Tell me, Mr. Doherty,' I said, 'did you by any chance know the widow Brady?'

A shadow crossed Mr. Doherty's face. 'I did that,' he said darkly.

'Well then,' I said, 'what age was she when she died?'

'She would a been seventy-two,' said Mr. Doherty, rummaging amongst the annals of the countryside, 'the night they cowped the oul' Ford comin' from Derrytrasna an' they all paralytic on their own poteen.'

'So she was killed in a motor accident?' I said.

Mr. Doherty refused to be dogmatic. 'Well, she was quarely failed when they took her out.'

'What was the matter with her?' I said.

'Her neck was broke,' said Mr. Doherty.

'I see,' I said.

''Twas a pity,' said Mr. Doherty. 'But d'ye know what I'm goin' to tell ye?'

I refrained from asking. I was going to hear it anyhow.

'Do ye know what I'm goin' to tell ye?' said Mr. Doherty, 'All that Brady poteen was *la*mentable.'

'Bad?' I said.

'*La*mentable,' said Mr. Doherty.

'It must have been,' I said, visualising the scene in the sheugh.

'*La*mentable,' said Mr. Doherty. He ruminated darkly. 'Do ye know what I'm goin' to tell ye?'

'What?' I said.

'Them Bradys,' said Mr. Doherty, 'they should a put the pethrol in themselves an' their oul' poteen in the cyar.'

'Fair enough,' I said.

''Twould a been better so,' said Mr. Doherty.

And that was that. On the way home I took a bottle of colourless liquid from my pocket and emptied it into a trout stream. The colourless liquid, guaranteed 'grand for the kidneys,' had been wished on me one dark night by a gentleman called Brady who assured me that his widowed mother, fortified by 'wee sups of it,' had reached the (locally) record-breaking age of a hundred and three.

'Is that a fact?' I said.

'It is,' said Mr. Brady. 'Last Halloween.' This time, I gathered, the elixir was intended not so much for export to Glasgow in butter boxes as for the entertainment of American soldiers in Derry.

PART FOUR
A Glare of Burning Tankers

Inishtrahull

The incoming tide slaps against the pier, flooding towards the upper reaches of the lough. Shags scurry past, necks outstretched, wing-tips almost touching the water, like stockbrokers rushing to town at a hint of commotion on the stock market. A seal sticks his sad, whiskered face out of green depths below the pierhead, snorts, then vanishes again, shattering plum-coloured reflections of the Inishowen mountains.

Down below the pierhead, in black forests of seaweed, sudden death but no murder. In green depths above the forest a band of violet fluorescence, an advance party of jellyfish swirling in from the Atlantic, surging in with the tide, like the lights of an under-water city. Each individual jellyfish glows at the heart of its violet transparency with a malignant pattern of red, like the red in transparent glass tubes outside picture palaces.

Sunset flares behind the Fanad mountains. The jellyfish procession, brilliant in the gathering darkness, waiting for an exact water temperature to unfold its regimental pageantry, forges gauzily through dark green depths, floating involuntarily with the tide, lighting up the water with its poisonous glare—unlike those shark-like shadows in the open Atlantic, out beyond the shore lights of Buncrana and the steadily-winking lighthouse at Dunree, that move without warning to the glare of burning tankers, setting the war at sea deep down below the level of the invertebrate kingdom.

Malin Head to Inishtrahull. At moments flat calm, then a wall of oily blue, threatening to breach the gunwale; the boat climbs dizzily, with a sideways twist, an upward-thrusting corkscrew motion, like a sea-gull side-slipping a wave crest. Inishtrahull thrusts its green humpback through the rollers like a submarine, then disappears behind the mist curtain. The wall of water that masqueraded as the horizon slides from us, racing eastwards down the channel between Inishtrahull and the mainland; replaced by another that springs into position behind it, like guardsmen forming ranks, as if the Atlantic is alive with energy, mustering its defences, in no mood to entertain whaleboats, no matter how thrustful their engines.

The scene stays monotonously the same: the wicked black cliffs of Malin, rock-stacks surrounded by what looks like ice cream; the green humpback of Inishtrahull; the blue-grey ocean mustering its forces, crashing its water-blows against the bow. The focal point is old James's apple-red face where he sits in the stern-sheets, one gnarled hand resting on the tiller, the other thrust for warmth in some crevice of his tattered coat. Old James is seventy-six and has been making this crossing for half a century, starting when Parnell was in trouble with the priests. His grey-blue fisherman's eyes look at you from so far away he doesn't seem to

85

see you. He sees holes in the mist that no-one else can see; sees, or rather senses, the set and run of the rollers so that he can steer without a compass and not be a quarter mile out when it comes to landfall on a small island lost in Atlantic mist. The boat is of the Donegal type, with a flaring bow and stern; when on rare occasions, she is caught by a following sea, old James, muffler, red face and all, rises eloquently past me as if in a lift hoisted by the power of rollers all the way from America. He looks like an ancient kindly seabird that has settled in the stern-sheets and taken to chewing tobacco.

We leave minuet-performing rock stacks and islands for the tide-rip between Inishtrahull and the mainland. A destroyer was lost here in the war. Which war? A war is just a war, something that every now and then strews oil drums, planks, chests of tea, torpedoes, unexploded mines, and the bodies of drowned sailors along the beaches. A mine blew the top off one of the Garvan Isles; everybody in the boat takes his affidavit; didn't the blast kill three of Johnny Mc'Inerny's sheep? 1914-18 that was. Along with the British destroyer that obligingly ran herself on the rocks, the massacre of Johnny Mc'Inerny's miraculously-grazing sheep is now locked in the treasure house of the Irish past, flanked by Finn MacCool and the Fenians.

Rock pinnacles slide past like paintings on a marine backdrop, to an accompaniment of sounds like *Fingall's Cave*, with a chorus of shags watching disdainfully from ocean-foaming rocks, and clouds of screaming sea-gulls. Then suddenly, screaming sea-gulls, foaming rocks, disdainful shags, are behind. We are alone again in our circle of subdued sunlight; rollers racing all the way from America. Old James adjusts his muffler, takes a bite out of his quid, stares at the mist ahead as if studying a chart with the course marked on it in red. Occasionally, when a particularly monstrous roller hoists itself out of the oily blue, then comes hissing at us, the gnarled old hand moves the tiller a trifle, tenderly, as Heifetz might move his fingers over the strings of his violin, and we surge, slide, and dance on our way again, with no water shipped and a queer vital sensation that seeps up through the thwarts into the bowels and charges the whole body with a fierce exultant joy. The only other living thing in sight is a sea-gull, immaculately white in a patch of sunlight, riding the onrushing walls of water as if the land had never existed.

A finger of sunlight stretches down from a gap in the clouds and touches the water ahead. At the stroke of a magician's wand, Inishtrahull appears on the starboard bow, lit by its spotlight from the clouds, a brilliant green gem set alongside the track of shipping to and from the North Channel. Old James shifts the tiller; the engine splutters; we smash through short slapping waves. Perhaps the spotlight will be switched off again, the magician wave his wand, Inishtrahull sink back into the ocean from which it has vividly emerged—an illusion created by its private shaft of sunlight.

But Inishtrahull is real, with the white tower of its lighthouse crowning a grassy knoll. A siren bellows at intervals, snarling at the mist curtains beyond the island, at seething tide-rips, sunken reefs, isolated tors that, like the pillars of a half-submerged cathedral, mark this ending of Irish soil in the Atlantic. Waiting for the impact of the siren, with only the subdued thumping of the engine to break the silence, we coast in calm water round the southern shore. Shags dive and re-surface; watchful heads of seals dot the translucent green of rocky inlets. Out here beyond the white horses of the channel, life begins anew; but not human life—only seals, shags, the quiet *washing* of waves in rocky inlets. Except for a clump of ruined cottages, thatch fallen in, from which men, women, and children have fled, it is as if the island blew its own siren and at nightfall kindled its own light: as if the sea-god had laid an enchantment on this green knoll in the Atlantic, with its bellowing siren, its white-shafted stump of lighthouse, its tumbledown cottages that look across the sound to where wicked black rain storms slant wickedly over the black elbow mass of Malin Head and long rollers from America crash in a tumult of white shell-bursts under wicked black cliffs.

We thump round the island, making for the landing place, a narrow inlet surrounded by sunken reefs and jagged pinnacles. Gaelic scholars differ about the meaning of 'Inishtrahull.' Some, struggling with its stubborn last syllable, translate it as 'the island with its strand or landing place on the far side'—an unsentimental Irish version of Barrie's 'island that likes to be visited.' Inishtrahull does *not* like to be visited, and if Gaelic scholars favouring the version that locates the strand or landing place on the northern or ocean side are right, then the Gaels, with their cat-like feeling for places, have invented a place-name as vivid as an Admiralty chart—sailing directions, topographical details, marginal illustrations, all rolled into one. For the landing inlet, the rocky, dangerous boat harbour we are making for, *is* in fact on the far side of the island, the side turned away from the mainland—with the channel to it leading through a sort of North Atlantic nightmare, an inferno of shattering surf, sunken reefs, colonnades of rock pinnacles crowned with sea-grass, like surviving pinnacles of long-submerged cathedrals: all projecting northwards into the Atlantic, in search of ships and wreckage; hence the lighthouse and the old devil of a siren that howls at the mist-compartmented ocean like a demented banshee, as if the banished, green-sodded island was in pain.

In war-time this green humpback shouldering the Atlantic lurked in the track of disaster. In October 1942 the 81,000-ton *Queen Mary*, carrying 10,000 American troops and travelling at 30 knots, crashed into and through her escorting light cruiser, the 4,500-ton *Curacao*, bisecting her as a butcher might bisect a carcase with a cleaver. Three hundred and twenty-nine officers and men either went down with the separated bow and stern sections, or were left struggling in the water. One moment the *Queen Mary* was towering over them; the next, from the viewpoint of the men in the water, she was disappearing over what seemed to them the horizon.

Further items in the Inishtrahull saga of thudding mines, blazing tankers, sinking warships, began beyond the Mull of Kintyre, with the sailing of a battered freighter from Glasgow. She sailed at the height of the bombing campaign, with a scratch crew, an assortment of amateur seamen scraped from the bottom of the war-time barrel. Somewhere in the Firth of Clyde she was attacked by a bomber. The first bomb wrecked the electrical system, plunging the engine-room in darkness. As the bomber swerved away, she raked the freighter's decks with her machine-guns, killing the captain on the bridge, pinning the first officer with a broken leg.

The freighter pounded on. Darkness fell. When it got light she was out of sight of land, engulfed in fog. The newly-promoted officers tried to fix her position, but there was no sun, and even if there had been, nobody could read a sextant. Night came down; they pounded on—for all they knew in circles. No lights appeared through the fog curtain; the ghostly island of Ireland seemed to have sunk without trace. Still they kept on, steering, as they thought, due west, making for Belfast Lough, a nicely-coloured haven on the chart.

This paid off. Towards evening of the second day, fog began to clear; land rose mysteriously from what they took to be the North Channel, backed by a tangle of blue mountains. To port was a small green island with what looked like the white tower of a lighthouse; ahead, a sea-lough, entrance overshadowed by mountains. They assumed they had been steaming all night in circles; that the green island was, as identified by the chart, the lighthouse island of the Copelands; that, in consequence, the sea-lough ahead was Belfast Lough. All this by guess and by God, according to the best navigation between pints in Liverpool's dockside pubs.

They crept, engines barely turning, into this mysterious fiord, shaping up like Ulysses to the mountain-guarded shores of Ithaka, and, just before sunset, dropped anchor alongside a bright red buoy. In the morning they would steam up towards Belfast, blow the siren; a pilot would arrive in a pilot-boat; the nightmare voyage would be over. Unfortunately the hills were the hills of Donegal, not Antrim; the red buoy that looked so inviting had been anchored there to mark two dangerous rocks near the entrance to Lough Swilly—Swilly More and Swilly Beg.

The result was that as the tide ebbed, the freighter sat down heavily on Swilly More; her fore section slid one way, her after section the other. Finally she broke her back, and quietly gave up the ghost, not a hundred yards from shore. But not before the dead captain, the wounded first mate, the press-ganged scarecrows of the crew, had been transferred to the lifeboats.

So ended the war-time voyage of the s.s. . . . . . . , its final phases watched with astonishment from Inishtrahull. There remain only fragments collected, partly in the bar of Bertie Barton's hotel at Portsalon, partly in the hills overlooking the red buoy and the expanse of blue-grey Atlantic stretching on towards Iceland—that empty arc where nothing seems to happen in peace-time but everything breaks loose, including burning tankers, in war. First (and this caused bitter comment amongst the watchers from the Fanad hills), the s.s. . . . . . was thoughtless enough to sink in deep water, at a spot where her cargo was all washed out to sea. Second, that the young man with the long hair and suede shores who, acting as navigator and lord high everything else, piled her on the rocks, was an ex-dance-band leader from Liverpool. Faced with conscription, he abandoned saxophones for a life on the ocean wave, bringing his suede shoes with him. No seaboots for him.

A spring evening on Inishtrahull. War still rumbles beyond the horizon. We start the long stagger and wallow back to the mainland. Six miles away, across the sound, ghostly white columns shoot skyward under the black cliffs of Malin. A cold wind blows in from the north, from Iceland and Spitzbergen, sweeping the ocean, so that by the time we are halfway across Islay has appeared on the north-eastern horizon, resting on the water like a faint blue cloud.

Dusk is falling as we make fast at Malin pier. A rocket streams up from Inishtrahull. Beyond Inishtrahull, flickering, faint-blue flares. A second whaleboat, opposite number to our own slips her moorings and thumps out into the gathering darkness, heading in the direction of the flares. A British plane, hunting submarines, has crash-landed in open Atlantic, out beyond the green humpback of Inishtrahull and its foaming apron of rock pinnacles.

More rockets; distress signals thud as if some one is slamming a distant door. War and the rumours of war have returned to Malin Head and its green knoll in the Atlantic—prelude to more oil drums, more oil-stained planks, more bodies of drowned sailors strewn along rock-ribbed beaches under the black and hungry cliffs.

October Afternoon at Glasnevin

Towering white clouds over Stephen's Green. Brass bands, *O'Donnell Abu* competing with *The Boys of Wexford*; also, unnecessarily, *Let Erin Remember*. Concussed by bassoons, full of 19th-century rhetoric, we jerk like a gigantic banner-bearing caterpillar round the corner of the Green, past the still bullet-pocked College of Surgeons. Saffron-kilted pipers add to the cacophany. Piloted by funereal brake-loads of stuffed shirts, we jerk our caterpillar way down Grafton Street. Irish democracy, up for the day from Cork, Kerry, the sad black mountains of Leitrim, spouts from lamp-standards, overflows from attic windows, waves green, white, and orange flags from roof-tops.

Bands reverberate from plate-glass windows in Grafton Street. If you can hear yourself think for *Let Erin Remember* fortified by *The Boys of Wexford*, you wonder what the man himself—the uncrowned king above in Glasnevin—makes of the stuffed shirts in the funereal brakes, the wildly waving tricolours; so far removed from his forest home at Avondale, the black day he came back to haunt the priests and the holy men, to light that eternal flame in *A Portrait of the Artist as a Young Man*. It is as if a dusty, battered edition of the French Revolution had been dug up from the green sod of Erin, scandalising the Widow of Windsor, affronting brassy-faced Unionists behind the plate-glass windows of the Kildare Street Club.

We jerk, still anachronistically thundering, full of hot air and 19th-century rhetoric, towards that window-less side-chapel of the Bank of England that once did duty for our Parliament House. But we don't storm it—don't even remember what Shelley said about it.* 'Freedom' is with the stuffed shirts in the funereal brakes; 'Liberty' in the rash of tri-colours. In the house of Irish politics are remarkably few mansions, and the brass bands are there to prove it. So we give the windowless façade of our *ci-devant* Parliament House another shattering dose of *The Boys of Wexford*—which, shades of Grattan and Flood! it receives in shattering silence—and march on, still flying slogans, still (when you can hear them) skirling with saffron-kilted pipers, past the cool rational front of Trinity and the statues of Goldsmith and Burke, across O'Connell Bridge (shades of the oul' Queen and that famous misprint), and on down the ferro-con-crete Nevski Prospekt of O'Connell Street, down past porticos of hotels and cinemas to the far end, to the westward-gesturing statue of the uncrowned king.

Here, after big-drum thumps, final shattering explosions from the brass bands, and a loud rattling of chains, the harlot Oratory is let loose from her cage, released from tin trumpets fixed to lamp standards—sent fluttering like flocks of pigeons over the heads of crowds that stretch in every direction out of sight. Words boom interminably, darting like in-visible swallows out of the tin trumpets. *Democracy*, *Faith of our fathers* (not Parnell's and, incidentally, not mine), *common heritage*, *glorious dead*—there should be a René Clair, complete with recording apparatus and film cameras rolling, setting all this down with ironic French pre-cision. Grand words, hollow sounds, boom up and down the street of the cinemas, reverberating from all that is left of Georgian grandeur, twisting, turning, like house martins returning to their nests. The patient sea of white faces stares upwards towards them, mutely, forbearingly, enduring all this harlotry without a murmur because it is the green-flag, brass-band tradition to endure it; because this demoded wind and fury has been going on so long in Ireland that nobody has the courage to get up and stop it.

A few yards away, the harp on his obelisk freshly gilded, oratorical birds from tin trumpets fluttering round his head, the uncrowned king stares into infinity, one arm mutely extended towards the west—also, *pace* the inevitable Irish cynic, towards Messrs. Mooney's somewhat rococo public-house. *No man*, says the gilt lettering on his obelisk, *has the right to fix the boundary to the march of a nation*. By the same token no man stems the flood of Irish oratory, now spouting like a black fountain of porter released from a cask. The little man with the rimless pince-nez (shades of *Le Million*!) on the roof of the superfluous air-raid shelter grasps his fluttering typescript; invisible words boom from tin trumpets, twisting like house martins. 'Jasus,' says a voice from the crowd behind me, 'he still has *furlongs* to go!'

*'They have turned the fane of Liberty
 into a temple of Mammon.'

But Glasnevin is better; the peace of death reigns in its cypresses, its yew-trees, its stretches of sad green turf. Green-uniformed soldiers fire volleys; commands ring out in Irish; *crash* go the lifted rifles; echoes charge like foxhounds in and out amongst gilt-inscribed angels, marble tombstones; wads from blank cartridges float down, a slow-motion snow-storm, to settle on the plain grey boulder with the simple inscription PARNELL. Now with harlot Oratory back in her cage, tin trumpets and brass bands silenced, the aristocratic ghost returns to haunt the stage-property round tower, the sad green turf, the dark-green yew-trees—emerges again this cloud-torn October afternoon with sunlight chasing shadows between the marble angels and tombstones—rises like a vin-dicated phantom from the pages of *A Portrait of the Artist as a Young Man*:

O, he'll remember all this when he grows up, said Dante hotly—the language he heard against God and religion and priests in his own home.
Let him remember too, cried Mr. Casey to her from across the table, the language with which the priests and the priests' pawns broke Parnell's heart and hounded him into his grave. Let him remember that too when he grows up.

As if we had ever forgotten, as if he is not still there, in the hearts of the Irish people, behind the cloud shadows, under the bright October sunlight, in odd ballads sung at country fairs, in the imagination of young dra-matists seated at battered typewriters in shabby attic rooms, in the pages of *A Portrait*—a haughty aristocratic presence at the mere breath of whose name it is still, fifty years on, as if some one had exploded a battery of depth charges deep down amongst the black sea caves and sunken wreck-age of the Irish mind.

Looking at those United States

I

GREEN DAWN FROM NOVA ZEMBLA

Night over the Atlantic. A last vision of the coast of Clare. Red sparks flit past the port windows. A young man in a dark-blue uniform emerges from the pilot's compartment, stares moodily at the illuminations outside, retires with professional gloom.

At midnight the plane shudders in a violent turn, one wing saluting brilliant Arctic stars. Below, a star-lit snow crater. Hekla in Iceland. The plane recovers, lowers its solemn star-saluting wing, zooms on like an enormous bluebottle in a darkened room, a bluebottle lit inside with reading-lamps.

Air brakes hum for landing at Kevlavik. Lights flash past the windows, suggesting a buried city. We climb out into freezing blackness like the inside of a refrigerator. A feeling of arrival at the world's end, of an enormous darkened stage where gigantic scenery is being shifted by invisible scene-shifters. A sliver of acid green, like the green in the flame of an oxy-acetylene welder, burns under the towering black scenery of the northeast horizon—flaring above the blackness of the ocean. It is the Arctic dawn, riotous at the ocean rim, rising as on a stupendous cinema screen from Nova Zembla.

Like children in a fairy story, we crowd into a lighted hut, anywhere out of freezing blackness. The hut is lit by electricity, jazz seeps from a wireless-set in a corner; a stout American clad only in white canvas slacks and a singlet, serves coffee at a buffet-counter—apparently American central heating reaches right out under the Denmark strait. The stout American in the canvas ducks is assisted by two flaxen-haired Icelandic waitresses, tarnished princesses of the frozen North. They wear tousled jumpers, tweed skirts that look as if they had been slept in, rumpled nylons that may at one time have been presents from the American air force but now sadly lack the glamour of the American female leg. One would be attractive but for American cosmetics; in the unshaded electric light her mouth looks like a slit in a letterbox. A sadly decadent type at the edge of the Arctic circle.

We stand round, drinking excellent American coffee, lost souls in a battered hut at the world's end. Beyond double windows, with one wing literally overshadowing the doorway, stands the gigantic metal bird that has just carried us from Shannon—lit by a glare of lights, with mechanics swarming over her. They have wheeled up portable floodlights and trestles, and are working at wing height, wearing heavy duffle suits with hoods over their ears, heavy gauntlets, mufflers. Icelandic dogs hang dejectedly about

in the floodlit space below the plane—ungainly little creatures, like miniature collies run to fat; little men bewitched in some Icelandic saga. Perhaps
the American way of life has done them wrong—it certainly has the
waitresses. Headlights appear, flashing far out on the endless steppe of the
airfield; presently a jeep drives up; out bundles a hooded figure, padded
like an Eskimo—one of the American ground staff, jaws endlessly champ-
ing gum. What sets these trolls and troglodytes of the Arctic night—the
stout magician at the coffee-urn, the gum-chewing Peer Gynt from the
jeep—serving in this outpost of American empire, this jazz-age equivalent
to Kipling's North-west frontier? Twentieth-century cogs go round, but
all that clatters out is a rattle of dollar signs, prospects of pay-packets back
in Brooklyn.

Somebody turns up cinema-screen effects from Nova Zembla, the unearthly green strengthens beyond the double windows. We drink more
coffee. The sky pulsates with engines; red and green navigation lights
multiply over the airfield. More planes arrive; more lost souls troop in to
be drugged by the sorcerer at the coffee-urn, like Russian convicts on their
way to Kamchatka. The hut, the convicts lined up for coffee, the half-dead
bodies propped against the buffet-counter: this ghostly canteen at the
world's end has an effect of *When We Dead Awaken,* of a scene from
Sartre's *Huit Clos,* of dummies dumped on a strategic chessboard half-way
between Russia and America. The magician at the coffee-urn dispenses
more American coffee; the flaxen-haired Icelandic waitresses hand out
packets of magic American candy, like trained dogs in a circus, not
understanding the purpose of the act; by Icelandic standards the proper
function of sugar is warmth in winter, not stuffing airline passengers
awash with coffee from the sacred American machine.

Six thousand feet below, a pale blue freezing ocean spreads to the
darker-blue freezing horizon. Oil leak in port engine cured:

> 'Climb to the last headland,
> The recognition
> Of wind and ocean,
> Beyond them only the long
> Wave and the long heartache,
> A long creed dying . . .'

The blur on the darker-blue horizon is Greenland. Beyond it, in suburbs
north of Boston, surviving in what was once Indian forest land, Thoreau's
'quiet desperation' lurks in the shadows beyond the Macy table-lamps, the
'long creed dying' is sluiced along with soap-suds in washing-machines or
thumps with sad reiteration from the icy interiors of still unpaid-for
refrigerators . . .

II

A SWIFT LOOK AT BOSTON

At the edge of Boston Common, a Presbyterian church with a black notice
board. On the black notice-board gilt lettering declares that a famous

divine will D.V. preach at both services next Sunday. Beyond the notice-board and the gilt lettering stretches the green expanse of the Common; beyond that again, distant buildings, shining with Canaletto clarity in the 'dry American light'—the light Henry James remembered from the fogs of London, fogs now re-created by Hollywood. I feel that when the 'Old Hundredth' thunders out from the church behind me, past the black notice-board with the gilt lettering, it sounds—in spite of that *Deus Volens*—more confident, more assertive than it did in our whitewashed meeting-house that looked out across the green-blue North Channel, and the heads of seals, to the long blue hump of the Mull of Galloway. Here in Boston they may be waiting on the Lord, but they are waiting in financial sanctity, in comfortable mahogany pews, confident, in the dry American light that filters through costly stained-glass windows, that the Lord has Boston on His special 'blue-plate' list.

Beyond the reassuring notice-board, Boston Common reanimates Boston history, its wooded heights and hollows not uncomfortably crowded with ghosts of the Revolution; the motto here, as in the 'blue-plate' church behind, moderation in all things. My most vivid impressions are of brilliant flower-beds, of a lake with a bridge over it, and on the lake small white pleasure boats in the shape of swans, propelled by men who sit at the stern or after-end of the swan and work the equivalent to bicycle pedals with their feet. A quaint conceit, an element of Nordic fairy tale, sweetening the facts of life on Beacon Hill—such facts (see the voluminous works of John P. Marquand) as rich old ladies living longer than rich old ladies ought to; dusty old lawyers fulminating in dusty old offices; vast male clubrooms full of enormous leather armchairs and that special Boston emptiness Henry James fled from—the whole Boston scenario, enormous leather armchairs, dusty old lawyers, and all, haunted by the ghosts of the Cabots speaking only to God, and to hell with lace-curtain Irish.

But that, past and present, by the way. The facts this sunlit May morning are the lake, the swan-boats, the brilliant flower-beds, a brass band playing in a tree-encircled bandstand, the musicians in the uniform of American Marines. In the intervals of the *pomp-pomping* band, a cavernous voice issues from loudspeakers in wooded glades, telling us to join the Navy and see the world, thereby chasing the ghosts of the Revolution, scandalising Jefferson and the Founding Fathers. It might (shades of Patrick Henry) be a scene in Hyde Park, London, on a May morning of the day before yesterday. The wooded parkland, the heights and hollows, the lonely tree-encircled bandstand, the uniformed bandsmen, the roar of distant traffic, the exhortations to join the Navy—all this, barring Henry James's 'dry American light,' is English social history repeating itself on the North American continent, a scene from Edwardian London translated into terms of revolutionary Boston turned rich and respectable, sunk in its mahogany box-pews and leather-armchaired clubs.

The London analogy repeats itself at lunch-time, in an old-fashioned Boston tavern in an alley off a roaring narrow street—the tavern once the scene of famous Harvard entertainments. Franklin Delano Roosevelt ate here in his salad days. Setting: dark wood panelling, elaborate mirrors, pictures of scantily-clad ladies with chiffon floating in all the right places, a rococo bar backed by handsome tiers of bottles—the bottles reflected, apparently *ad infinitum*, in plate-glass mirrors. My host remarks that during Prohibition the proprietor maintained his rococo bar and his mirror-multiplied wines and spirits intact, in the sure and certain hope of resurrection. Judging by the tumult at the bar, his faith was justified.

For lunch, a delicious cheese soup, a bottle of well-chilled Graves, broiled lobster fresh from the Atlantic, cheese, biscuits—a European meal, a sunset touch from the English nineties. The bar, the mirrors, the tiers of reflected bottles, the Graves, the lobster, the pictures of bosomy ladies with chiffon floating in the right places, the memory of the band recruiting on Boston Common—given an off-stage jingling of hansom cabs, we might be lunching in a tavern off the Strand, stoking up, back in the golden days of Edward, for a matinée performance of Gilbert and Sullivan.

At the pictures. A real 'crystal' screen mirroring murderous work in Chicago saloons—mirrors splintering, sub-machine-guns chattering. This 'beer baron' classic is followed by another revival, Loretta Young in *The Farmer's Daughter*—a nice brittle American fairy tale, with all the bad men coming to suitably bad ends. A gentleman whom, in my Irish ignorance, I take to be some new-fangled brand of American Fascist, is thrown out on his ear through the stately iron gateway of a stately (that is, plutocratic) American mansion into the snow. To the approval of this Boston audience, his hat is then crumpled and thrown out after him. *Im Mittel Westen Nichts Neues*—classical American violence on classical American screen.

Thoughts for the New England notebook. First, the cinema wasn't a cinema at all, but a converted theatre—a sidelight on Boston. Second, the 'beer baron' war, with mirrors splintering and sub-machine-guns chattering, seemed just as far away in Boston as it would have in Belfast, as if the Atlantic is less of a frontier than the Appalachians. Boston audiences watching Chicago gang warfare on the screen react like astonished spinsters peering out through lace curtains at nasty violent happenings down what was once a nice respectable street. I'm told (in the lobby of ny hotel) there are still tea-time gatherings of old ladies in the neighbouring towns like Salem whose conversation rarely recognises anything more recent than the Revolution. Fortunate old ladies whose church clock still stands at an early Georgian ten to three! For them New York (where I shall be tomorrow) is just a rackety collection of skyscrapers at the mouth of the Hudson, with, beyond it, the red-light district of Hollywood in siren lands along the Pacific, and, still further threatening the tea parties of old ladies in Massachusetts, Irish-named senators snarling in the thickets of Washington.

THREE SLAIN IN LOVE NEST

The plane for Chicago stands at its loading platform under a lofty echoing roof, a Pullman car with wings. Outside, in the streets of New York, it is raining, with a gusty wind amounting at moments to a gale. Inside, under the roof of its terminus, the DC6 bounces in a glare of floodlights as mails and newspapers are loaded. All that's missing is a clang of milk cans, a soft hissing of steam. The passengers in the lighted belly of the DC6— nearly all with neckties displaying tropical vegetation—take it all for gospel; unload brief-cases, slump back in adjustable seats, switch on reading-lamps, crackle newspapers, unfold colourful magazines that look like garish versions of the American Koran.

Deathly silence, as if all committed to mental home. The inmate in front unfolds his copy of the Koran. It has two messages: Personal Hygiene: eupeptic gods and goddesses grin toothily from toothpaste advertisements, surrounded by ghastly swarms of toothily-grinning offspring, all in a state of highly-coloured asepsis in bright newly-painted apartments—like looking through plateglass into a cupboard on Olympus. The second text is Transportation: bronzed, aristocratic-looking gentlemen with neat white toothbrush moustaches stand on darkie-hovering porches of white-pillared colonial mansions, ready to step into chromium-grinning automobiles about the length of the *Queen Mary*. Like a scientist on the Amazon puzzled by the plates in his textbook, I look round in dismay. Maybe we haven't reached America yet: the little men under the reading-lights, tropical vegetation and all, bear no relation to toothpaste gods toothily grinning in aseptic apartments, or toothbrush-moustached aristocrats descending from the porches of white colonial mansions.

Newspapers are less uplifting. Headlines shout in thick black type about blasts, quizzes, probes, arson, murder, and sudden death by stepping off skyscrapers—apparently we're lucky to be alive; the gem in New York's evening crown being a story headed THREE SLAIN IN LOVE NEST. This peep into the home life of America is illustrated by gory flashlight photographs of corpses strewn round a cold-water flat in Brooklyn; no hint as to which corpse with face smashed in was the intruder, or whose nest it was before the flashlight cameras. The corpses, photographed with great accuracy, from as close up as possible, evidently form part of the great American death wish; all along the belly of the DC6 shafts from pencil reading-lights pick out worshippers holding aloft their icons of the blood-stained scene, like communicants in a cathedral.

Tense religious silence. Maybe the photographers were having us on with tomato juice? Then, punctual to the minute, with the worshippers under the reading-lights still at their blood-stained devotions, the DC6 trundles sedately out from under its train terminus roof, accelerates through aerial shunting yards that would have delighted H. G. Wells; finally, taking the bit in its beak, roars up into the night.

We bump and bang through darkness. Lights of cities appear and disappear below. At intervals the whole sky lights up; violet flames stream from the wing-tips. At one point, when the bucking nearly breaks my backbone, I hear the pilot shout to the co-pilot, 'Boy, what a bump!' No reaction from the robots under the reading-lights; they just lie back in adjustable armchairs, ties loosened, studying the love life of film stars, peering religiously at blood-stained corpses with faces smashed by automatics, swallowing advertisements for automobiles with fins like whales; catching up on their home work of blasts, quizzes, probes, arson, murder, rape, seduction of little girls, bodies of blondes in wardrobes, and what the house detective found behind the door in 2006. Death may have come for the arch-bishop, with the doll in 2006 but all that stuff going on outside the windows is just hooey, not for real metropolitan he-men with hair on their chests plus time to study to-morrow's tabloids to-night.

The lights of an enormous city appear, stretching out of sight. Chicago —some incredible number of miles across according to the knowing gentleman in the seat across the aisle, a witness modelled when he started from New York on advertisements for men's wear in the glossies. It is just after midnight; we have bumped, banged, and bored our way through the upper air a third of the way across the continent. New York (where with wailing of sirens they're probably removing the three slain in love nest), New York is just yesterday, New York is old boots. Chicago, here we come. In the words of the knowing gentleman tipped back in his armchair across the aisle, 'Brother, what do ye know!'

Below, sky-signs wink, traffic lights switch from red to green, talking a secret language of their own. Life down there on those rain-reflecting boulevards, in the craters between those skyscrapers, must be driven by the same kind of clockwork now controlling non-existent traffic; we seem to be hovering over, about to descend upon, a vast light-blazing fun fair where everybody has gone home, leaving the dodgems still switched on, dead men still ringing the cash on the tills. The last thought that occurs as, carrying its cargo of print-sodden corpses from the upper air, the DC6, still bucking viciously, slides steeply down towards a providental black space, is how much wiser we would all have been, and how much more like human beings, if as parties of the first part we had all set out from New York in a covered wagon. A sad, violent world down here; just as sad up there, aloft in the lighted belly of the DC6.

We hit the tarmac with a vicious bump. An avalanche of New York evening papers (blasts, quizzes, probes, unphotogenic corpses, and all) slides off laps and seats into the aisle. They lie there like a dirty rash and we all stamp on the faces of the THREE SLAIN IN LOVE NEST in the rush to get out. Remembering those violet flames, the ghastly, undignified attitudes of the THREE SLAIN IN LOVE NEST, it feels like a 20th-century inferno, something Dante never dreamed of, even in the horrors, including Chicago's black stair-rod rain.

IV
CHICAGO NIGHT'S ENTERTAINMENT

Dusk. Panorama of lighted skyscrapers. Driven to a lakeside restaurant, in a blaze of headlights, four cars abreast and the devil take the hindmost, as if everybody's house was on fire, not just the widow Leary's cowshed. On our left, the architectural fig-leaf Chicago created to hide utilitarian crudity —the famous lake-front palisade of skyscrapers and apartment houses, all lit up like Christmas trees. On our right, the pale green ocean of Lake Michigan, stretching northwards to Canada.

Hollywood chariot race, punctuated by police whistles. We emerge on the lake front, pull up with a Keystone squealing of tyres. The restaurant is on the ground floor of a mammoth apartment house; shades of Raymond Chandler, you need gumboots to wade through the carpet in the lobby. After the M.G.M. chariot race on the boulevard I expect glass bricks, acid colourings—the usual 20th-century bright, chatty looney-bin or psychiatric home. Nothing of the sort: the restaurant interior is straight out of *The Merry Widow* or an antiquated French comedy in an anti-quated Paris theatre seen from the back of the crumbling stalls—red brocade curtains, chairs and settees upholstered in the same material. Sardou, Brieux & Co probably ran accounts here. Bourgeois of the western world, unite; we have nothing to lose but our overstuffed furni-ture!

Elaborate meal. Grapefruit, unrecognisable fish out of Lake Michigan, side-excursions into Europe, Middle West specialities, including corn-on-the-cob; down the home straight with ice cream and enormous cups of strong, creamy coffee. Outside, a cold wind from the lake buffets the bro-cade-curtained windows; inside, the temperature mounts; the atmosphere gets more and more like Vienna: red brocade curtains, rue St. Honoré upholstery, over-furnished interior, rich heavy food—all Austrian or central European; all we need is a string orchestra playing Strauss waltzes. But if being shut in behind thick curtains in the centre of a continent is redolent of central Europe, it is central Europe laced with something heavily and stuffily mid-American, something at once *farouche* and pro-vincial, as if whole regiments of irritable Mr. Deeds had just arrived in town; as if the whole restaurant is just a couple of degrees below flashpoint for shooting up the chandeliers. I think of young Mr. Henry James practising involution in his notebooks; how at the mere mention of Chicago he suddenly sounded like a Victorian clubman writing to the *Times* about peasants hacking off cows' tails in Ireland, or a Roman patrician casting a cold eye on table manners in Gaul. He never actually used the words *hi barbari*, but you could see them all lit up across his mind, like a notice calling for a doctor in a cinema.

From the restaurant, full of coffee and ice cream, to the ballroom. Maybe young Mr. Henry James had something. Young men in white tuxedos not so much revolve as sway about minute patches of dance floor, clutched in the arms of young women doing their best to look like adver-tisements from the more decadent American magazines—some already drunk. The marble pillars, the sinfully-discreet darkness, the spotlights, the white tuxedos, the wailing saxophones, the *thump thump* of jungle-haunted drums—all this is Rome with the skids under it; a celebration in the Colosseum complete with torches, slave girls, and barbarian music from Cappadocia.

But this Chicago version has threatening undertones of its own. There is violence in the air, as if the entangled couples, frustrated by what Shaw called 'the perpendicular expression of a horizontal desire' (with, in addition, in the tactful formula of our Irish police, 'drink taken') might, out of some frightful provincial boredom, suddenly stop pretending to dance and start to wreck the ballroom—suddenly, in the spirit of their forefathers from the neighbouring prairies 'shooting up' the saloon. In the interval before the explosion, before six-shooters start firing, police clubs swinging, watching the young barbarians at play, an Africanised hint of a classical theme from their jungle-haunted band reminds me of a wisecrack from a recent thriller when a gentleman waltzing in a San Francisco ballroom to a hotted-up version of an air from the Pathétique Symphony implored his partner not to be alarmed if she heard a strange whizzing sound—it was just Pyotr Ilitch Tchaikovsky revolving in his grave.

We abandon chandeliers, mirrors, marble pillars, spotlights, darkness, the *thump-thump* of jungle-haunted drums. Nothing new out of Africa, except Chicago love potions. Outside; a startling smell of fresh air from the lake; under the stone-canopied entrance, a honking, rain-streaming herd of automobiles hurls itself at the *porte cochère* with an effect of an infuriated herd of elephants charging a stockade. Gasoline fumes accumulate, car doors bang; all the gilded youth of Chicago seems determined to fight its way into its 20th-century Colosseum at the exact moment we have decided to fight our way out; and the later the arrival, the more 'drink taken' in search of lost time.

We crash out with a rending of bumpers, swish through rainy darkness with Lake Michigan looming like a spectral green ocean beyond the boulevard lamp standards. We are on our way to 'the Club'—words pronounced with proper Anglo-Saxon reverence. Another stone-canopied entrance, another herd of infuriated elephants. We plunge in out of wind and rain. The entrance hall is positively Pompeian, with lofty pillars that lose themselves in the shadows of a chandelier-encrusted dome. I feel enshrouded in the past, about to be entombed in a buried city, uncovering layers of Chicago to the point where I wouldn't be surprised to find a notice-board under the lofty dome announcing lectures by Socrates. Instead I am shown skittle-alleys and bathing-pools. We inspect an enormous empty ballroom, switch on lights in a library like the interior of a cathedral—a vast apartment bursting with books, but no readers—this on our way to the one department that seems to be doing real business, a sombre, richly-decorated bar, gleaming with table-lamps, shadowy with alcoves. Here, as in Dublin, the alcoves are for drinking, not the art of love. Here the art of drinking is treated with proper reverence: dim

102

religious light from table-lamps, a bar counter as chancel, white-jacketed bar attendants as priests; the whole shadowy interior charged with that static electricity, that thundery masculinity, that results, probably from friction, when men, and especially American men, play at being something the way they once played at being Red Indians—at Elks, or Masons, or Shriners, or Buffaloes, or Christians, or Oneupmanship, or who's got the biggest motor-car, or just doing one another down in the ordinary way of business. The male worshippers at this shrine, the combatants in this Chicago game of Indians—as far as I can be certain in the dim religious light—all seem to be over six feet high, average weight 200 pounds, all got up like outsize advertisements from *Esquire*; everything, including the furniture, is on the gigantic, pantomimic scale Arnold Bennett once noted in a London club where the nail-brushes in the lavatory were the size of deck-scrubbers on a battleship.

At midnight we leave this rich, shadowy interior where gigantic business men are still playing Indians or Shriners or Buffaloes in one of the shadowy, table-lamp-lit alcoves. We are on our way to the night plane for Los Angeles, another high-spot for playing Indians, and scalping everybody all round. The scene under the chandeliers of the entrance hall still suggests a buried city; the magnificence of the architecture extinguishes the human beings beneath; the marble pillars, the chandelier-encrusted dome, are still living a life of their own, contemptuous of happenings on the tessellated pavement far below. This time Socrates is definitely out; the only sounds in this enormous palace of callisthenics are a faint clattering of skittles from a distant skittle-alley mingled with plungings and splashings from the swimming-pool. The colossal library without readers is, apparently, closed for the night; the gigantic ballroom dreaming like a stage-set without actors; only the bar and the alcoholic games of Red Indians still carry on at full blast.

Outside, the lake front skyscrapers are lit up like Christmas trees. From one bronze-glowing illuminated skyscraper tower a searchlight beam goes soaring towards the stars, probing at the clouds, like a child reaching towards a darkened ceiling; the image fits this city that in some endearing way has never quite grown up; Chicago's reach still exceeds its grasp. That bronze-glowing skyscraper pinnacle, that groping searchlight beam, are my last clear-out pictures. Towards dawn I wake in the Los Angeles plane and look out of the window. We are over the Arizona desert. Real desert, pale red and threatening in the sunrise—trailer for the unrealities of Hollywood. Staring down at it, I have the greatest difficulty in believing that my Chicago night's entertainment was real—that the corn-fed giant on the shore of Lake Michigan—with all its domes, temples, art galleries, skyscraper towers, and positively Pompeian palaces—ever existed, was not a product of my travel-strained imagination.

V

THROUGH THE HOLLYWOOD LOOKING-GLASS

The old lady in the hotel corridor gives a magnificent performance as Queen Victoria. She advances in a dignified manner, elegantly dressed in black, wearing a large black picture hat liberally, but not too liberally, blossoming with artificial flowers, leaning on the arm of a handsome young man, presumably stand-in for the Prince of Wales, supporting herself on a fragile ebony cane—an aristocrat of birth or great wealth, or both, a breath from some blossoming time in the Californian nineties. As she advances she bestows majestic greetings on the hotel servants—including young coloured women operating vacuum-cleaners—and they, as if hired for crowd bits by M.G.M., drop old-fashioned (probably Spanish-originating) curtsies in reply.

The whole scene, including the hotel corridor, is Metro-Goldwyn-Mayer. It leaves me wondering what the star of the production, the Queen Victoria of the boulevards in the black picture hat, makes of Los Angeles today, blaringly present beyond the revolving glass-doors of the hotel lobby; speculating by what magic she turns back the Californian clock, revealing, somewhere behind the juke-box noise and glitter of the Californian present, secret places, traces of the old Spanish dignity, of life on the *hacienda*. Perhaps if you escape from down town Los Angeles, crash through blocks of white-sugar offices and apartments, roar through surrounding clutters of sugary white villas—what Mencken called fifty-nine suburbs in search of a city—you eventually find some doorway leading to the Spanish past.

No Spanish doorway. A friend calls in his car; plunged into darkest Africa, we hurtle into Los Angeles rush-hour traffic, heading for the ninth inferno, a dinner date in Hollywood. Once the thickest jungle, the sugary white office blocks, the avenues of waving palms, is behind, it is like roaring through a mad builder's yard. Item: the eating-house got up to look like a bowler hat; item, Graumann's Chinese theater, with teenagers lounging round its doors in shapeless toreador pants that hang halfway down their calves, looking like Chinese coolies or stevedores out of a job. So many electric signs flash and wink that nobody bothers to read them; evidently the mad builders have been joined by a convention of demented electricians. Young men slouch along pavements clad only in singlets and trousers as shapeless as, but slightly longer than, their sisters': total effect, a South Sea island metropolis where, in the poisonous wind from the Orient, there ain't no Ten Commandments, where a man can raise, and quench, any particular thirst he has a fancy for, with no holds barred, including nymphets of fourteen. It is Raymond Chandler country, haunted by a sad satiety, a threat of violence. See recent drawing in *Punch*: little girl in ultra-modern schoolroom holding up her hand and wistfully inquiring, 'Must we *always* do what we want?'

Sun drops into Pacific. Rendezvous in fashionable Hollywood restaurant said to be infested with film stars. No stars: this leaves host disconnected, like astronomer on foggy night. The dinner goes its Hollywood way, floated down on floods of alcohol, all think-pieces barred. Followed by bottle party that rages like a forest fire in a small house set high amongst pine woods—whose house, whose party, never appears on screen. We sit on a wide first-floor balcony, high above the tops of pine-trees—ice tinkling in tall glasses, distant sky-signs spelling out words and sentences (C-A-T, cat) below the dark rim of the Hollywood hills, telling us the facts of life in California, instructing us what to eat, drink, and wear. All straightforward words of one syllable, like the blackboard I saw in a county Down school on which a future Hemingway had written in large chalk letters: JACK HAS A CART AND HE CAN CART BRICKS AND SAND. That young man would have gone far in Hollywood—no nonsense about philosophic depths!

Then, as if there are not enough stentorian red, green, and blue lights already—including searchlights searching for something (possibly THE MEANING OF LIFE)—an aeroplane buzzes like an intoxicated bluebottle across the deep blue velvet of the sky, spelling out words in coloured lights on the undersides of its wings and fuselage, advertising a film *première* in Graumann's Chinese Theater—illuminated flying-machines instead of elephants down Main Street. Instructed by pentecostal red and green lights of the plane, I gather that all is not well with the one true church that is in Hollywood; that something has interrupted the holy apostolic succession of motion pictures. Shades of Charlie Chaplin! Equally agitated shades of Mary Pickford! O blue fishponds of television! It is like arriving in Mecca the night the bed falls on the Koran, the night the Pope take off on his *ceilidhe* to Portadown.

Horn-rimmed spectacles glitter, cracks grow more sulphuric. Like being in Italian medieval city, surrounded by acolytes from outer Hollywood shrines, by script writers, experts on historical backgrounds, cute secretaries who, prompted by Scott Fitzgerald's *Last Tycoon*, specialise in falling out of office closets completely nude—promising start to their careers. The conversation never strays from the main Hollywood channels, sounding to my ignorant ears like a bench of bishops confronted by heresy. Not a bathing belle, not a swimming-pool, not a Mack Sennet Beauty, not a nice juicy lump of scandal in the whole melange: just the frustration of presenting talking pictures to a world besotted by icy blue screens flickering in the front parlor, dinette, medieval lounge, or what have you. *O tempora, O mores.* Only random flickers from that old-time religion: goodbye Charlie of the perpetual rainstorms, the constant *delirium tremens*. The liluminated flying-machine, still flashing its authorised version, its un-revised gospel, still buzzes uneasily overhead, banging about under the Hollywood stars like a disillusioned bluebottle under a ceiling, no crumbs left on the table.

Below, like a small boy calling attention to himself at a party, the blazing bowl of Los Angeles blazes back with mindless profusion at its lofty dome of blue velvet sky; the robot skysigns spell out their equivalents to C-A-T, cat under the dark rim of the Hollywood hills, jazz trumpets blaring in a floodlit glasshouse, the extroverted West shouting adolescent catchwords at the Pacific. I feel like an old man exhausted by a children's party; get a sudden violent longing for the sad dark mountains of my native land. At midnight, when the drink has begun to die, I am returned like a missing goldfish to my empty glass bowl of a bedroom down in the blazing goldfish bowl of Los Angeles, minus an article for the glossy magazines; back to the image of the old lady in the black picture hat who advanced, leaning on her ebony cane, not only down the hotel corridor, but straight through the Hollywood looking-glass and out the other side, back into the Spanish-American world before moving pictures were invented.

VI

REFLECTIONS IN THE CALIFORNIAN NIGHT

Los Angeles. Union station, a white-walled garden, imaginary music by Granados. Floodlit turf, Spanish archways, alcoves, marble benches under shade-trees. Yet this Spanish beauty, unmarred by orange peel and paper bags, merely magnifies the underlying restlessness and melancholy of American life. Set against the gleaming coffee-percolator, the kitchen like a dream by Escoffier, the bath-tub like a municipal swimming-pool, is emptiness, empty deserts to the south-east, empty spaces beyond the Rockies, poisonous winds from the Pacific—the murderous unease that lurks in spine-chilling cellars below the house that Chandler built.

The night express for San Francisco. Outlined beyond Spanish archways, immaculate in pale green, waiting to thunder north towards the green forest sanity of Oregon. White-coated negro porters, a sort of Californian praetorian guard, man the entrances to her sleeping-cars. No flush bank roll, no ticket for this glossy-magazine, expense-account equivalent to a gilt coach.

My compartment glitters with chromium-plated taps, switches, gadgets for controlling ventilation. As an Irish immigrant, I test everything—switch on and off, adjust temperatures and degrees of light—before I tackle the whiter-than-white, antiseptic-looking bed. There is a lavatory-bowl that emerges from the wall as prelude and introduction to a lavatory-bowl when you pull a lever. The blue-print materialises, the thing takes over for itself, starts a phase of jerky evolution, like a flower unfolding on a cinema screen. You watch like a mad scientist. The last phase is actual lavatory-bowl, as opposed to the *idea* of a lavatory-bowl. I pull the lever several times, just for the hell of it. *Eine kleine Nachtmusik* on the road to San Francisco. And as the county Antrim butler who had been told to pour the gardener a small whiskey said in the act of pouring, 'It's all ye're goin' tae get!'

With philosophy plus science producing lavatory-bowls from original sketches for lavatory-bowls all down the train, we click-clack through the Californian night, each in his white-painted cell, each with his noumenon or *idea* of a lavatory-bowl. In the intervals of frightening bad Communist wolves by switching on roof-lights, bedside lights, blue night-lights—not forgetting the god-like process of creating lavatory-bowls where there had been no lavatory-bowls—we all go to bed in our white-enamel interiors like hospital patients due to be wheeled into operating-theatres in the morning. American *Angst*, where are ye! Give me a good, old-fashioned European wagon-lit every time, dusty red curtains, mahogany whatnots, suspect yellow water-bottles, and all!

(Mem. I remember previous journeys up and down this crazy state of California, down to San Diego, up to San Francisco, then on through the forest country of Washington and Oregon, finally by sea through island-studded channels to Vancouver Island. On one journey south to San Diego and the Mexican border, I was involved in a bus accident at La Jola (pronounced Spanish-fashion) unaware that forty years later I would be staring at La Jola on a television screen, watching my American folk hero exorcising booze, tobacco, and air-conditioned nightmares by tramping the beaches, mesmerised by long Pacific rollers rolling in from where-ever Pacific rollers start rolling. The folk hero was Raymond Chandler, taking an hour off in the desolate period just before his wife died—hero for me because he wrote such hard-hitting English—used his eyes, set down what he saw, knocked the mandarins of Bloomsbury and Chelsea Village for six. Pages from 'The High Window' should be set for Eng. Lit.)

Last night I was in a Chandler interior in a plutocratic suburb of Los Angeles. A big house that matched the big house in *The High Window*— the same stuffy, mummified atmosphere, the same vast Metro-Goldwyn-Mayer gilt tables and standard lamps. In the shadows of an enormous lounge like the nave of a gilt Metro-Goldwyn-Mayer cathedral stood the gigantic figure of an Irish Catholic bishop; he looked in the plutocratic gloom left by the gilt table-lamps about six foot eight, and broad in proportion; everything grows big here, including Irish Catholic bishops. Whether big is best is another matter. In the stuffy, mummified interior of this Los Angeles mansion where the bishop loomed like a giant in a Spanish folk tale, I began to long for the forest gloom of Oregon. I also understood where Chandler got the stuffy sinister atmosphere of his West coast thrillers, of this enormous, sun-dried, overheated state where everything flourishes except the human soul, and the result is instant religion, packaged for export along with canned grapefruit:

> 'Sister Aimée MacPherson
> Was a most insatiable person:
> I don't think Christ
> Sufficed.'

Dawn. No more blue night-lights. No more communist fairy tales. My image of San Francisco, a certain sea-food restaurant. That and a bottle of red Californian wine on a white tablecloth. Symbols for the Athens of the Californian north. Where the Mormons cease from troubling and the Holy Rollers are at rest.

VII

LOOKING DOWN AT NORTH AMERICA

Night over the Rockies. The hostess fixes a length of rubber tubing to a valve, then hands me the mask at the other end. I sit in a fantastic dream, inhaling oxygen—fantastic snow peaks beyond the windows, dimly-lit interior of cabin, thin shafts from pencil reading-lamps shining down like experimental theatre spotlights on inhuman, robot figures that hold masks against their faces; the purring of the engines as they lift and drag us through this vast blue tank that is night over the Rockies; a tank where snow peaks emerge as from the depths of an aquarium, a science-fiction nightmare through which we are painfully swimming, not thinking too much about the rock-teeth that any minute may rip our oxygen-dream wide open, not thinking of the chasms between the snowpeaks, or what lies thousands of feet below in the unseen, unimaginable depths from which, like water lilies in a pond, the jostling snow-teeth rise; depths where bones might lie till Doomsday. Somewhere overhead, a moon is riding behind clouds, its brightness sluicing down at intervals with an effect of theatrical limelight filtering down through water, its shifts and changes illuminating the gigantic stage below where order is still painfully thrusting up through chaos.

A last effort from the inhumanly-purring engines; the water-lily snow-peaks sink into the blue tank of night over the Rockies; the nightmare scenery slides downward in tremendous folds and creases that, separated by dark shadows, are the beghinnings of valleys. This is the watershed of the American continent; in the state of Montana, the Missouri has started its two-thousand mile journey to the Gulf of Mexico—making for St. Louis and the junction with the Mississippi. Missouri, Mississippi, Ohio —channels of American history. As if in confirmation, the lights of a township suddenly blaze like a casket of jewels in the darkness of a canyon thousands of feet below, an outpost of history after the inhumanity of the Rockies.

Below, colossal land waves surge down from the watershed to the prairies. The darkness is chased westwards; the dawn comes up like thunder over the Atlantic and hurtles to meet us across the shelf of the American continent. We are swimming in golden half-light over the grass-lands of Colorado. Soon with a honking of air brakes we are coming in to land at Denver.

Up on the grasslands. A tin shack serving coffee. Nothing happens; the air is clear as crystal, the blue wall of the Rockies glorious.

Bursts of activity. Planes arrive, planes depart. Inhabitants of Denver bang car doors, descend from planes—vivid, uninhibited citizens who laugh, and talk, with a little extra something, as if the crystal-clear mountain air and the enormous background to their lives had released a secret store of energy; as if every gesture and intonation had to be magnified in order to carry under this lofty American sky, against the gigantic drop-scene of the Rockies. I think of the Abbey players playing (of all things)

Riders to the Sea in (of all places) the London Colosseum back about 1911. The colossal distances of the Colosseum did them no good—reduced them as seen from the top circle to cheese-mites under a microscope—whereas up here on the grasslands of Colorado a tendency to overact is just reaction to the scenery, a device for protecting the ego from the colossal scale of the grasslands backed by the Rockies.

Towards noon I set out again. A small two-engined plane that hops out of Colorado into Nebraska, taking up and setting down farmers' wives at small dusty airfields, like a bus running through a rural district in Ireland; everybody gathers at the dusty airfields to watch us arrive, speculate who is aboard and why—finally watch us struggle into the sky again before settling down to sleep or the afternoon's chores. In this mid-American analogy the bus becomes a small two-engined bi-plane, a sort of conversational grasshopper that whirs a few hundred feet into the sky and down again over an enormous checkerboard of states—transport service and afternoon's entertainment rolled into one.

At times the absence of a pattern in the landscape frightens me. The farmers, or rather, the farmer-mechanics, who gather at the airfields are *on* the land, not *of* it. We have left the area of winter wheat and are, I suppose, over part of the great corn belt; all I can make out from the air is a vast dun-coloured, faintly green untidiness stretching everywhere to the horizon. No farmhouses, no trees, no crossroads; nothing we would call in Ireland a 'townland.' Where the small gatherings at the airfields—work-worn farmers' wives, farm mechanics in dungarees—come from or disperse to remains a mystery. Yet somehow, in some mysterious mechanical fashion, the land is being cultivated. This for most strangers is *terra incognita*, the great heartland of North America; travelling over it upsets all European, movie-fed notions of blazing boulevards, thousand-eyed skyscrapers, clangorous cities. We drone on for hours through the hot sleepy afternoon with nothing in sight but earth, earth, still more earth; agricultural anonymity all the way to the horizon.

At last a break in the monotony. A river, muddy-coloured, pale green over the shallows, wanders south-eastwards across the line of our flight. A small town straddles its willow-grown banks, sets me thinking of Tchekhov—of vast landscapes, of lives lived on apparently never-ending steppes by the banks of rivers that flow sluggishly towards enormous horizons. Then when the river is past I remember it must have been the Missouri. Nevertheless, Missouri or not, I cling to my Russian *mise-en-scène*, my equation of Russian and American land-masses. When I was a small boy I spent hours staring at the map of Russia, dreaming of beards, blood-red sunsets over the Kremlin, jingling sleigh rides with property wolves in pursuit; now nothing interrupts my recollected dream, not even the flat American voices of the pilot and co-pilot 'chewing the fat' in their stuffy little cockpit. As Goethe remarked, beware of what you long for in youth; in middle-age you get your bellyful—right down to Sioux Falls substituted for Novgorod; stuffy bi-plane for sleigh.

The landscape changes, growing faintly tidier as we drone on to the north-east. The typical red barn, beloved of American landscape painters, shows up at last; we have droned our way across the corn-belt into Minnesota, and the hand of the Swede is manifest in the way things look from the air.

Evening. A string of lakes set in dark forest land, white houses grouped by water's edge. Beyond the lakes, a cluster of skyscrapers, like reversed automatic pencils—Minneapolis, American metropolis of the Swede. Facing it, on the opposite bank of the Mississippi, the twin city of St. Paul, stamping ground of Scott Fitzgerald. Looking down at neat summer homes on wooded islands and promontories, at white launches that leave V-shaped trails on the water, at yachts anchored alongshore or moored to jetties, I remember a friend's description of Stockholm. It is as if the Swedes had brought their European story with them—had imprinted it on the landscape of Minnesota, merging it with the overtones of Lake Minnetonka, the falls of Minnehaha, memories of the forest lands that once hid Hiawatha.

VIII

A SLIGHT ENCOUNTER WITH HENRY LONGFELLOW

What I plan in Minneapolis is to write a short monograph on Scott Fitzgerald, the young man from the other bank of the Mississippi—stressing what I saw from the plane over Minnesota. Even allowing for American lakes, woods, and prairie lands behind him, no wonder Fitzgerald had a passion for Europe. Europe had transplanted itself into the lakeland and forest surrounding St. Paul; hence, with hardly any change of key, those haunting European scenes in *Tender Is the Night*, scenes with the grey mystery of a Monet painting: Amiens with its 'little trolley-cars of twenty years ago,' its 'faded weather like that in old photographs'; that unforgettable picture of Somme battlefields where 'infinitesimal portions of Wurtembergers, Prussian Guards, Chasseurs Alpin, Manchester mill-hands and Old Etonians pursue their eternal dissolution under the warm rain.'

But I'm not allowed to forget Minneapolis. First the famous flour-mills, dominating the skyline like a North American version of the Parthenon. Having acknowledged this monument, I am driven out to inspect an old fort and a modern military barracks on the banks of the Mississippi. Looking at a military barracks in Minnesota is like looking at a fire-station in the Arctic; you feel that if the brigade is ever wanted it will be a long way from the fire. Somewhere beyond the woods, lakes, and flat lands to the north is the Canadian frontier, an imaginary line across a map—an invisible feat of triangulation beyond which the same North American phenomena of sexy magazines, hot-dog stands, flamboyant petrol-stations, well-stocked refrigerators, more or less harmlessly repeat themselves. I wonder what it is like to look out through American eyes on this 'wind's sweep' that according to the poet MacLeish is the North American continent and know nothing of Europe except that it is very old, very picturesque, and always starting bloody wars.

110

Then through scattered woods, past tree-encircled lakes on the shores of which god-like young men and women lie sun-bathing, to see the Falls of Minnehaha. All there as Longfellow described them in *Hiawatha*, except that, as Longfellow had never been to Minneapolis, he had to do his describing from a photograph. The famous falls descend as a thin trickle from some not very impressive rocks, flowing away along a rocky, tree-lined channel that seems at first glance to have been intimidated into continuing its literary function by means of municipal concrete—folksy tales from the Minneapolis woods embalmed for booksie-wooksie girls from 'out of state'—all with cameras, nearly all with blue rinses. In an interval of snapping lenses, I observe the scene from a row of iron railings against which are leaning flotillas of brilliantly-painted, exotic-looking bicycles, the property of uproarious American small boys. And here I begin to get at cross purposes with my American host. He is suffering from such an overdose of the present that he is interested only in the past; whereas I, as a European, have had such an overdose of the past that for the moment, here on the soil of North America, with all those brilliantly-painted bicycles to examine, I don't want to hear any more about it—especially a past represented by Henry Wadsworth Longfellow and his falls described from a photograph. I am, in short, more interested in the design and construction of North American bicycles than in the Falls of Minnehaha. After all, I never knew Minnehaha, whereas the uproarious small boys and their bicycles are very much present, some of them performing hair-raising balancing acts—acts reminiscent of rolling drums and flooding limelight in yesterday's music-halls. I try, not very successfully, to conceal this morbid interest in the present, and, out of politeness to my host, do my best to talk breezily about Hiawatha and Minnehaha, without, however, altogether concealing the lamentable fact that I remember very little about them, and am now not too certain whether Minnetonka was just a lake or one side of a human triangle. I can see that my host has tagged me with the Teutonic label of 'not serious,' than which nothing worse can happen to you on this, in part, Teutonic continent.

We then emerge from the forests of the past, and, abandoning Hiawatha (on my part very thankfully), motor back into Minneapolis for dinner at a sea-food restaurant. A sea-food restaurant in Minneapolis sounds like the Swiss Navy or the Horse Marines. Nevertheless, there is an excellent sea-food restaurant in Minneapolis, where, having first braced ourselves at the bar, we follow up clam chowder with broiled lobster, and wash the whole lot down with strong creamy coffee—by which time Henry Wadsworth Longfellow is just an also ran. The proprietor assures me that the lobster I have just eaten was fresh out of the Atlantic, and, in company with other lobsters fresh out of the Atlantic had been rushed halfway across the continent in a special refrigerator tank-car, by express freight. I feel like a Roman senator well primed with shellfish from the Tyrrhenian sea. Round the wood-panelled walls of the restaurant are mounted a number of terrifying stuffed fish, of a frightful size and ferocity, all staring down at us out of wickedly-gleaming glass eyes and, understandably, not much liking the look of us. Like the French poet's lobster, they know the secrets of the deep. Just name your fancy, say the wickedly-gleaming glass eyes, but whether it's lobster Neuberg or call-girls with secret telephone numbers, remember you pay for it.

Fortified by sea-food, coffee, Walter Mitty dreams, we emerge into downtown Minneapolis, where skyscrapers are already dressed up as illuminated Xmas trees. Winter must be crisp and invigorating up here when the cake-ice consolidates on the Mississippi and snow-storms drift south over that trigonometrical fantasy that is the Canadian frontier. With its passion for education, its famous municipal orchestra, its climate of electric energy, Minneapolis is a starting point for that journey in which you never arrive—the search for what it is like to be an American.

IX

SHOSTAKOVITCH SYMPHONY

Dinner at 4,000 feet over Lake Michigan. Drone through golden haze over a green-blue sea. As the eastern shore emerges from the haze, the hostess serves coffee and dessert. Below, a white sandy beach bordered by hilly country with dark clumps of trees. White summer cottages shelter in woods by the water's edge. Yachts and motor-launches moored alongside wooden jetties.

Below us as we leave the lake behind (it is over 300 miles long and, on average, 70 wide), two sleek, racy-looking ships travel north with 'white bones in their teeth'—U.S. frigates or destroyers, reminders that the Americans have a naval tradition all their own, with memories of naval battles, fierce winter storms, and sea-going problems that breed a hardy race of fresh-water sailors. I think of *Thunder Rock*, the play that put the Great Lakes in the theatrical limelight, and how these waters were once the main gateway for immigrants into the heart of the new world. Somewhere on the opposite shore, out of sight to the south, Chicago sprawls beside its green-blue ocean, its ghettos hidden behind its theatrical palisade of lake-front skyscrapers, its docks and piers all set for salt-water trade from the Atlantic.

We cross the eastern coastline with its wavy edging of white sand, drone on over undulating country with low green hills crowned by dark woods. This is the main body of the state of Michigan, the spatulate peninsula that thrusts northwards into the Great Lakes. Somewhere under the port wing-tip is Grand Rapids, a good American name for a town, reminiscent of the Mandrake Falls from which the pixilated Mr. Deeds, armed with his tuba, set out to conquer the metropolitan wilderness of Manhattan; the guide to the wild dark woods of Manhattan being, if I remember aright, an essentially good-hearted blonde called Arthurs; so that everything worked together for good for them that loved the Lord, box-office included.

Which brings me back to Grand Rapids, to the green spaces with dark woods below. Somewhere ahead, hidden on the far side of this fertile peninsula that seems on the map to be floating on blue lake water, is Detroit, fourth (or is it fifth?) great city of these United States, and the devil take the hindmost.

But Detroit, for all its size, seems to be hiding behind the landscape. We land at an enormous airfield, stagger drunkenly about on a maze of bumpy concrete runways. As the French poet remarked of the albatross—*ses ailes de géant l'empêche de marcher.* The words WILLOW RUN blare in stentorian lettering from the end-wall of a gigantic hangar. *Genius loci*—Henry Ford, the man with the blue-prints for peace that turned into machinery for war. What never occurred to the egregious Henry was that history is not so much bunk as a peculiarly un-American form of irony!

Then from Henry Ford and the blue-prints of Willow Run, to the ruins of Berlin. Are the words 'Willow Run' inscribed in letters of fire in the German brain? Probably not. Nobody in Germany seems to have paid attention when Bismarck chalked up on the German blackboard the central political fact of the 19th century—the fact that North America spoke English. It is still a fact of the 20th, now slightly tempered by icy winds from Tartary. Nevertheless it explains the ruins of Berlin.

In search of Detroit I climb down from the mechanical bird, like an archaeologist exploring a dead civilisation. Dusk. The nearest things to open country between Willow Run and Detroit. Dead. We hum on a road like a concrete ruler across flat lands divorced from the story of humanity —buffer states between rival industrialisma; sad, haunting no-man's lands blasted by poisonous gases; backdrops with tall chimneys outlined against wrathful sunsets. The New Twilight of the Gods—libretto by Henry Ford Jr., score by Shostakovitch, whose symphonies sometimes sound like Diesel engines thumping sadly to themselves in empty, echoing sheds.

Maybe he thought he was writing it for Magnitogorsk; actually Shostakovitch was writing theme music for Detroit. From the synthetic cell of my 16th-floor Detroit hotel bedroom I look out at vistas of gigantic concrete honeycombs. At dinner, 16 floors down in the hotel restaurant, I feel like a not too industrious bee enclosed in a succession of synthetic honeycombs, with no possibility of escape. I sit facing enormous wall-paintings of Cadillac, Radisson, and other *coureurs de bois* trading with the Indians in green shadowy forest clearings. These gentlemen with their red, eighteenth-century faces, their bulging eighteenth-century calves, have about as much relevance to twentieth-century Detroit and the restaurant in which they are exhibited as the skeletons of primeval monsters remounted in metropolitan museums. An iron curtain has descended between machine-belt America and the shadowy green world of its primeval forests, and to paint murals on it suggesting that the one has descended from the other is a dangerous form of romanticism—the Machine has intervened, hence Shostakovitch's symphony with its lonely Diesel engines thumping in corrugated-iron sheds. Even the diners in the restaurant seem aware they will never return to the green forest world depicted round them; the twentieth-century puppets are busily jolting themselves into insensitivity with cocktails, automatically adjusting themselves to the assembly-lines of Detroit machine-belt entertainment.

The real iron curtain is between Detroit and the forests out of which it grew, not between Detroit and its opposite number beyond the Urals. They, *pace* the leaders in Detroit's morning newspapers, are twin souls, Tweedledum and Tweedledee, threatening us like gigantic shadows on a screen.

X

SATURDAY EVENING POST

Interlude in Pullman sleeping-car. Still under African spell. Nothing changed in twenty-five years: the airless African gloom; the water-spigot with attendant cups in the corridor; dark-green curtains like jungle vegetation behind which you meditate on your latter end and listen to other people snoring; white-coated monsyllabic negro attendants whom years of travelling at close quarters with the white man have reduced to rancour and a more than African melancholy.

Buffalo. Convulsive clashes and bangs. The dark-green sarcophagus moves off pretending this is not Africa but North America. Snoring starts again fortissimo. Reflect it was a long way for Africans in white coats to be buried in these travelling tombs.

Syracuse. Pleasant lively town with avenues of overarching elms and one of those magical Indian names—Onandago county. Who, with the possible exception of William Faulkner, would not opt for Onandago county?

An excellent hotel, with, in its basement, a marble-gleaming, softly-lighted bar where the more sybaritic inhabitants of this Greek-named city crowd round the bar-counter, and a small string orchestra (one saxophone) embroiders the uproar with snatches of be-pop, honky-tonk, or what have you. I notice an American habit that interests me. When you have paid for your drink, you do not invariably collect your change and put it in your pocket; you leave it lying on the counter—presumably on the assumption that you will soon be having another drink, or out of *panache*, as gamblers leave their winnings on the table—to show you are certain of your place at the conveyor-belt of society.

Or is this a relic of the '49, when you plonked your nugget or your bag of gold dust on the counter and stayed there till you had polished off the lot? Certainly the wads of high-denomination bills on the counter of this Syracuse bar seem too imposing to be tips. Maybe this is another facet of the frontier mentality below the glittering surface of American life—like the automatic pistols, revolvers, hunting rifles, shot-guns, etc., in the floodlit windows of the stores. Apparently, like the piles of dollar bills on the counter, some sort of firearm is *de rigueur*, like a refrigerator or a television set.

More stuffy catacombs, more Pullman sleeping-cars. I emerge from behind dark-green curtains, a body resurrected from the tomb. The train is rumbling through a pass in the Appalachians. It is a New York Central train and the scene in its breakfast-car is an exact reproduction of a recent cover illustration for *The Saturday Evening Post*. The same white-jacketed negro waiters (a good deal more genial, according to the *Post*, than the Pullman-car attendants farther up the train!), the same gleaming silver coffee-pots, the same portions of grapefruit, the same bacon and eggs, the same gaily-coloured packets of cereals.

Yet there are variations. In this New York Central version, rumbling down from the Appalachians into Massachusetts, the passengers look less eupepetic, less insanely pleased with themselves and the state of the Union than they did on the cover of the *Post*. They fit in fact into reality, into the scenery streaming past the breakfast-car windows—the Massachusetts countryside where farmhouses merge more snugly into the green of stony uplands, send down deeper roots into soil, landscape, and history than the farmhouses of the Middle West and the forest lands round the Great Lakes. Watching the little stone-walled farms reel past, I realise that back in that pass over the Appalachians, at the point where the train began to pick up speed again, we crossed the Great Divide of American history. The mountain barrier of the Appalachians is nowhere very high—not much over 5,000 feet at the peaks—but for nearly a hundred years its wooded passes were the frontiers of what amounted to a nation, long enough to stamp it as indelibly American. Beyond the wooded passes were trackless forests, Indians, scattered French colonists, *coureurs de bois* like the red-faced gentlemen in the restaurant murals in Detroit; this side, the side down which we are rolling towards Boston and the Atlantic ocean, were the original colonies, growing into a nation, still looking backwards to Europe. Hence this morning's slight departure from the garish suburban optimism of *The Saturday Evening Post*—the more nervous, introverted types dealing with grapefruit and coffee while stony mountain farms reel past the windows. The giant U.S., offspring of those original colonies, now sprawls from Atlantic to Pacific and beyond, but the descendants of the original *accoucheurs* present in this New York Central breakfast-car seem a trifle worried—sorcerer's apprentices who set the broomstick to filling buckets with water and now can't make it stop.

XI

ROBERT FROST COUNTRY

The edge of the Atlantic north of Boston. Pleasant wooded country: white-painted houses grouped at cross-roads, amongst lawns of well-cut grass, already smelling of the Atlantic and the rock-bound coast. A salty freshness in the air, grass theatrically green. Between the road and the sea, screened by thick plantations, guarded by un-American stone walls, the summer homes of wealthy Bostonians: magnificent mansions fronting the Atlantic, with ornamental iron gateways, and long winding drives that disappear amongst privileged lawns and plantations. John P. Marquand country. More accurately, *former* homes of wealthy Bostonians, now windfalls for churches, hospitals, clinics for drying-out alcoholics, etc.

Mist thickens from the Atlantic; grass grows greener, moisture drips from trees. They grey mist, the stone walls bordering the road, the black trees dripping moisture, the lush green of the grass, the occasional glimpses of the blue-grey Atlantic, the strong, languorous air—western Ireland repeated this side of the Atlantic. Then with the fishing town of Gloucester, the Irish illusion disappears—a lively town, thronged with visitors in summer, famous for its fishing industry, its schooners that range as far as Newfoundland, its canneries. We visit one of the fisheries, where a modern, Diesel-engined version of the standard Gloucester schooner is lying at a wharf; then follow the chain of processes by which the cod dumped in tubs on the wharf are converted into canned food—cans with brightly-coloured labels ready for the shelves of supermarkets. I think of Kipling's *Captains Courageous*, of the troubles and lawsuits he encountered in Vermont; how the whole experiment of transplanting himself and his family to America ended in disaster. This distracts my attention from the business in hand, and earns me a rocket from the earnest gentleman with the steel-rimmed spectacles who is explaining the transfiguration of unattractive cod on the wharf into colourful cans on the shelves of *Saturday Evening Post* super-markets.

(*Mem. I must remember I am in Massachusetts and watch mechanical processes with respect. Not to do so is to be labelled, as efficiently as the cod in the cans, an egghead, a Communist, a poet, or worse.*)

In the train to Albany. I sit at the window of a day-coach, watching the grey-green Massachusetts countryside. Rain is falling; little wooden towns along the line, with dripping shade-trees, wet-shining automobiles parked outside drug stores. This is Robert Frost country:

'The land was ours before we were the land's.
She was our land more than a hundred years
Before we were her people. She was ours
In Massachusetts, in Virginia,
But we were England's, still colonials,
Possessing what we still were unpossessed by,
Possessed by what we now no more possessed . . .'

including the rain now dripping on automobiles parked under the dripping shade-trees of Main Street:

'I have been one no dwelling could contain
When there was rain;
But I must forth at dusk, my time of day,
To see the unburdening of skies,
Rain was the tears adopted by my eyes
That have none left to stay.'

No wonder that severe and intricately simple poet lived and worked in New England. He must have been quarried out of the rock that thrusts through the green of New England fields, and this landscape under frost and snow must be signed with his Puritan austerity.

116

The train climbs, panting, into the foothills of the Appalachians, feeling its way towards the gap through which, three nights ago, I rumbled in that olive-green tomb of a sleeping-car that, with its atmosphere of unburied dead, had *Saturday Evening Post* written all over it. The track up here in the foothills wanders through stony hill country and scattered woods. A wooden house, distant cousin to a manor house in Europe, dreams in an isolated glade, with, roaming the fields in front of it, a black-and-white pointer nosing for game—a sporting print from the New England day-before-yesterday, cover illustration for a print by Robert Frost:

> 'Careless and still
> The hunter lurks
> With gun depressed,
> Facing alone
> The alder swamps
> Ghastly snow-white.'

Up here, in tumbling streams we are repeatedly crossing, the sport is fishing; every stretch has its solitary figure, hip-deep in waders, whipping away at the rain-pocked surface. We rumble slowly upwards through narrow, alder-lined valleys: more tumbling streams, more solitary fishermen:

> 'It is turning three hundred years
> On our cisatlantic shore
> For family after family name.
> We'll make it three hundred more
>
> A hundred thousand days
> Of front-page paper events,
> A half a dozen major wars
> And forty-five presidents . . .'

then the land opens out, with distant prospects of wooded ridges and open spaces of cultivation. We have surmounted the gap in the Appalachians and are running downwards towards the valley of the Hudson.

XII

Under the Shade-Trees of Saratoga Springs

The main street of Albany runs steeply up from the Hudson, flashing with electric signs, to the State Capitol, tree-embowered, crowning the green *place* at the top with a strong suggestion of Paris. This little town has deep roots in American history, so deep that the ramifications extend into Europe as well—as witness the wallpaper in my hotel bedroom. It has a rustic scene, with water-mills and shepherds sitting in the shade of trees, repeated *ad infinitum* over its plain white surface.

It reminds me of a stuffy little hotel beside the Paris markets that in spite of its grandiloquent title, *Hotel des Empereurs*, had the usual smell of drains on its winding stone staircase. Or perhaps a small family hotel in Amsterdam would be nearer the mark—this attractive little town on the hillside overlooking the Hudson was in fact founded by the Dutch. Albany, deep in rolling green savanna that was summer camp ground for the Iroquois, is both capital of New York State and landmark in American history, including literary history as temporary pasture for the James family on its way to produce Henry who, on his own confession, couldn't have too much gilt.

A tree-shadowed road lined with white suburban homes leads out of Albany towards Saratoga Springs—setting for recent unpublishable happenings, secret history not for general release, certainly not for *The Saturday Evening Post* or the Daughters of the American Republic. Along it not so many years back a small band of American Communists advanced to seize the State Capitol, met determined police opposition at a certain cross-roads pointed out to me, and fled over the fields into the woods, to disappear into the underworld and those shadowy caves and grottos where the bogeymen live at the back of every good American mind. All this light-years after that short-circuited bishop, Henry James, had left Albany to pontificate in Boston and New York.

In Saratoga Springs, beyond the Mohawk, on a wide green plain dotted with spinneys and prosperous farmsteads that has the look of English parkland, a perfect piece of period architecture—a disused hotel with balconies and the kind of thin elegant pillars once shown in illustrations of American classics, or in back numbers of *Harper's* and *The Atlantic Monthly*.

No amount of American *Angst* about parking problems gets me past this hotel; for me it *is* Saratoga Springs, raffish background and all. I see the famous State bath-houses in the green environs; I see the famous race-course; I see strings of famous racehorses being led along pleasant, tree-shadowed suburban avenues; but nothing equals that hotel with the elegant, in fact the classical, pillars and balconies. It has character; it has a certain effrontery; it has something deeply American that crops up only in patches—in the old red-brick streets of Annapolis, in Williamsburg, Virginia, in odd corners of Philadelphia, in the cosy provinciality of Albany—a purely American rhythm and pattern, the sort of thing men die for on battlefields.

Other American phenomena this fine summer afternoon are bevies of young women on their way home along suburban avenues from tennis. They wear the shortest of shorts; their main efforts at concealment are sunglasses; darting in and out of sunlight under the shade-trees, they look as elegant as, but far more purposeful than, the racehorses—illustrations for a transatlantic version of Proust's *A l'Ombre des Jeunes Filles en Fleur*. The young men of the neighbourhood are, I assume, intensely interested in what Anatole France (and he ought to have known) called the 'centre of gravity' of these young women. If not, desire has failed, locusts have eaten the green heart of Saratoga, and the stories about that hotel with the elegant pillars must have been part of the Great American Myth that began in 1777 when they beat back Burgoyne on the road from here to Albany.

XIII

AMERICAN MYTHS

Long ago, from a train in the Hudson valley, I saw the blue contours of the Catskill mountains, and longed to be there. Now in fulfilment of Goethe's dictum on youthful longings, I *am* there, in the middle of them, surrounded by a series of low green ridges and a patchwork of dark-green woods. A twisting mountain road climbs past the woods, past a grey, stony-shored lake (used by Murder Inc. for dumping bodies), on between more green ridges, more dark blanketing woods. Somewhere in these green uplands are reservoirs for New York city; also, in July and August, the summer homes of those two tribes with a not-so-secret affinity, the New York Jews and the New York Irish.

Along the tree-lined road are white-painted hotels, some with swimming-pools. Then instead of hotels there are clumps of wooden shacks, buried in the shady edges of woods or congregated round cross-roads stores. This is where the New York Irish emigrate in hot weather; whole districts up here have Irish names and resound through stifling summer nights to the rhythmic thumping of *ceilidhe* bands from lighted cabins or cross-roads dance halls.

An Irish-named bar in wood shadow. Through a window above the bar I look into steeply-shelving forest. The bar-counter lurks beneath another kind of shadow: the head and antlers of a deer, flanked by a pathetic collection of stuffed stoats, squirrels, badgers, foxes; the squirrels paralysed in the act of climbing property branches of property trees; all staring down at us with, reasonably enough, glaring antipathy in their glittering glass eyes. Alleged Irish whiskey 'on the house'; also, in association with, and almost arising out of, the Irish whiskey, a wheezy piano badly played by an Irish-named gentleman with a battered straw boater and thick, pebbly glasses who looks like an assistant gunman from the Bowery. First thought: what's he doing up in these woods (*nous n'irons plus aux bois*) when there are, presumably, lolly-laden laurels to be lead-punctured in New York?

Watching the gentleman in the straw boater, listening to his showers of wrong notes in the treble, I take a violent skunner at the well-known human race as typecast by Hollywood; their shenanigans in these mountains—white-painted hotels ('What's it matter so long he love his old Momma?'), pale-green swimming-pools, gunmen in straw boaters strumming pianos, crucified stoats, badgers, foxes. The time to come up here would be in the dead of winter when the green swimming-pools would be empty or frozen over, the gramophones, radios, pianos, and *ceilidhe* bands silent, the old Irish mothers safely locked in winter quarters, *in hibernis*, on Third Avenue; and the real story of the real inhabitants would be told by prints and run-ways in the snow, by the real street-plan and directory of the forest rides. With that I raise my glass of suspect Irish to the silent, glass-eye-glinting company of stoats, squirrels, badgers, foxes, etc., nailed to the wall above the bar-counter. Some day we will pay for this. Meanwhile, God help them, they have fallen in with a shower of rascals, the kind of rascals who pollute good Irish whiskey; and Rip Van Winkle, if he should ever be back in these parts, will find his wooded mountains sadly changed. God between us and those glass eyes on the wall!

Sunday morning in Albany. From the window of my hotel bedroom (the one with shepherds sitting under shade-trees) I look out over huddled roof-tops to the Hudson valley. A ship's siren reverberates amongst roof-tops—reminder that beyond the swirling currents of the Hudson, the Atlantic begins a hundred and fifty miles down-river at the docksides of New York.

I switch on the bedside radio. Tinkly chimes, advertisements for department stores—stuff for white-anglo-saxon protestant Sunday mornings. A famous divine, a veteran of World War One, pumps out 'muscular Christianity,' variations on a text by the War Department—'they were expendable.' The secret of life is to be expendable and expended—this to a reunion of veterans of World War Two. Look not to the ants; look to that famous American, Mr. X., who only yesterday burst his boiler in a last fabulous, headline-making explosion. Go ye and do likewise; keep your safety-valves lifting; keep pounding away on the battlefield, the football field, the stock market—all, according to the voice that breathes over station 2RXZY, scenes of commendable American activity.

I consider this without moving from the bed. The voice, I imagine, emanates from a large, stout, well-groomed, well-manicured gentleman bursting from pulpit or rostrum; once an heroic obstacle behind the scrum; now, by extension, a formidable buttress for things as they are, a 250-lb backstop for God and America.

Silence. More tinkly chimes, asterisks for more white-anglo-saxon advertisements. I listen drowsily. Again the ship's siren on the Hudson. From the railroad tracks branching west for the Great Lakes and the Rockies, north for Montreal, the long African wail of a locomotive—barbaric, infinitely sad, emphasising the emptiness of North America. Surburbia may be eating out North American forests; vast emptiness remains, raising its tinny voice in my bedside radio, substituting its phoney sermons, its tales from cornflake packets instead of the Vienna woods! O God, O Montreal!!

XIV

FAIRY TALES OF NEW YORK

At first the bank of the Hudson is marshy, with scattered plantations. A freighter bound for Albany looms beside the train windows, nosing against the current, bringing a breath of the ocean. The river here is narrow, with white lighthouses and navigation marks in mid-stream.

Then the flood widens, with glimpses of towns, villages, tree-embowered country houses on the farther shore; ferry-steamers sliding helplessly as they fight their way across. Low green banks give way to precipitous rocky shores. Over there, backed by the swelling blue contours of the Catskills, the land of Washington Irving with his myths that might have come from the Hartz mountains—the Catskills now withdrawn to the remoteness of 'blue remembered hills,' not breathing a word of Irish cabins thumping with *ceilidhe* music, white-painted Jewish hotels, blue-rinsed Yiddischer mommas, pale green swimming-pools, spectacled New York gunmen playing wheezy pianos in forest-shaded saloons.

We rumble slowly round a bend. The Hudson widens to a lagoon. Small grey-painted warships, about the size of British frigates, rust at anchor, resting between wars. The valley narrows to a rocky gorge. Wagnerian cliffs, the famous Palisades, justifying comparisons with the Rhine. Carrying the Rhine *motif* still farther, a white-painted, many-tiered river steamer pushes slowly up to Albany—the sort we watched from the darkness of the one-and-ninepennies, dream vessels thronged with amorous ghosts heading out of town, clattering with deck restaurants, resonant with four-piece bands playing 'The Sidewalks of New York.'

Then, on cue from river steamer, a long grim wall surmounted at intervals by machine-gun turrets. Sing-Sing. More celluloid fairy tales, flickering shadows in suburban picture palaces, riot squads, warders with sawn-off shotguns, screeching sirens—vicarious crimes committed in the darkness of the Gaumont and the Majestic—arson, mail van robberies, safe-blowing, sudden death. The train, with all this on its mind, puts on a spurt, flings Sing-Sing behind it with a long, menacing wail from its siren. New York, here we come. We flash through suburban stations, under graceful concrete viaducts, familiar background for fairy tales. New York puts on its act as glittering entrance foyer to North America; this time the backstage version; a stage-door, back-alley welter of scrapyards, concrete docks, concrete fly-overs, shunting-yards, mammoth blocks of tenements, threatening red-brick buildings that look like mental homes, head-shrinking clinics, laboratories for drying-out alcoholics. Strings of washing fly from rusty iron fire-escapes, celebrating New York tales of father's pants will soon fit Willie; gangs of small boys play baseball with pathetic exuberance in canyons between mountainous apartment blocks; cops twirl batons at intersections like cartoons from *The New Yorker*, poker-faced, men who wouldn't be surprised at anything, not even if King Kong surfaced from this metropolitan jungle, emerging all lit up with bath-tub gin, chanting, 'Oh, say can you see?'

The train, not without reason, ducks underground into a tunnel lit by dirty electric lights, grinds to a halt in clanging darkness. From the abyss below Grand Central station the ascent, as in the more literally-minded hymns, is sudden and dramatic; dingy iron staircase to floodlit magnificence, to an immense pleasure dome of marble, rows of ticket windows inviting with unearthly fluorescence, news-stands overflowing with the love life of film stars, the houris who will some day reward the faithful; crowds ecstatically surging as to some kind of resurrection; authoritative voices rebuking them through loudspeakers; a stout matronly woman in a hat playing an organ in an organ-loft. Heaven as imagined by Aimée Semple MacPherson.

I circulate under the marble dome like a soul in Hell, unable to hear what the stout lady in the hat is playing on the organ for authoritative voices issuing instructions through loudspeakers. Still in a daze, I shoot like a ball in a roulette wheel into a passage. The passage, of imitation marble, ablaze with brilliantly-illuminated shop windows, is a real *Alice in Wonderland* burrow, the New York equivalent to the tunnel down which Alice fell, and from the walls of which, while falling, she attempted to abstract a pot of marmalade, even if the pot was empty.

But this New York passage doesn't stop at marmalade. Float in at one end in your Freudian underwear and, provided you have the correct currency in your underpants, you can float out again at the other in a gent's natty suiting, complete with overcoat, umbrella, galoshes; if necessary, suitcase containing silk pyjamas (spelt here 'pajamas,' which somehow simplifies matters), dressing-gown, luxurious carpet slippers. Or maybe you had forgotten your hunting-knife, your complete hunter's outfit, including gun, cartridges for gun, tent, coil of rope, tent pegs, mallet for knocking in tent pegs, or your patent cooking-stove operating on solid fuel—all, no doubt, invaluable in the wilds of Manhattan, or, if headed in the opposite direction down the *Alice in Wonderland* passage, the Adirondacks.

The opulent passage, blazing with shop windows, ends at the basement entrance to an hotel. Here, attended by a New York white rabbit, watch in hand, there is business with an elevator button. One minute would have taken us up the stairs, but to climb—still worse, to be seen to climb—stairs would involve New York loss of face, and with all that Red Indian equipment lurking behind plate-glass windows, no faces must be lost. Meanwhile, waiting for the elevator, we sternly resist the brilliantly-lighted shop windows; firmly refrain from leather grips or suitcases, silk shirts or pajamas, patent cooking-stoves or collapsible canvas wash-basins, coffee percolators or neckties suggesting tropical vegetation, that, for fear we might have missed them farther back behind the looking-glass, here repeat themselves in riotous profusion, in heaped-up floodlit munificence for us playboys of the Western world.

At last, with the New York rabbit on the verge of apoplexy, the elevator arrives. We are translated to a vast hall with twisted sugar-candy pillars we might have had in pantomimes at the Belfast Grand Opera House, but are really architectural ingredients of the hotel lobby, and are in fact inedible. This Walt Disney fairyland is crowded with chain-gangs in the uniforms of *Esquire*, *Harper's Bazaar*, and other 20th-century fantasies; the main difference from Sing-Sing being individually-controlled heating in the cells and a horrible proliferation of bell-boys expecting tips. As Mort Sahl remarked of a cover illustration for *The Saturday Evening Post*, 'This cover shows this kid getting his first hair-cut, and a dog is licking his hand, and his mother is crying, and it's Saturday night in the old home town, and people are dancing outside in the streets, and the Liberty Bell is ringing—and, hey, did I miss anything?'

The answer is, he did. There's no Liberty Bell ringing in little old New York to-night, at least not at 42nd Street, and he should have put the young men behind the registration-desk in this sugar-candy-pillared hotel lobby in the act. They are characters in the great *Saturday Evening Post* illusion; they wear dazzlingly, almost unnecessarily clean shirts; they set down our names with superbly-glittering fountain-pens. They are in fact choristers and censer-swingers of the Great American Machine, and the Great American Machine seen close up is, for us European villagers, haymakers, etc., a terrifying sight. Here in this floodlit, sugar-candy-pillared setting for *Scheherazade* is a high temple of the Great American Machine—the trouble being that in this American apotheosis of the mechanical there is still no financial Reformation to deal with the consequences of the Machine or the popes and cardinals of High Finance.

Conversations with Jan Masaryk

A flag-draped reception room in a Belfast hotel. Jan Masaryk speaks to the P.E.N. club about Mussolini and his famous circus horse—a superb piece of pantomime; how he, Masaryk, when in Rome, was commanded to get up at 7 a.m. to watch Mussolini ride. The arena was a Roman riding-school, the horse a white horse that, with due attention to protocol, could be trusted not to put a hoof wrong, even when carrying sacks of potatoes or dumpy little Caesars. The pantomime is all the more ludicrous if you know that Masaryk, the man condemned to the spectator's gallery, is an expert horseman.

Later, apropos Russian diplomacy that consists, with Andrei Vyshinsky as the worst offender, in 'bawling out' your opposite number like a lighterman, Masaryk remarks in his fluent, colloquial English, with just a touch of central European irony, 'Nowadays, if you don't call a man a bugger right away, they say "This fellow has no diplomatic vocabulary!" '

Promenade-deck of the *Queen Mary*. Panorama of New York harbour. In the foreground, Andrei Vyshinsky, like an evangelist on the pier of a seaside resort. The flapping black suit, the shock of white hair lifted in the wind, the arctic smile, the glad, explosive handshake—it only wants *Jerusalem the Golden* performed, slightly off-key, as cornet solo; the rattle of a collection-box; a placard announcing that the wicked will be turned into some refrigerated Marxist hell.

The second night at sea, accompanied by Miss Vyshinsky, he appeared in the cinema and sat down bang in front of me. There were empty seats all round but Mr. and Miss Vyshinsky (Miss Vyshinsky very plain and dressed like a mid-Victorian governess) elected to plump themselves virtually in my lap. And there we remained, a highly critical trio in a desert of stuffed shirts and Peter Arno blondes, while moonbeams from the larger Hollywood lunacy glittered on the screen and the *Queen Mary* wallowed majestically in the following seas. The Vyshinskys watched the screen; I watched the Vyshinskys, especially Mr. Vyshinsky, who seemed to be enjoying himself immensely, if not in the manner, or for the reasons, the cinematic czars intended.

The first item was Walt Disney's *Make Mine Music*. This was coldly received by all three, Russians in front, capitalist stooge in dinner jacket behind. As far as all three were concerned, the idea of a whale singing soprano never got off the ground—this, we concluded, must be some sort of Anglo-Saxon joke, beyond our combined Russo-Irish comprehension. Not so the masterpiece that followed—short scenas that brought down the Russian side of the house—an illustrated album of Russian snippets, a Russian salad devised, mixed, and decorated à la Sunset Boulevard, full of Russian broths of boys battering balalaikas. At the sight of it, Mr.

127

Vyshinsky seemed to have a stroke: tears streamed down his face and he performed, single-handed, the Hollywood operation known as 'rolling in the aisles'.

This did not surprise me: American nonsense about Russia was, I supposed, the dead spit of English nonsense about Ireland; here, in mid-Atlantic, the screen was simply dishing out leprechauns à la Russe, translating the English school lesson about Ireland that began, 'The Irish are a merry people and very fond of pigs' into 'The Russians are a dangerous people except when playing balalaikas', projecting it on the blackboard in the *Queen Mary's* cinema for the education of Peter Arno blondes.

Which was, I suppose, as near the great Slav soul as you can get, starting from Sunset Boulevard instead of Dostoievsky. At any rate it set the frosty-eyed Vyshinsky letting down his frosty back hair. As long as the Sunset Boulevard broths of boys went on walloping their balalaikas, his back view was the back view of a man enjoying himself—having a night out, a holiday from death cellars, corpses, shots in the back of neck, coffins carried out at dawn, death-trains starting for Siberia. It was, for one Hollywood-illuminated moment, as if the Sunset Boulevard boys had knocked a small, precarious hole in the Iron Curtain: the gentleman with the frosty hair in the seat in front suddenly turned into a nice, jolly little man, very kind to his plain, Victorian-style daughter—a joker who had put thousands of miles of first-class travel, not to mention endless bottles of diplomatic champagne plus mountains of *petits fours*, between himself and those gruesome executions, those mechanical shots in the neck, those corpses slid out at dawn. Or was it just that, hidden in the discreetly-expensive darkness of the *Queen Mary's* cinema, surrounded by expensive blondes, he no longer heard his Master's voice!

So far in the manner of the *New Yorker;* now for Kafka. On the last night, with shore lights flashing in the English Channel, I was talking to Masaryk in the bar. From where I sat I could see Vyshinsky framed in a doorway, the wind from the coast of Devon ruffling his evangelical white hair. Masaryk, who didn't see Vyshinsky, was in brilliant form, talking like a Chopin fantasy interspersed with intervals of Grock.

Later I left the bar and made a tour of the promenade deck, watching the distant lights. At one point, in a moment of truth, I got a glimpse through a lighted window into the main lounge, where English shipping company decoration had gone skittishly modern—like a herd of elephants dancing a fandango; for even more asphyxiating analogies see Evelyn Waugh. In an enormous, dropsical armchair Jan Masaryk sat staring straight in front of him—as we say in Ireland, 'thinking long'. An orchestra was playing; beside him sat a beautiful woman. But there was no conversation. Masaryk just sat there, slumped in the mammoth armchair, staring straight in front of him as if the ship had suddenly been invaded by ghosts.

I thought of the first time I saw him, in that flag-draped reception room of a Belfast hotel—the day he gave us his immortal pantomime of Mussolini and the white circus horse. His face, now that I saw it in repose, was the face of the elder Coquelin, as I remembered it in an illustration—like the blank surface of a pond, waiting for light to irradiate it, the actor's mask *par excellence*.

Later, news of his death. Before I switched on I was reading George Santayana's *Persons and Places*, at the point where he speaks of the capacity to see clearly as sometimes paralysing the will, but at the same time setting the personality free to make exquisite fun of things the mechanically-minded regard as deep and serious.

That was Masaryk's dangerous gift, and it caught up with him in the Cerninsky palace. From the moment he landed from the *Queen Mary* he must have been moving in a claustrophobic nightmare, a sort of Kafka mousetrap enlarged to the proportions of palaces, marble corridors, ministerial offices—except that Kafka never invented anything so suffocatingly sinister as that lonely pilgrimage up and down marble staircases that led to the shattered corpse below the palace windows. Whether the Party killers were at work or not, does not matter; the Kafka nightmare consists in the fact that the night I watched him through a promenade-deck window in the *Queen Mary*, Masaryk, with his appalling clarity, was probably foreseeing some such end. That night, with potential murderers crowding beside him in the bar, haunting the decks and companion-ways, queueing alongside him at the purser's office, the trap was already closing, the journey to that final defenestration in Prague just begun.

Twilight of the German Gods

I

A mountain peak in the Vosges. Below, in the valley of the Rhine, patches of woodland loom like seaweed under water, spreading in grape-bloom purple to the smudgy black line of hills that marks the beginning of the Black Forest. The Rhine itself is invisible except where in the last sunlight of a winter evening it shines at one bend like a streak of silver.

Night falls. The silver gleam of the Rhine is extinguished. Up here on the Hochkönigsberg, in the shadow of the Wagnerian Schloss at the summit, Wilhelm II, Emperor of Germany used to shoot wild boar amongst the pine woods, probably with a rifle supported by some patent contraption because of his withered arm. He never stayed the night in the Wagnerian scenery at the summit; just banqueted in the banqueting hall that was heated by colossal log fires burning in colossal fireplaces; looked out over the heartland of Europe and the grape-bloom valley of the Rhine; sprayed lead at a few inoffensive wild boar, or at any rate wild boar that were never allowed to become offensive; and departed again down the mountain road to Strasbourg, then a gastronomic gem, *pâté de foie gras*, Alsatian wines, and all, in his imperial crown. For this annual assault on the Hochkönigsberg an enormous retinue of rangers, foresters, game-keepers, huntsmen, chief huntsmen, housekeepers, kitchen maids, scullions, butlers, chefs, major-domos, and what not, was either maintained at the castle or else transported up the winding road through the pine forests almost into the clouds; not to forget the gold plate for his Imperial Majesty's table.

Now scattered snowflakes swirl round the battlements. The danger to-night is not the *furor teutonicus* but the ice age from Tartary, the sudden drop in European temperature that, behind the rampart of the Vosges, back there in light-twinkling Paris, translates itself from snowflakes to smudgy black print in the columns of *L'Humanité*. From somewhere far off, faint and fragile in the frozen air, a sound that might be a peal of bells or the ghostly memory of bells. I remember the prize for French I won fifty years ago at the Academical Institution in Belfast, back in what seemed the cozy, unpartitioned Europe of Wilhelm of the withered arm and the frantically protestant moustache. It was a fat little leather-bound volume called *Les Oberlé*, its story set here in Alsace against this pine-clad background of the Vosges; in it somebody heard the bells of Strasbourg echoing amongst the mountains as from a sunken cathedral. But the bells tingling to-night in the frosty mountain air are not the bells that echoed in *Les Oberlé*. To-night, with Germany divided and Europe ending in the blackness beyond the blackness of the Black Forest, they sound like bells on a frontier. The clocks of Christendom still strike, but *diminuendo*—muffled by ideological snowstorms sweeping from the Vistula to the valley of the Rhine, and beyond the Vosges to where at this moment fellow-travelling presses thump out the pages of *L'Humanité* in Paris—fresh ammunition for the cold war.

II

Heidelberg, former backdrop for *Lilac Time*, lies in its wooded valley, lit by frosty winter sunlight. All that is missing is the sound of an orchestra tuning up on the banks of the green-tinted Neckar. That and a chorus of students in coloured caps, the ghost of Heine, the lilac blooms of yester-year.

But below in the town, beyond the rose-red bridge over the green-tinted Neckar, nobody is bothering about Heine. Or for that matter, about lilac blooms of yesteryear. American soldiers wander uneasily in narrow, tram-clanging streets, still smelling the charred corpse of Hitler from that bunker in Berlin, still sickened by the stench of concentration camps. We visit a Weinstube down on a quay by the sunny, green-tinted Neckar. It has narrow wooden tables, spotlessly clean, but with nobody eating at them. It has a tinny wireless-set blaring from behind a zinc-covered counter; a sad-faced waitress still distracted by a rendezvous with death; a death's-head of a host with mad staring eyes. The host with the mad staring eyes looks like an ex-Nazi stormtrooper; he has the same daft, doped expression as the creatures we saw being smoked out of that Nazi wasps' nest in the Hotel Majestic, Paris, in that unforgettable French film, *Le Journal de la Résistance*. From the moment we enter, the mad, staring host never takes his eyes off us. The effect is like being

130

watched by a dead man. But then perhaps he *is* dead; perhaps some ghastly moment of total war was the end of him; perhaps what now stands behind the zinc-covered counter is a *Doppelgänger*, a glassy-eyed automaton. Behind him, with all the treasures of German music to draw upon, the tinny wireless blares out a German version of a current 'Family Favourites' hit in Britain—*Mocking Bird Hill*, Bach and Beethoven banished for the Common Man. The only other visitors to the Weinstube seem to be a colourless young couple who sit, without moving or uttering, in a corner. They are neither eating nor drinking; they just sit there, motionless, plunged in melancholy, as if waiting for a bad dream to dissipate itself—waking the corpse of the Germany that was.

Then, as our eyes become accustomed to the darkness—like the darkness of a Dürer engraving—we discover, in a shadowy corner beyond the motionless couple, an old grey-haired woman lying drunk over a table, with the sleeves of her worn cardigan rolled up to show the red, swollen arms and calloused hands of either a washerwoman or a charwoman. Beside her sits a stout, quiet man, perhaps her husband, who, every now and then, without saying a word, touches her gently on the shoulder. Perhaps he is trying to comfort her in some terrible sorrow, a son lost or maimed in the frozen wastes of the Russian campaign. But in spite of the quiet dignity and devotion of the man, the sight of a drunken woman is a shock—shattering sheltering myths about Germany, letting loose a regular Walpurgisnacht of suffering in the darkened corners of the Weinstube. All this time the death's-head behind the bar keeps his sightless gaze turned in our direction, marking up some dossier on the *Ausländer*, and the feebly imitative wireless blares out *Mocking Bird Hill*.

The sad-faced waitress stirs herself from her encounter with the dead. An excellent lunch appears by Teutonic magic on the bare, scrubbed table—bowls of soup; the inevitable but delicious *schnitzel*, sizzling in a mass of exquisitely-cooked vegetables; cheese; goblets of golden Rhine wine, fit for the Teutonic gods. Stimulated by food and wine, we begin to to talk, even venture to laugh—but always with a sensation of making merry in a house of mourning, with the body upstairs. The body upstairs may, of course, have committed suicide, but that does not detract from the solemnity of the mourners in this Dürer-shadowed Weinstube. Meanwhile the skeleton behind the bar watches us with his fixed, unwinking stare; the young couple, still silent, still drowned in melancholy, register every mouthful, every sip of wine. Only the drunken old woman and the quiet, dignified man, absorbed in their private sorrow, are exempt from curiosity. The rest watch avidly, as if visitors from outer space had just arrived in Heidelberg for lunch.

Outside, on the quay by the green-tinted Neckar, it feels, in frosty winter sunlight, as if lilacs will never bloom in the dooryard again—certainly not *wie einst im Mai*. We climb into our large, shiny, status-symbol American motor-car; thread narrow, tram-clanging streets. American soldiers still lounge disconsolately at street corners, a stage army behind which somebody has let down the wrong scenery. A ruthless autobahn leads towards Strasbourg—across a wide sandy plain flanked by dark regiments of pine-trees behind which a frosty red winter sun is in the act of setting—across the shattered Siegfried line where colossal concrete bunkers lie up-ended, fragments from the cavern of the German mind. Ahead, the blue wall of the Vosges and the chandeliers of Strasbourg; behind, the ogre's tomb, the black ending of the fairy story with the ice palace beyond the Vistula, the wide sandy plain that, pine-trees outlined against red sunsets like Prussian regiments on the march, stretches back with hardly a break into Eurasia, to Moscow; beyond to Tomsk and Vladivostock. The lights of Strasbourg twinkle beyond the Rhine, promising crystal chandeliers and light Alsatian wine; the last barrier falls, the last dark-blue-uniformed German clicks his heels. Behind us, separated only by an iron bridge, Germany feels like an enormous haunted room, a vast Gothic stage-set in which curtains turn into apparitions, cabinets to elemental beings; where the east wind blowing out of Tartary frosts the window panes, blurring the faces looking in from the dark; where the verb *werden*—the most overworked verb in the German language—conjugating itself like a contortionist in a music-hall, points like an enchanted dwarf from one brassy Wagnerian climax to the next; forward, that is, from the last one, the scene at the bunker in Berlin, when, to imaginary Wagnerian accompaniment, the evil magician, having set everything else on fire, was himself set on fire with war-department petrol. No wonder that, along with the *schnitzel* and the wine, there was a smell of death in that tavern on the bank of the icy green Neckar. The twilight of the Wagerian gods had begun.

PART SEVEN

Island of 18th-Century Ghosts

Last Journey on the Sligo, Leitrim and Northern Counties

At five minutes after the advertised time the little green rail-bus chugged, a trifle bumpily, out of Enniskillen's railway yards. I noticed that a pane of glass in the side of the driver's cabin had been mended by plugging it with a crumpled paper bag. It had been a big day in Enniskillen, the day of the cattle fair; but already, one minute out on our journey west, we were rattling along a sort of private green lane. At the iron bridge over the Erne, I looked back and got a last glimpse of Enniskillen framed between tree trunks, rising like an Irish Venice from its lagoons, its skyline crowned by eighteenth-century cupolas and that north-western equivalent to Nelson's Pillar, the Lowry Cole monument.

Soon there were no cupolas or monuments. We were out in a wild dark stretch of Fermanagh, with enormous vistas of untidy sky and vast black plains that had once been forest. It's true there *was* a station called Florencecourt, calling up visions of a justly famous Georgian mansion. But nobody got on or off at Florencecourt, and there wasn't a pillared portico in sight—nothing but untidy sky and far-spreading black plain. This was western Ulster in the act of becoming western Ireland.

The transformation accelerated with every mile along the shore of Lough Macnean. The view across the lough was infinitely sad, infinitely subtle, a symphony in black and silver, with the black mass of Cuilcagh mountain (beyond which the Shannon rises) as back-drop across the water. We traversed a narrow neck of land between the upper and the lower loughs; halted at a solid-looking station of grey stone where the platform name-boards dramatically announced 'Belcoo and Black Lion'. Then, rattling and vibrating, we began to climb, leaving on the right a long blue arm of Upper Lough Macnean surrounded by fresh green belts of afforestation, and so on into the desolate upland emptiness of Glenfarne and the grey-stone station of the same name.

At Glenfarne a Customs man climbed into the rail-bus, took a good look at all three of us, then climbed out again. We chugged on deeper into the Irish Republic and the lonely heart of Leitrim. I began to wonder how the driver, down whose neck I was breathing, ever hoped to penetrate the wild tangle of mountains that kept springing up along the western horizon; how he and the railway line between them thought they were going to win through to the Atlantic.

The answer was evasion. We evaded the mountains and the mountains evaded us. A tangle of untidy black peaks slid mysteriously to the right, and we were up on a plateau, clattering past water hydrants and a jumble of locomotive and wagon sheds into the station at Manorhamilton. An imposing signal box gave at any rate the impression of a vast, complicated junction—the Swindon or Crewe of the Sligo, Leitrim, and Northern

Counties—the Slow, Lazy, and Never Comfortable of the wags. Alas for vanished glories, alas for imposing trains of eight-wheeled Victorian coaches drawn by equally imposing 0 . . . 6 . . . 4 tank engines rejoicing in such names as 'Sir Henry', 'Lissadell', and 'Lough Gill'. The first-class carriages had fussy little curtains, odd bits of mirror, and photographs of lordly interiors full of marble pillars and potted palms, that turned out on inspection to be the entrance halls and lounges of first-class hotels —to the end that the 'quality' might feel at home. Those carriages wanted only maids in starched caps and aprons serving afternoon tea, and the illusion might have been complete. Now the lordly little trains of eight-wheeled coaches have been replaced by cattle specials moving through the night, bumping and clanging between the black and lonely hills.

Beyond Manorhamilton we began the long descent to Dromahair, Collooney, and the Yeats country. Grey December dusk was falling. Near Dromahair we ran for half a mile through a magnificent avenue of beeches, as if down the private avenue to a gentleman's mansion. Far below, in the gathering dusk, the spire of Collooney church punctuated the last stage of the journey.

Nobody got in or out at Collooney, and a philosophical taxi driver drove philosophically away, as if he had never expected that anybody would. We chugged on deeper into the Yeats country, towards Ballysodare. It was here, at Ballysodare, on the shore of a landlocked arm of the Atlantic, that an old woman translated for him the Gaelic ballad about the young man who gambled away his bride. 'The Host of the Air' Yeats called it, and into it, by some magic of his own, carried that magic of the Gaelic mind that is never very sure which world it is talking about—this world, or the next, or the one beyond that again:

> O'Driscoll scattered the cards
> And out of his dream awoke:
> Old men and young men and young girls
> Were gone like a drifting smoke;
>
> But he heard high up in the air
> A piper piping away,
> And never was piping so sad,
> And never was piping so gay.

It was dark now; with memories of the female relative who said, 'There was always a want about poor Willie' rattling in my head, and the lights of Sligo shining in the distance, we chugged on past Ballysodare on the main line from Dublin—smoothly, like a small badly-lighted ship sailing safely up a dark estuary after the hazards of the ocean.

At 6.15 next morning, in the bitter blackness of December, I climbed aboard a rail-bus at the Sligo terminus. The guard looked at me in astonishment. It was the same guard. It was also, judging by the crumpled paper bag stuffed in the cracked side panel of the driver's cabin, the same rail-bus. At 6.20, with flashing of lanterns, we were off on our journey, back through the tangle of mountains to Enniskillen. A section of the track ahead was lit by our not very brilliant headlights. We slid into darkened stations which, at the moment of our arrival, were suddenly illuminated.

Nobody got in or out. A bicycle was delivered at Ballysodare, and left there, propped in solitary state in a small brightly-lighted waiting-room. We slid into more darkened stations which promptly lit up to welcome us. I sat alone in the forward end of the rail-bus, my overcoat collar about my ears, a small bottle of the 'craytur' in my overcoat pocket. For me all these switches were being switched, all these stations being illuminated, all these stationmasters were waving lanterns, all that Irish whiskey had been left in bond.

Between Collooney and Dromahair a rabbit bounded ahead of us along the track, its white scut flashing in the glow of the headlights. Fortunately we were climbing what railway men call a 'bank,' and the rabbit won by several lengths. At Manorhamilton we slid to a stop and the driver switched out his headlights. In the silence that followed, our opposite number, a comparatively luxurious Diesel rail-car, chugged in from Enniskillen. As far as I could make out in the half-light of the dawn, there was nobody on board except the driver and the guard.

But business was looking up on our side of the tracks, for Manor-hamilton produced a small dark man on his way to Liverpool, who immediately fell upon me with the frenzied curiosity of a Robinson Crusoe discovering an outsize Man Friday. Where was I going? Belfast. Did I live there? Yes. An expression of mingled wonder and commiseration flitted over his face. Obviously I was a trifle astray in the head. Why leave the gorgeous palaces, the gay lighted boulevards, of Belfast to go wandering through the county Leitrim?

And where was he going? Liverpool. To work? No, just for a holiday. It was now my turn to conceal a sense of wonder. Then, on reflection, I saw the point. Fair enough. If you could go from Liverpool to Manor-hamilton for a holiday, why not the other way round? I was suddenly converted, suddenly became an enthusiast for Liverpool. I thought of Merseyside by night. Towering buildings honeycombed with light, the roar and clatter of the elevated railway, lighted ferry boats, floodlit funnels of liners, the sound of ships' sirens—it was a sort of poor man's New York but cheaper if you stayed with your relations.

The small dark man and I got on like a house on fire. I told him about the rabbit and was relieved at the way he took it. Sure enough there did be rabbits in these parts that had escaped the myxoma-whatever-you-called-it. I patted the wee bottle in my overcoat pocket, relieved that the rabbit was a real rabbit; above all that it had survived the myxoma-whatever-you-called-it. Having escaped worse, it deserved to escape decapitation by internal combustion. What about foxes? Ah, now that the rabbits were so scarce, the foxes did be wild. Looking out at the bare black hills of Leitrim in the half-light I was not surprised. I would be wild myself.

The dawn came up over Lough Macnean in a riot of red, green, and turquoise. It blazed in the sky; it blazed in the water. Even the small dark man from Manorhamilton, elated at the prospect of Liverpool, was silent.

We shuffled along in low gear, driving a sheep before us up the track to Enniskillen; this was not one of those railways where you tear ahead regardless as long as the lights show green—in any event the driver probably knew the owner of the sheep. Eventually the sheep decided it wasn't going to make it as far as Enniskillen, and we rattled on again, only to halt at Belcoo and Black Lion—one of those long, silent, contemplative pauses during which, without the sound of steam escaping from the engine, you feel you ought to be saying your prayers. The small dark man from Manorhamilton spent it counting his money, making sure he had enough to reach Liverpool.

Then on again along the shore of Lower Lough Macnean, with the remnants of the riotous dawn still blazing in the water. Pale winter sunlight seeped over the flat black land of Fermanagh that had once been forest. In a quiet, country fashion of their own, passengers had been slipping into the railbus at wayside stations, so that now we were doing comparatively big business. At Glenfarne we had picked up a statuesque, Titian-haired beauty on her way to do a day's work or shopping in Enniskillen. Behind her a small boy was being conveyed with by no means shining morning face towards something unpleasant like a school or a dentist's. Behind them again, three hefty farmers from West Cavan were talking cattle.

We rattled over the iron bridge; there again was that fascinating vista of Enniskillen, framed between tree trunks, rising from its lagoons like an eighteenth-century print strayed from the library of a Georgian mansion. In more senses than one that print-like, eighteenth-century vista was the end of the line—now in next to no time they would be tearing up the tracks.

View Day at Mount Panther

We bumped up the long, twisting, tree-shadowed drive and parked in an enormous stable yard. The coach-house was pure 18th century, complete with campanile and elegant clock-face. At the other end of the yard the mansion reared its starkly reasonable 18th-century posterior, like a cliff —no attention to frills. No Gothic nonsense, as Squire Weston remarked in *Tom Jones*. Just insert your window frames in proper functional order and leave the rest to compelling rectangles of wall space. After all, if you were an 18th-century country gentleman, what would you be wanting with back windows anyway, except to see if the chaise was ready, or that saucy-looking new milkmaid was alone in the byre.

We went in by the back door. Half-a-crown to see the 18th-century ghosts, and very reasonable at 1s 3d per skull. But there were no ghosts, just tweed-clad furniture hunters in search of mahogany sideboards, and a scattering of local farmers. The famous Mrs. Delany's name was flourished by an arty-looking young man with long hair and a catalogue, but she never materialised, backed as she might have been by Johnsonian thunder. Instead of ghosts there were chandeliers—chandeliers in glittering 18th-century ranks as one apartment opened into another: chandeliers and gilt-framed mirrors reflecting still more chandeliers. I kept thinking of the space dimension that made those enormous gilt-framed mirrors possible; the time dimension that meant, not only a long day's journey to get here from Belfast, but punctiliously-organised expeditions with cases of wine in the boot every time you set out to call on your neighbours at Castle-wellan. No wonder you talked in Johnsonian periods, polishing up your phrases on the way; no wonder conceits glittered like crystal chandeliers; that conversation ordered itself like the Wedgwood patterns on the walls of Mount Panther's 'blue drawing-room.'

Outside, rain was falling through the dank green afternoon. Just the weather for 18th-century phantoms, for ghostly echoes from the London literary scene, rumbles of Johnsonian thunder—clinking of teacups as Irish colonial exiles reconciled themselves to the deep green solitude of county Down. But there was no Johnsonian thunder, no clink of teacups, and the scene beyond the lofty, small-paned 18th-century windows—including a tantalising vista of Dundrum bay insinuating itself towards the dark barrier of the Mournes—was just a wet Irish autumn afternoon: the Irish present glimpsed through clear, 18th-century glass, the kind of glass on which Swift etched those still-reverberating 'words upon the window pane.'

But there was no Swift, no Yeats, only familiar ghosts from yesterday. I remembered my friend Richard Rowley, the poet of the Mournes, telling me that from somewhere amongst the dank green pastures and wet, mournful woods I was looking at through lofty 18th-century windows he had picked up a fragment of verse about Mount Panther and had rushed off to share it with his friend Lynn Doyle (Linseed Oil—Lynn C. Doyle), the man from Downpatrick who invented a place called Ballygullion and never looked back afterwards. The fragment went:

> The lovely Miss Armitage
> To her last resting place was borne
> 'Neath the sycamores of Mount Panther
> In the Kingdom of Mourne . . .

and along with the vision of rain falling over the dark-green desolation of the woods beyond the 18th-century windows, it left a picture of Rowley rushing into a small 20th-century bank interior and reciting it to a figure leaning sardonically on a mahogany counter.

'Isn't that lovely?' said Rowley (a linen merchant whose real name was Williams) when he came to the bit about the sycamores and the Kingdom of Mourne.

'It is,' said Doyle (whose real name, barring all jokes about linseed oil, was Montgomery), 'but it's unfinished.'

'How do you mean it's unfinished?' said Rowley.

139

'It doesn't give the full address,' said Montgomery alias Doyle. 'It should go:

> The lovely Miss Armitage
> To her last resting place was borne
> 'Neath the sycamores of Mount Panther
> In the Kingdom of Mourne, townland of
> Cloghram, barony of Lecale (Upper).'

To which, telling the story afterwards, Rowley always added, 'Mind you, he wasn't a Downpatrick man for nothing!' To which again, looking out of Mount Panther windows at the rain falling, the wet woods, and the dank green afternoon, I now add, with chandeliers and gilt-framed mirrors all round me, that neither was he a bank manager for nothing—it was there in the confessional of little county Down bank parlours he got the sardonic detail that went down in a succession of children's exercise books and finished up as *Ballygullion*.

A Moon Like Green Cheese

The Lagan towpath. Beyond a humpback bridge, a church spire, rising from tree-tops. A resolutely Protestant spire, outlined against winter sunset, witness to Ulster history. Rooks threshed noisily in the plantation by the churchyard; below the humpback bridge the canal reflected lemon-yellow sunset. Overhead, masses of grey cloud sailed in from the Atlantic, passengers across the green wastes of Ireland, threatening rain in the night.

Beyond the canal, the moon hung like a lantern over the dark woods of Ballydrain. Not just an ordinary moon. A pale green moon, like an enormous green cheese. We walked on, pretending not to have seen it. But there it was. Somebody, perhaps for a joke, had hung a moon like an unsmiling green cheese over the canal and the thick black woods round Ballydrain House.

Then, as if a theatrical green moon wasn't enough, there was a wild, clanging burst of melody from the sky. It was the carillon in the church tower playing a well-known Christmas hymn: jerkily, with one of its notes about a quarter tone flat. Flat or not, with the green moon and the lemon-yellow water under the bridge, it was magic.

It stopped. Silence. Even the rooks in the plantation stopped cawing. Then it started again. Another wild burst of melody, clanging away over the woods, the Lagan valley. We set out for the churchyard, round by the hump-backed bridge. What genius had chosen this moment of December sunset, of lemon-coloured sky and water, of unsmiling green moon hung over the winter purple of the woods, to broadcast melody from a church tower? Something stirred at the back of my mind about carillons—something read long ago about the real experts coming from Belgium. I rehearsed a few phrases in French. *Monsieur, je vous félicite. Un effet magique*!

140

We reached the churchyard, waited amongst tombstones. Wild melodies poured overhead, with just an occasional jerk. Then just as twilight settled over the valley and the canal, and even the rooks in the plantation had begun to call it a day, the music stopped abruptly—like a record that had played itself out.

We waited reverently in the dusk, our gaze on the door at the bottom of the belfry, the green moon just visible above the belfry pinnacles. Very soon now we would see the great man himself, the genius who had compounded this miracle of church bells and winter dusk, this *son et lumière* lit by green-cheese moon and lemon-coloured water. And right enough, after an interval, there was a pounding on the belfry stairs. Not just the measured tread of an old gentleman with a beard, a frockcoat, and pince-nez—a trifle hesitant about the next step; this was more like the uproar we made on the bare-boarded staircase at the Academical Institution when the bell had gone for recess and we weren't too certain the baker's cart might not be away. A rushing sound, a crescendo of clattering footsteps, and out from the little door at the bottom of the belfry shot four small boys—followed, after an interval, by a small, yapping wire-haired terrier.

'Was it you who were playing the carillon?' We included the wire-haired terrier, who had lined up along with the rest, panting, with his tongue out, as if he had just done a hard afternoon's work.

'Yes,' said the tallest. He might have been, at the most, fifteen.

'But isn't it very difficult?'

They stood there, diffidently, concert stars delayed in the green-room, only wanting to get home to their tea.

'No, it's easy once you know how.'

'And what about him?' I pointed to the wire-haired terrier. 'What does he do?'

'Oh, he just gets in the way.'

'And what about the rector?' I said, making a proper nuisance of myself. 'Does he know you're playing the bells?'

'Oh yes,' said the spokesman. 'He lets us play any time we want.'

And that was that. We all said good-night and went our separate ways. They were nice, well-mannered boys who illustrated what it's like to be young in the second half of the twentieth century. No false modesty, no hanging back, and just produce the piece of mechanism we can't master! At the same time they turned a spotlight on the rector, who must be a man worth knowing.

Leaving the carillon-players and their wire-haired terrier, we returned, by way of the lych-gate and the humpbacked bridge, to the sunset-reflecting canal. In the churchyard behind us were the graves of Protestants massacred in the 1641 rebellion; in the church a wall-tablet commemorating a young man killed in the charge of the Light Brigade. Before he went to be a dragoon he lived in the big house beyond the canal, amongst the dark woods of Ballydrain over which there now hung a solemn-faced moon like a green cheese. We walked on with the yellow sunset behind us, aware of omens, towards a bitter winter of frost and snow—the coldest for half a century—and a horrible fright the night we thought the rockets were going up over Cuba—wondering what deadly instruments the young campanologists might be controlling before their slightly uneven rendering of *Hark the Herald Angels* reaches the farthest stars and some fanatical idiot of the sort that ordered the charge of the Light Brigade goes stark raving mad and pushes the wrong button. Meanwhile, in the sunset hour, a sound of propitiatory, *Portrait of the Artist* bells streams up towards the solemn green moon from dismal steeples all over the green island. Perhaps Joyce's picture of the Jesuit hell was right. Except that in the modern world, hell-fire, instead of a nice blazing coal-fire red, would be a cold, ghastly green like the light from a television-set or that ghostly moon hung over the woods of Ballydrain that may, for all we know, still be looking down at the bodies strewn in the wake of the Light Brigade.

Requiem for Louis MacNeice

An iron plaque with the name, low iron railings, a patch of rough grass. The sea is invisible from the grave, shut off by the wall of the churchyard. But it is there, below, about a mile from the church on the hilltop, the Irish Sea that was the problem of his life, part of what W. R. Rodgers called 'the old account-books of earth:'

> Only a green hill
> And a man with a spade
> Opening the old account-books of earth
> And writing paid.

Beyond the churchyard wall, the railing-enclosed patch of grass, and the iron plaque, the castle lies buried in dark woods—privileged, Anglo-Irish, evocative backdrop for an Anglo-Irish poet. The castle blanketed in dark woods; the woods advancing up the leafy avenue to the gate in the churchyard wall; the Anglo-Irish spire pricking above its rampart of Anglo-Irish plantation—fitting illustration for his life and times; if he has risen from his iron-railed enclosure to meet his Maker, they will agree about a job well done, the perfect final curtain for his sardonic Anglo-Irish comedy. He always loved trees, saw them with the miraculous eyesight of the poet, felt in his heart the wounds inflicted by the thudding axes:

> They are cutting down the trees on Primrose Hill.
> The wood is white like the roast flesh of chicken,
> Each tree falling like a closing fan.

Now the woods crowd towards his grave, advancing from castle to churchyard, an army with banners. In the barley field beyond, part of the Anglo-Irish scenery, a pheasant squawks, crashing as if by clockwork, in short frenzied flights. A fox slinks through the churchyard shrubbery, flaming along the churchyard wall. If there is heart-break in this scene, it is the clamour of the pheasant breasting through the barley, sounding her klaxon at a hint of the fox, not the heartbreak of the poet on the wrong side of the Irish Sea:

> And as I go out I see a wind-screen wiper
> In an empty car
> Wiping away like mad and I feel astounded
> That things have gone so far . . .

Now the wind-screen wipers have wiped away all that marching through Kensington with rolled B.B.C. umbrellas under self-conscious red flags, those red-faced retreats from Moscow when the tell-tale shots in the back of the neck could be heard in furnished flats off the Fulham Road:

> It's no go the Yogi-man, it's no go Blavatsky,
> All we want is a bank balance, and a bit of skirt in a taxi.

Now unrelenting Irish headstones stand round his railed enclosure. Beyond the churchyard wall, haze thickens over the Irish Sea, strengthening the veil of mutual incomprehension that hangs between his two islands. No resting place over there, no real hearthstone here:

> I was the rector's son, born to the anglican order,
> Banned for ever from the candles of the Irish poor . . .

self-exiled, too, except on Rugby international nights, from Dublin's flat-faced terraces and all that 18th-century grandeur along the Liffey:

> This was never my town
> I was not born or bred
> Nor schooled here and she will not
> Have me alive or dead.

Instead the harvest fields of Down have him, the last of a line that began with Sheridan and now comes to a full stop amongst green basket-of-eggs hills and whitewashed cottages in the Ards peninsula. It was a stroke of genius to bury him in this plantation-guarded churchyard at the top of the long, tree-lined avenue, within sight, but for the churchyard wall, of the Irish Sea and the mist that shuts us off from Scotland. What they should have written on that iron plaque planted in the patch of rough grass was his *credo*—the last lines of his *Eclogue for Christmas*:

> Goodbye to you, this day remember is Christmas, this morn
> They say, interpret it in your own way, Christ is born.

So down the lane where the last blackberries are ripening, down to the mist-veiled sea beyond which Scotland broods unseen, leaving the unbeliever who believed, the exile torn between two islands, home at last in the churchyard at the top of the hill, shadowed by the anglican spire, the Anglo-Irish woods that crowd towards his grave like an army with banners. The only sounds in the lane are the crashing of the Anglo-Irish, castle-incubated pheasant through the barley, pursued by the presbyterian fox, and, beyond green basket-of-eggs hills, the whirring of a combine-harvester, still binding its sheaves, still gathering its late harvest, busy with 'the old account-books of earth.' There remains the background music of that iron-railed enclosure on the green hill, the sound of the wind in the trees.

Skeletons from an 18th-Century Cupboard

Up there in black, sea-indented Donegal, a steep hog-backed peninsula projects into Lough Swilly. A perpetual backlash from the Atlantic swirls round its rocky snout; behind, the sharp-spined Urris hills, punctuated by patches of scree, plunge down to where the Atlantic explodes in white shell-bursts round the rock-base of the peninsula—with northwards, out beyond the lofty stacks of Dunaff and Fanad, nothing but empty ocean all the way to Iceland. Here, in the shadow of the Urris hills, on smooth green turf behind the concealed guns of Dunree fort, lay the third (reserve) battalion of the Irish Fusiliers.

It was autumn 1914. The lough smelt of herring. On Sundays the band still played below the rows of honey-coloured tents on the headland. There were long sweaty route marches up the valley of the Owenerk river to where Slieve Snaght reigned in the heart of Inishowen, with the men singing:

> You'd be far better off in a Home
> You'd be far better off in a Home
> Far better off
> Far better off
> Far better off in a Home.

Derry and its pubs were out of sight, the nearest spot for an other-ranks booze-up main street Buncrana; officers the bar, complete with barmaid and gilt-inscribed mirrors, in the Lough Swilly Hotel. Then one misty October morning, still in our rows of honey-coloured tents, we woke to find the lough dotted with warships, much as Athenians must have found the fleet at Salamis. It was the British Grand Fleet under Jellicoe, taking time off from Scapa Flow, spread over the roadstead between Buncrana and Rathmullan, forty ships in all, including auxiliaries, repair ships, store ships. There was a sound of bugles; picket-boats slid to and fro like shuttles; anti-submarine nets were laid across the narrows below the fort; white-faced crews were landed and marched about the mountainous Inishowen by-roads; bumboat men did a roaring trade in dead rabbits and, concealed below the rabbits, poteen. As far as the merchants and publicans of Buncrana's utilitarian main street were concerned, this was Christmas: thousands of customers, hard cash, raging thirsts, all miraculously translated from the North Sea.

Then fog came down, blotting out the Grand Fleet, shutting shop on the bonanza. I rode the rocky seven miles along the lough shore, stabled my horse in the tumbledown yard of an hotel in Buncrana. Fog or no fog, I was looking for my brother, navigating officer of H.M.'s now invisible light cruiser *Birmingham*. I found him by injecting still more drink into an already drunken bumboat man and setting off from Buncrana pier in a leaky rowing boat laden to the gunwales with dead rabbits, rabbits covered with fish scales and already awash in salt water. The drunken bumboat man had only one eye, and as a cousin of mine declared of a man who made a pass at her, that was a bad one. It also turned out, when the pier-head light disappeared in the fog, he had only one oar. Nevertheless, as the chairman at the Scottish concert remarked, we found *Birmingham*, in a pea-soup fog, out of a fleet of forty vessels spread over a four-mile road-stead. We found her by the simple expedient of running into her side, not very fast, propelled by a one-eyed boatman drunkenly sculling with a single oar.

Once on board, apart from the fact that nobody was supposed to know where *Birmingham* was, plus the problem of what to do with a drunken boatman in charge of a boatload of dead rabbits flavoured with fish scales, everything went like wedding bells. Assembled in the wardroom for a war-time reunion, somebody 'rattled the ivories' of the asthmatic, sea-going piano; we sang, or rather bawled, a succession of those part bawdy, part cynical, part sentimental ballads beloved by the 'silent service.' Sometime towards midnight I seem to remember my brother playing Raff's *Cavatina* on his violin, he being of the real sea-going tradition in so far as he played the violin and at one stage kept a parakeet in a cage. The mere fact that he produced the violin at all was evidence of a considerable party, in Irish terms a 'hooley.'

Considerable or not, it ended at midnight. At midnight the fog lifted; the one-eyed boatman (who in the interval had sold his entire boatload of long-dead, fish-scale-flavoured rabbits and been lavishly entertained, at my brother's expense, in a service pantry) was carted by a posse of Marines and dumped, semi-conscious, on the half-awash floorboards of his coracle. We, the 'quality,' then went ashore in a picket-boat, with my brother at the wheel—towing the rabbit boat, no longer in ballast, behind us. I remember that it yawed wildly and that from it, under the reviving in-fluences of sea air and salt water, there rose maudlin strains of *The Bold Fenian Men* and *Who fears to speak of '98, who blushes at the name.* From the point of view of the 'quality' in the picket-boat the wires were getting a bit tangled. Jutland was only nineteen months away, and not long after Jutland my brother was to be washed overboard from the foredeck of the light cruiser *Southampton* and drowned in the North Sea, ending up as an oil painting in a gilt frame, a posthumous portrait of an Edwardian naval officer, heavy gold epaulets, one white-gloved hand on the hilt of his sword, the other clasping his cocked hat. But for the moment, the night of the Homeric party in *Birmingham*, the night he played Raff's *Cavatina* on his violin, he was just a face lit by the binnacle lamp of the picket-boat.

The night after the Homeric party in *Birmingham*, nineteen months before telltale German star-shells burst and glittered over the North Sea, the Grand Fleet emerged from its bolt-hole behind anti-submarine nets in Lough Swilly, set its course for Scapa Flow. It was a magnificent sight seen from the cliffs below our camp at Dunree, long lines of warships filing through the narrows below the fort, each ship illuminated in turn by searchlights.

I stood watching through field-glasses. In the normal way when you look through field-glasses (especially brand-new glasses by Karl Zeiss of Jena) you see the normal world governed by the normal laws of optics—in this instance the Grand Fleet steaming through the searchlight-illuminated narrows. But the laws of optics did not apply; what I saw through my Zeiss field-glasses was a gap in the Time Curtain; when the Grand Fleet reached the entrance waters of the lough, and with my brother navigating the leading cruiser *Birmingham*, was settling on its course for the open Atlantic, there was suddenly a patch of brilliant light on the water, flickering like Greek fire under the Fanad cliffs, and accompanied by, or itself originating, the Greek fire, what looked like an 18th-century frigate. It seemed to be moving *through* the files of the Grand Fleet, flitting through armour-plated hulls as a ghost might flit through a brick wall. At the same split-second were sounds of battle, sounds of battle as they might be heard in a dream, mock detonations without the sound of guns.

I looked right and left, but none of the officers beside me, some, like myself, watching through field-glasses, seemed to have heard or seen anything extraordinary. Later I put the incident down to too much port, and hardly thought about it again. There were other things in the foreground. I served in the trenches in France and Flanders; was slightly wounded by a German 'sausage' bomb at Armentières; then, escaping the slaughter at the Somme and Gallipoli, finished by sweltering (maximum temperature at Athens, 110 in the shade) in the Struma valley throughout the summer of 1916, waiting for the Bulgarians to descend from the Rhodope mountains.

The denouement came in county Cork. In the summer of 1917, invalided from Macedonia with malaria, I was transferred from hospital in Derry to a convalescent home for officers at Glengariff—unaware that I was caught up in the backlash of revelations at Lough Swilly. Glengariff harbour is an opening off Bantry Bay, and the mention of Bantry Bay releases ghostly trains of association in most Irish minds, ancestral memories of Napoleon, stop-press news of yesterday that the French were 'on the say.' My trouble was that, like most Ulster Protestants, I knew nothing of Irish history beyond vague notions of Brian Boru and the battle of Clontarf. What had happened in Ireland during the Napoleonic wars was out, taboo; in fact the Irish 18th century was pointedly omitted as a kind of Unionist *dies non*.

Now the catechism of the 18th century was about to be reprinted. While we 20th-century wounded and convalescent officers sat at lunch or dinner in our convalescent hotel, looking out over the wooded shores of Glengariff harbour towards the deep blue waters of Bantry Bay, we were apt to discover that war in Europe and the Near East was being complicated under our noses by subterranean war—more accurately, by phases of open war—in Ireland. The unfinished business out there in Bantry Bay had been resumed. Easter Week was not a matter for open discussion round the mess tables of Anglo-Irish regiments. As far as most senior officers were concerned, the Rising was just something sudden and nasty—like a gas explosion next door—headlines about hoodlums with no seats to their trousers—a scandalous affair best brushed under the mat. A lot of odoriferous Liffey water was to flow under O'Connell bridge before I realised that, first as lieutenant, then as captain, in the Royal Irish Fusiliers I had been fighting part of the same anti-imperialist war as the men in the General Post Office in Easter Week—we against German imperialism on the continent of Europe; they against English imperialism in Ireland—which made them in the last analysis my comrades in arms, closer than some snooty customers with toothbrush moustaches and phoney English accents encountered in the lounges and bars of that repair shop for broken-down officers and gentlemen in Glengariff.

As for my viewpoint in the summer of 1917, I had been isolated when firing broke out in Sackville Street—first in a hospital tent on the outskirts of Salonika, looking across the green-blue Thermic Gulf to the snowy peak of Olympus, then on the eastern shore of the Chalcidic penisula—so that the whole thing seemed like a bad dream after a lobster supper in Jammet's. It's true that on my two-day journey down the length of Ireland, from Lough Swilly in Donegal to Bantry Bay in county Cork, I had seen the ruins of the Sackville Street down which Oliver St. John Gogarty was later to let his imagination wander—the ruins of Sackville Street and the shattered shell of the General Post Office. But there again, on the analogy of a sudden gas explosion, the whole thing was a matter of newspaper headlines; for me no 'terrible beauty' rose from the ruins until it was pointed out to me later by William Butler Yeats. At that moment, in the summer of 1917, wandering about Dublin in uniform, waiting for the train to Cork, all I remember is that from some hidden window a sniper had a shot at me; by this time I was fairly well educated in the sharp *crack* of a near miss, the dull thud of a bullet hitting a wall.

But down in the deep south, on that fairy-tale seacoast of Glengariff, with excursions by canoe to the lotus-eating island of Ilnaculin in the harbour, and expeditions through a haze of Cork Distillery whiskey to Killarney, not only the war in Europe but Dublin and its Ypres-reminding ruins retreated into the background. Up there to the north, Nelson might be brooding on his Pillar, overlooking the Joycean trams and the devastation of the Post Office—unaware that in the winking of an historical eyelid he himself would be a shattered torso on the pavement below, part of the rubble of Irish history. Meanwhile, down in the deep south, with all that gorgeous West Cork scenery waiting to spread itself on the advertisement pages of British luxury magazines, we convalescent officers of World War One lived our luxuriously sheltered lives—looking out through protective sheets of Anglo-Irish plate-glass at the Irish world around us, waited upon by either obsequious or cleverly time-serving Irish waiters with what amounted to our four square meals per day.

Sometimes, like happenings observed from a stage-box, Irish reality managed to break through, reality reminiscent of Somerville and Ross. Excursion steamers arrived from Bantry, brass bands blaring, green flags waving, at the jetty below the hotel windows. Processions from the steamers formed up and marched away into the hills, with occasional *pomp-pomps* from the bands. One day I noticed that the bands, the tramp of feet, the banner-tops moving unsteadily past the windows, seemed to disturb the waiter who was handing me my upper-class cold ham and salad at lunch-time. I asked him what the fuss was about. He looked at me in astonishment. 'A gentleman like yerself, sir, shouldn't be troublin' his head with such matters.' I said I was not troubling my head; I was merely curious. 'But them's the Shinners, sir!' he said, as if announcing Beelzebub and all his works. 'Them's the Shinners from Bantry.' 'Well, what about them? Isn't that what this war in Europe is all about—the rights of democracies and small nations?' To which I remember adding, as a post-script to the bit about war in Europe, 'I suppose you've heard of it?' 'Ah ye're a great one for a joke, sir!' he said, rearranging the napkin on his arm. 'Will ye take the fruit salad to folla?' This tactfully conveyed that my reactions were unsuitable for an 'officer and a gentleman' (terms by no means synonymous in that dining-room); and it took me a long time to get back on an even keel with that particular waiter.

I would have been even farther adrift with that particular waiter (to whom I gave the name of Hannigan in a sketch afterwards published in the *New English Weekly*) if he had known that in the evenings, instead of getting well tanked up like a proper 'officer and gentleman,' I was studying Irish history in the hotel library; for Hannigan certain occupations were indicated for the soldiery and studying Irish history was not one of them. Nevertheless, I spent most evenings in the library, a long, narrow room, lined from floor to ceiling with books, with a small-paned, low-silled window that looked out over the wooded shores and rocky inlets of Glengariff harbour. It had the musty smell of old books, and stacked on the shelves, mouldering with the rest, was an enormous two-decker edition of *The Autobiography of Theobald Wolfe Tone*. I had only the vaguest notions about Tone; like the founder and first editor of *The New Yorker* at the mention of Marcus Aurelius (or was it William Blake?), I might have inquired, 'Who he?' But those enormous musty volumes fascinated me; here, in addition to the history of my native land, was the 18th century, pure, sparkling, new-minted from Paris, set down in scintillating prose by a young man finding it bliss to be alive in revolutionary France—interviewing Napoleon in his study, drinking in taverns with Tom Paine. Wolfe Tone, I decided, whoever he might be, had a sparkling mind, and was in addition what we call in Ireland a 'lovely man;' if he had not been an Irish rebel and therefore, by that very fact, shut off behind the paper wall Britain had erected (and to this day partially maintains) against all things Irish except witty mockery *à la* Somerville and Ross, his autobiography would long ago have been accepted as a source-book of European history and the revelation of a first-class mind.

There were glimpses of the classical furnishings of Napoleon's study in the rue Chantereine, Paris; revolutionary spectacles at the Opera; then an

148

account of the French expedition to Ireland of 1796, and its failure to make a landing in Bantry Bay ('Oh, the French are in the Bay, they'll be here without delay') only a few miles from the musty-book-smelling library where, in August 1917, I sat reading Tone's account of storm and frustration as seen from *Indomptable*. One picture shines at the back of my mind like a detail from a classical canvas in a picture gallery—Tone's description of the snow-covered mountains of West Cork seen from the quarterdeck windows of *Indomptable*; the nearest he got to his native land. Those snow-covered mountains remained like a snow-powdered landscape in a crystal ball—the same mountains that formed a high-peaked purple barrier to the south-west when we broken-down and wounded officers of World War One looked at them from Ilnaculin, the Greek-templed island in Glengariff harbour where we spent long summer afternoons poodle-faking and drinking tea.

But for me the outstanding passage in Tone's autobiography was the account in the appendices of the *second* French expedition, when in October 1798, a small French squadron, including *Hoche* as flag-ship, was overhauled by a larger British squadron somewhere between Tory Island and Horn Head; finally, after a long stern chase, shot to pieces off the mouth of Lough Swilly. When I heard that, the jig-saw fell into place—in 18th-century fact there *had* been a naval encounter near Fanad Head; at the exact point where I had seen the strange light on the water, had heard the sound of guns as in a dream, had seen the white sails of a frigate ghosting through the armour-plating of the Grand Fleet—at that point in October 1798 the battered frigate *Hoche*, with Wolfe Tone on board and about to be captured in his French uniform, had been towed up Lough Swilly, passing on its way through the narrows at Dunree, under the cliffs from which we officers of the Irish Fusiliers had watched the searchlight illuminated Grand Fleet set out on its voyage towards Jutland in October 1914. What I had seen was the aftermath of a naval engagement of which I had never heard—a hundred and sixteen years after it had happened.

The sequel was that twenty years after the night I sat in the library at Glengariff reading about the engagement at Lough Swilly I started to write the life story of the prisoner in the shattered *Hoche*, using the materials of his autobiography, linking them with passages of my own.* Historically speaking, a thousand years are but a watch in the night, a hundred years like the striking of a grandfather clock, and while writing the book I found myself talking to a man who had talked to a man who had seen Tone land at Buncrana pier. I had gone to stay at an hotel overlooking the entrance waters of Lough Swilly, and there one night at dinner an old gentleman, a member of a family known in Buncrana for generations, told me he remembered talking in his youth to the family gardener about the scene when the French prisoners landed from the battered *Hoche*. The gardener described it as if it were yesterday (which in the light of history it was), including in his description a word-picture of Tone stepping ashore at Buncrana pier in his uniform of a *chef de brigade*. Tone,

Patriot Adventurer, 1936.

he said, was small and long-nosed, and walked 'with his head down,' as if anxious to escape recognition. As well he night; he was on his way to the Provost's prison in Dublin barracks, and beyond that the silence of his tomb at Bodenstown.

From the silence of which tomb, and that last vignette of Tone stepping reluctantly ashore at Buncrana pier, to Derrymore House, county Armagh, on a wet August afternoon of 1969. So wet we did nothing but stand in the 18th-century drawingroom, looking out through enormous floor-to-ceiling 18th-century windows at the rain coming down like stair-rods on the drive and the paddocks; that and a slight discolouration of the mist where Slieve Gullion should have been. I always suspect that mountain, with its thickly-wooded flank looking down on the plateau of what was once the Irish-speaking Meigh, of being up to something. What it was up to yesterday behind the stair-rods and the mist discoloured where Slieve Gullion should have been, I couldn't say. Probably welcoming home the Fianna from putting the fear of whatever Irish gods remain into Chichester-Clark. That and the discouragement of Anglo-Saxon hyphens!

What we saw beneath a crystal chandelier that descended like a sound of music, was the table at which the so-called Union between Ireland and Britain was drafted. It stood in the elegant hall, outside the drawing-room door, and it was ghastly; just what I would have expected from that combination of thugs and sentimentalists who organised the 'merger,' the same kind of thugs and sentimentalists who operate the realms of High Finance. It stood there on its thick, swollen podium, balancing itself on three swollen feet shaped like dropsical shamrocks—the kind of horror you imagine when your temperature is 101; like a seaside postcard of fat women bathing, associated with degradation and dirty work. It may have been an ingenious piece, misbegotten by-blow of a well-known 18th-century cabinet maker in Grafton Street; I only hope he got back to proper cabinet-making, and tried to forget. Against the 18th-century elegance of its surroundings it stood out like a bad deed in an early 19th-century world, the last ugly piece of self-destruction and throat-cutting on the part of the Anglo-Irish about to sell their Irish heritage down the river. It smelt of Castlereagh and that mask of murder on its way for Theobald Wolfe Tone.

The man that hath no flair for elegant furniture, let no such man be trusted with the drafting of treaties. As if in confirmation there is a brass plate fixed to the under-carriage of this monstrosity. It carries the signature 'H. M. Pollock,' one-time Minister in the Northern Government, and is brazen enough to take the name of that decent, unsuspecting man George V in vain. Believe it or not, the founding fathers of Northern Ireland at first failed to realise they had by right a share in the museums and art galleries of Dublin, and when at last they did realise it, spent the money-equivalent on police barracks—a characteristic gesture! Still worse, they were insensitive enough to use this monstrosity of a table in Derrymore to perpetuate their end of a 'Union' that had already collapsed in the ruin inherent in its fraudulent beginning; an occasion at which George V—

150

trusting soul that he was—was there to hope the said founding fathers would now run away and live in peace and Christian harmony, not only with their Catholic neighbours but with the original owners of the soil. My unPresbyterian view—uncharacteristic of 'Ulster' Presbyterianism—is that nobody could live in peace and Christian harmony by the light of anything signed at such a bollox of a table. And if 'bollox' is not a nice word, I'm sorry, but it exactly describes that 'arrangement'—I can't call it anything else—with its unbelievable feet in the shape of shamrocks that stands in the elegant 18th-century hall of Derrymore House and still pollutes the air with the stink of its transactions.

Then, with that wet August afternoon back-view of 'Unionist' history, we shot up the road to Camlough in the rain. From Camlough, with a minimum of gear-changing, we shot on up the mountain road above the narrow lough of the same name. Beyond the chasm of the lough, Slieve Gullion was at its tricks, hiding whatever it was at beneath its cloak of mist. And whatever kind of hooley the Fianna were having up there by the cairn, there was plenty to rejoice at. The end of throat-cutting Anglo-Irish mergers—both of them—had been as disastrous as the table at which they were signed. In Dublin the wreckage had been lying around for nearly fifty years, reduced now to the last pathetic snob-appeal of 'Royal' in the names of cocktail bars and hotels. As James Joyce remarked in *Ulysses* apropos that Edwardian study where the walls were lined with pictures of Royal racehorses and mistresses, 'No doubt reasons of space prevented His Majesty . . .'.

As for the other part of that transaction at the monstrosity of a table, away over the mountains behind us as we shot up the road above the lough, in Ypres-reminding districts of Belfast, Hell Fire enough, as we used to say, to frighten the French; better Hell Fire than we heard about in Sunday school. Over there beyond the mountains, a hail of petrol bombs, paving stones, and jagged bits of metal, all served up with short, sharp bursts of machine-gun fire. Carry the word of God down Ravenhill Road and up Divis Street—One Faith, One Crown, One Fuehrer—loud Protestant Hallelujahs of shattering glass. Third Rome, where are ye? Book of Revelations, where are ye? Carry the word of God to the water mains and the transformer stations; lift up your voices unto the (Castlereagh) hills, ye sticks of gelignite. Sit on your behinds in your mahogany box-pews, in your savage red-brick city, waiting for missionaries from the Congo, all set for Bible-thumping in the North Atlantic, and it will surprise you, not only what the Lord has done, but what, according to Protestant scriptures, he started forty-eight years ago at that ghastly table with the Jehovah's-witness tablet screwed to its under-carriage. The gears were grinding from the night the ghost frigate slid, with a booming of inaudible guns through the Grand Fleet at Lough Swilly and—telescoping history, like the old gardener remembering—Wolfe Tone stepped ashore in his *chef de brigade* uniform, straight into the jaws of Anglo-Irish murder-masks in Dublin. Somehow, with petrol-bombs exploding in Belfast, those snowy mountains of West Cork seen through the stern windows of *Indompable* in Bantry Bay seemed suddenly nearer.

151

Goodbye Royal Terrace

Oscar Wilde said the nineteenth century was invented by Balzac, and the nineteenth century included Royal Terrace, first shown on maps of Belfast in 1847, when Balzac had three more years to run, if by that time he was capable of running, what with matrimonial troubles and money pouring down Parisian drains. Certainly there was something distinctly Balzacian about Royal Terrace, vast, seething inside, if not with disorderly passions, at least with bourgeois ambition and ponderous conglomerations of Victorian furniture.

I used to visit Number One, starting about 1908 with the new electric trams. The bell tinkled far down in the basement, a baited hook groping in the depths. What came up was usually Rose, black-avised, with a dark shadow of what the Americans call *mus*tache. Rose said I was bigger than ever, and the Lord knew when I would stop. Then two massive flights to the first floor and what was known as the back drawing-room, which makes this the passing of the first-floor back. On your way you passed enough cracked paintings to fill an art gallery. In addition to being cracked, they were dirty, so dirty you couldn't see what was in them, and the dirtier they were, the better the Doctor liked them. There they were, in ancient gilt frames, floor to ceiling up the staircase, dirty gilt frame to dirty gilt frame, with military precision; enough cracked gilt frames, as we still said in certain parts of Belfast, 'to frighten the French.'

All I ever made out under layers of grime was the faint outline of a ship with unnaturally stiff sails, sailing at an unnatural angle over stiff-looking waves. You could just see it sailing through the dirt and Balzacian gloom of the staircase, and the Doctor prized it as the jewel of his collection. My conclusion was that the Doctor, steel-rimmed pince-nez perched precariously on nose, had never been to sea. Possibly not even to the seaside. Living in Royal Terrace was occupation in itself; from basement to attic, gas jets included, like exploring the Himalayas.

One expedition was to the breakfast room, in which I never had anything but high tea. The breakfast room loomed over the mews at the back, and high tea was, in summer, a running battle with black battalions of flies on the tablecloth and the jam, the flies straight from the stables and the horse manure in the mews below. We were less fussy in those days, and we survived; at any rate the hardy ones survived; certainly if you survived high tea in that Royal Terrace breakfast room, you had a chance of surviving the Great War, more especially its Eastern and near-Eastern ramifications. The Doctor used to peer through his steel-rimmed pince-nez at the regiments from the mews carrying out manoeuvres on the tablecloth and jam. He just looked at them thoughtfully. Possibly he was planning an addition to his museum and art gallery on the staircase, though God knows how he would have crammed it in.

In any event he had left his stethoscope in a mysterious back region known as the 'surgery,' and was therfore, medically speaking, off duty. Honoré de Balzac certainly had a hand in that 'surgery,' and if illustrations had been required, Daumier was the man for the job. The only one of its

152

show pieces I remember was a diabolical-looking instrument for passing up the urethra to relieve the bladder. It leered out from its lair on a glass shelf in a glass-fronted cupboard like a shiny instrument invented by the Gestapo—no puns intended.

Aunt Polly reigned over the back drawing-room, clad in purple, clutching Yorkshire terriers. Wherever you sat down in the back drawing-room there were Yorkshire terriers yapping from below. Aunt Polly (just a courtesy title like Aunt Lizzie) said I was getting bigger all the time, and the Lord only knew when I would stop. Aunt Polly was always waiting for the 'men' to want the back drawing-room for bridge. According to Aunt Polly everything the 'men' did was right. Provided you had certain anatomical fittings, you couldn't put a foot wrong. Whatever the 'men' said went over big; they just sat there in their Balzacian studies, surgeries, libraries, and what have you, laying down the law, and Aunt Polly swallowed every word they said, hook, line, and sinker.

In the evenings, while the new electric trams spluttered below on the Lisburn Road, the 'men' sat under the gasolier in the back drawing-room playing auction bridge, looking, with their steel-rimmed pince-nez and bits of beards, remarkably like a Renoir painting. The 'men' were the Doctor and his medical cronies. Where Aunt Polly went during the sessions under the gasolier, I never knew. She just tactfully disappeared before the 'men' started firing medical back chat over the card table. The 'men' said I was bigger than ever and would soon be playing for Ireland. Now that they've sliced the end off Royal Terrace to make, of all things, a Coras Iompair Eireann hotel (Edward Carson, where are ye?), I still see them sitting there, still round a green table, floating in thin air, still floodlit by the gasolier, just the height of where the first floor back drawing-room used to be, with iron balls knocking things down all round them, still looking, with their steel-rimmed pince-nez and spectacles and their wee bits of beards, like a Renoir painting, and not a sound out of them except 'No trump!' or the latest news about somebody's prostate.

That's the way I see them every time I pass what's left of Royal Terrace. And if anybody notices strange nineteenth-century figures intruding into the stream-lined circulation of the new (God save us!) Coras Iompair Eireann hotel, they can put in their complaints in triplicate to the new glass-fronted manager's office where new twentieth-century machines do be clacking away about nothing in particular. Computers or no computers, I shall be surprised if their new all-electric Coras Iompair hotel isn't heaving away all night with nineteenth-century ghosts, including (are ye listening, alanna?) visions of Rose hoisting coal scuttles from the basement, complete with traces of black nineteenth-century mustache, and shades of Honoré de Balzac all over the place, still toiling away in his nightshirt at the *Comédie humaine.**

*But not much peace for either Rose or Honoré: a 500 lb bomb blew up the basement and lower floors of the Russell Court Hotel the same day William Whitelaw held that vague, windy conference in Darlington.

Aunt Florrie as Film Star

Last night, in the necropolis of a Belfast cinema, I saw the ghost of my Aunt Florrie. She was flitting about, Anglo-Indian bust and all, in the scene where scarlet generals fox-trot to a scarlet military band in the film version of *Oh! What a Lovely War*. And if it wasn't my Aunt Florrie (by marriage, on my mother's side), it should have been; for the last time I saw Aunt Florrie, she was having a lovely war in the chandelier-blazing dining-room of the Hotel Splendide, Marseilles.

Hotels Splendides were my Aunt Florrie's speciality. Hotels Splendides, red plush, gilt, crystal chandeliers, and, under the chandeliers, red-tabbed, field-booted military males. As a military male I was a wash-out. No red tabs, no highly-polished field boots, and as far as my shabby field-service uniform was concerned, I wasn't welcoming the chandeliers. I had just emerged after three draughty nights in a troop train from Amiens, and in spite of efforts by my batman to remove the mud of Armentières and Bois Grenier from my breeches, I wasn't a patch on the young cavalry subalterns who once circulated round Aunt Florrie in Poona like planetary bodies round the sun.

'Dear boy!' I was gathered to the Anglo-Indian bosom. She seemed a trifle depressed by my appearance as flood-lit by the chandeliers. Her companion, a small red-tabbed staff officer, wasn't enthusiastic either. War was getting out of hand when, as Disraeli remarked of a sailor's life, it interfered with the toilet.

'And where are you off to next?' inquired Aunt Florrie.

'Couldn't say, Aunt Florrie. All very hush hush.'

'Nonsense,' said Aunt Florrie. The hush hush was for Aunt Florrie like the scent of rabbit for a terrier. The hush hush was, in fact, Aunt Florrie's speciality; she just protruded her Anglo-Indian bosom at it, and it vanished like snow off a ditch.

'What division?' said Aunt Florrie, sounding like a sergeant-major.

I murmured the number of my division, very red in the face. I had been warned that such talk was dangerous. *Les oreilles ennemies vous écoutent.* And where better than in the chandelier-blazing dining-room of the Hotel Splendide, Marseilles, in the Orient-Express atmosphere of late November, 1915, with Townshend bogged down on the Euphrates and top-secret arrangements for evacuating Gallipoli already in operation?

'Wait,' said Aunt Florrie. 'We'll soon find out.'

Discarding red tabs, she plunged away in search of green; finally settling on a neighbouring table where a po-faced green-tabbed major was inspecting pêche Melba through an eyeglass. At the sight of Aunt Florrie's cleavage, the eyeglass fell into the pêche Melba; the po-faced major surrendered, horse, foot, and guns.

'Serbia, dear boy!' Aunt Florrie announced, returning triumphant from the wars—Anglo-India concentrated like a tableau from Madame Tussaud's in the Hotel Splendide dining-room.

And Aunt Florrie was right, or in terms of the Splendide, *avait raison*. Serbia it was, except that unrelenting Balkan ranges combined with several million anopheles mosquitoes to intervene. But we kept heading there to begin with, and if we weren't *spurlos versunken* on the way, that was just the luck of the Irish. *Oreilles ennemies* may have been listening; even if they were, Aunt Florrie's reaction would have been to let loose a squadron of Lancers. Indeed, looking back at that night in November 1915, with all its historical cross-currents, I see that the preliminary rushes of *Oh! What a Lovely War* were already being shot in the Hotel Splendide dining-room. Marseilles, with my Aunt Florrie, scent, *décolletage*, feather boa, and all, already one of its period-stars.

An Irish Fusilier Remembers

I

FARE THEE WELL LONDONDERRY

Down through fifty sweet-scented Inishowen springs, fifty dark turf-smelling Inishowen winters, back to the glen where the sound of our Protestant bell floated up steep green Inishowen mountains; down through the turf-reeking square at Clonmany where the same dog, or its great, great grandson several times removed, still sleeps outside Macauley's pub; down the tree-lined road to Lenan and the little lancet-windowed, honey-coloured church where the regimental band played at Sunday church parade, deluging the hymns with reverberations from the trombone, loosening protestant flakes of whitewash from the ceiling, snowflakes descending on the brass of regimental instruments below.

Now the church stands locked and shuttered. Ten thousand tides will flood Trawbreaga bay, a hundred thousand Atlantic rollers come charging at Dunaff Head, more charlock and ragwort gather in the churchyard, greener moss accumulate on the roll-calls for reveille, and it will have sunk back into the bogland of Irish history. No-one will remember its neat lancet windows, its emphatic little Protestant tower with the slatted louvres that allowed the sound of its Protestant bell to wander out through the greenery of the glen, past monastic ruins, up steep green mountainsides to curlew-haunted Inishowen boglands above. No more regimental bands to bring down whitewash; when we regimental dead awaken there will be just stones amongst the nettles.

At the turn of the road, where the Atlantic starts to unroll its sometimes grey-blue, sometimes slate-green carpet all the way to Iceland, the old whitewashed manor house that served as orderly-room, battalion headquarters, and quartermaster's store, still dozes beside the burn, overhung by steep green mountains, deep in green tree-shadow that once sheltered monks—the English for Clonmany being Monks' meadow. On the road outside, watched by whitewashed gateposts like miniature round towers, we fell in with a clatter of rifle butts for route marches, up the road to Clonmany and the square where the dog lay sleeping, up to the gaunt grey Catholic chapel at Ballyliffen; down the road towards Lenan fort and the blue-grey or slate-green entrance waters of Lough Swilly, breathing the thick, indigestible Donegal air, all the way from Iceland. From the ranks, along with an acrid smell of stale stout, rose our stale-stout-inspired substitute for the monks' chorus. Pacing in the shadow of the glen, in and out past grey monastic walls, they may have sung the *Gloria*; *we* sang:

> You'd be far better off in a Home
> You'd be far better off in a Home
> Far better off
> Far better off
> Far better off in a Home

No *jour de gloire*, no *Deutschland über alles*. Just a smell of stale stout, a clatter of rifles, and the monotonously-repeated assertion that we'd be better off in a Home. Which, in the afterlight of our destination and those trainloads from Clonmany station, was the understatement of the century.

The time was 1917. At first the train ran through a cleft in the mountains, rocked sleepily along the stony shore of a long narrow lough where the colonel went fishing. Usually a heron stood amongst the reeds on the farther shore in long-legged imitation. *Click, clack, clock*, went the wheels, bearing us out of Inishowen, out of this world; that train track through that cleft in the mountains was the entrance hall to the machine-gun bullet in the brain, to untidy remnants after 'sausage' bombs. Slieve Snaght, mist-enshrouded, slid sleepily past the windows; the train, gathering speed, ran out of the cleft in the mountains, the entrance hall to the next world, flung the narrow lough behind it, began to rattle downwards at a kind of bumpy hand-gallop towards the slate-green or grey-blue corridor of Lough Swilly; the orderly *click, clack, clock* of its wheels suddenly incoherent, riotous with a sudden sinister mirth.

At Derry we marched with a subdued clinking of water-bottles, a *thump, thump* of entrenching-tools, past ancient walls and monuments, past the sham-Gothic Guildhall, across the bridge to a sound of bugles from the barracks, while behind us, echoing over the Foyle, the Guildhall clock measured out fragments of life and time:

> Fare thee well, Enniskillen,
> Fare thee well for a while,
> All round the borders of Erin's green isle;
> When the war is over
> They'll return in full bloom,
> And we'll all welcome home the Iniskilling Dragoon . . .

for Enniskillen substitute Derry; for 'full bloom' shell-shattered remnants.

159

Later the sound of the men singing in battered third-class compartments:

> You'd be far better off in a Home
> You'd be far better off in a Home
> Far better off
> Far better off
> Far better off in a Home . . .

while beyond the blue inlet of Lough Foyle, the many-folded hills of Inishowen, crowned by the darkness of Slieve Snaght, were suddenly translated by some magic of the north Atlantic light into an earthy green paradise never likely to be regained.

II

THE BOOMING OF THE GUILDHALL CLOCK

Back there in the Glen camp, Clonmany, not far from the sheltering darkness of Slieve Snaght, we were, in 1917, like Samuel Beckett's dustbin characters, crammed in, with nothing to say. Reservists, ex-handloom weavers, machine-minders from Lurgan and Portadown, with no worldly possessions beyond the abrasive khaki uniforms they stood up in, the bulging packs they bore like regulation crosses on their backs, the pieces of death-dealing or death-defying machinery that clattered when they walked, 'Where he was it was warm and dry. Yes, and they crucified quick,' wrote Beckett two wars later. In 1917, in the interval before *their* crucifixion, the ex-handloom weavers and machine-minders—waiting for machine-gun bullets with their names on them or shells that came whinny-ing in recognition—made half-hearted attempts to break out of their symbolical morgues, W. D. huts, barrack rooms, prison houses, and dust-bins; attempts ending in pathetic moments of truth, face to face with the adjutant in the orderly-room, formerly the dining-room, of the white-washed manor house in the glen—the manor house so sunk in green tree-shadow that once sheltered monks that the malefactors lined up for judge-ment had a half-legendary quality, as if pushed backwards into history.

'What was he up to, sergeant?'

'He was creatin', sir.'

Which was a bloody lie for a start. The dustbin reservists were not, God help them, creating anything except, on Saturday nights, a rough house in Macauley's pub. What was facing them was the sinister journey from the glen, along the shore of the stony lough—'You shall be taken thence to the place of execution'—transportation from Clonmany station, rifles, packs, entrenching-tools, identity discs (especially identity discs!), across two seas to France and Flanders, to long, straight poplar-lined roads that led towards gun-muttering horizons, towards final doss-houses in the muddy walls of trenches, or neat, dress-by-the-right rows of white crosses in military cemeteries with only your identity disc to distinguish you from what had been gathered up in the next dustbin, to say who you were in the first place if you ever were in the first place. It was not warm, it was not dry, and crucifixion depended on the Pontius Pilates in chateaux well back out of gunfire, the brass hats with lashings of 'fruit salad' where their good intentions should have been.

From the harvest of white crosses, back to Derry and Lord Dunsany's ghost—white clouds mirrored in the Foyle, sycamores on the Waterside brilliant green. Peering in Ebrington barrack gates, I remember his lordship scandalising scarlet majors by appearing on parade with long hair sticking out below his uniform cap and an infuriating air of poetic detachment. '*Strornery* fella!' was the verdict in our Irish Fusiliers mess; with vitriolic addenda from scarlet, port-soaked Boer-war majors.

Lord Dunsany's ghost, hair projecting under cap, battering the barrack square with enormous, unsuitable boots, brings back scarifying memories —the autumn casualty lists of 1914, the wild melancholy of the Londonderry Air played in slow time by saffron-kilted pipers at military funerals, the fresh green of Donegal seen through iron-barred barrack-room windows as from iron-barred windows in a condemned cell. That and the Guildhall clock booming beyond the Foyle, *boom, boom, boom,* measuring what might be the last autumn of our lives, like a miser counting change.

Now beyond the barrack gates, new khaki-clad English regiments clash and clatter on the barrack square, their clockwork precision punctuated by the *pomp, pomp* of a regimental band. Farther down the river, at the opposite quayside, a Russian grain tanker is unloading, with strings of gaily-coloured flags fluttering from her masts and derricks, celebrating some Slavonic feast day. Clatter, rattle, *bump* go the winches, while from the barrack square, surfacing above the plantations of the Waterside, competing with the final clashing of the military band, soars the suffocating sound of a recruit to the British army learning to play the bugle.

In the shadow of the Guildhall I turn out of ancient habit into the bar of a near-by hotel. Nothing is like what it used to be, so says the barmaid, looking distastefully at her deserted kingdom.

'There's not half the drinkin',' she says, 'like there used to be in the old days when the young officers did be here in the war-time.'

Omitting the question which war-time, I agree. Things, including whiskies like Watts Tyrconnell named in advertisements on gilt-lettered mirrors, are not what they used to be. As if in confirmation, an enormous booming breaks out from the Guildhall clock overhead, rattling the glasses in the deserted bar. The dead stand round us, listening. Here in the heart of this old city like a Balzac novel turned to stone, the booming of the clock, the reiteration of the hour, sounds like the commotion of the outer world penetrating some inner shrine of Madame Tussaud's where history has turned to wax—the six o'clock news stirring cobwebs in the palace of the Sleeping Beauty.

The dead still listen. In the silence that follows the booming, to a faint clattering of winches from the quayside where the Russian tanker is unloading, and stifled sounds of the bugle from the barrack square on the wooded heights of the Waterside, things go on becoming not what they

161

used to be, punctuated by the booming of the Guildhall clock. More has been shattered than plate-glass in Derry super-market windows. 'No Pope here!' it says on shattered red-brick walls in Belfast, to which, from time to time, some philosopher has added, with fresh whitewash exclamation marks, 'And a bloody good judge too!'

Here in Derry, along with Watts Tyrconnell whiskey, yesterday has vanished like water under the Craigavon bridge, vanished along with Thomas Babington Macaulay's processions, London Guildhall banquets, ritual closing of gates against ritual 17th-century ghosts. Nowadays it's not so much a matter of Macaulay's 'imperial race' hurling its defiance at the Bourbons, as the new-style 20th-century Bourbons (that is, the inner cabinets of the great oil and chemical monopolies in alliance with the moneylenders) capturing and enslaving the 'imperial race.' As the barmaid testified against her gilt-lettered backdrop of yesterday, nothing is like what it used to be. Time not only for fresh whitewash but for revolutionary question marks. Time for us Protestants to whitewash on Derry's walls in letters several feet high, ARE WE SURE WE HAVE IDENTIFIED THE REAL TWENTIETH-CENTURY POPES?

That's what I thought, but not what I said to the barmaid. To the barmaid, when the Guildhall clock had stopped rattling the glasses on the counter, I simply remarked that things were not what they used to be. Which, after two world wars, shattered plate-glass in the Diamond, and the new (as not foreseen by Macaulay) RUC—English-armoured siege of the Bogside, was the understatement of the year.

III

AUGUST MOON OVER LILLE

I walked down the street in my second-best uniform, a flask of weak whisky and water (Jopp's Aberdeen whisky, 4s 6d a bottle) in my haversack, my new .45 Colt automatic in the holster on my Sam Browne, belt and holster glittering with boot polish. The women were at their doors, watching the stranger on his way to work. Clocking-in time, the equivalent to lunch-box and tools strapped round me with expensive leather straps.

Well, good luck to him if he gets past the tart at the bottom of the street. Some never came back. But not many. It was not a dangerous part of the line, unless you stuck your head over the parapet. At the bottom of the street which I remember as a sort of Jean-Paul Sartre entrance to Hell, Armentières (*linges, toiles, dentelles, distillerie, forges*) ended and the communication trench began. What went off here was the occasional whizz-bang. Sure enough one whizzed over, followed by its belated bang— went whizzing back towards the working men's wives gossiping in the evening sunlight and the tart situated at the strategic point where the street ended and the communication trench began.

The only shot fired in anger that night. A Saxon regiment in the trench opposite, twenty-five yards away at the nearest point, and nobody looking for trouble. An enormous harvest moon hung over Lille, and later there was an impromptu concert. From the trench opposite. A magnificent operatic baritone singing 'O pure and tender star of eve'— performance loudly applauded from both trenches, so loudly he had to sing it again.

That and the harvest moon were halcyon summer, before trouble began. Somebody threw a jampot-bomb too many; the regiment opposite, Prussians now, not Saxons, sent a colossal 'sausage' bomb sailing back, obscenely somersaulting over the scarlet poppies in no-man's-land, leisurely descending with a loud *crump* and a blast that drove your belly back to meet your backbone. A bull's-eye, right into the entrance of a dug-out I was just leaving—a scene I afterwards painted in the London *Spectator*. In those days German 'sausage' bombs were filled with anything that came handy—old gramophone needles, rusty nuts and bolts, the sweepings of factory floors; some minute fragment of this particular *Wurst* is, I suspect, still wandering about the back of my neck.

After that no more 'pure and tender star of eve' (*O du mein holder Abendstern*) while the pregnant August moon hung over Lille where the story in our trenches was that the dynamos were still running, supplying Armentières with electricity—or maybe it was the other way round; I can't remember which. What I do remember is imagining a sort of sinister Alice-in-Wonderland door at the bottom of that sunlit Armentières back-street. Beyond it, women gossiping at street doors about babies, whose husband was double-crossing whom; the business of life generally; this side this insane world of masculine logic where fragments of rusty iron-mongery went whistling through the air. I also imagined the fat German who pulled the lanyard that let off the bomb that sailed through the sunlight over the poppies in no-man's-land and nearly finished the lot of us. I imagined him as stout, tightly buttoned in a dark-blue uniform, like the German soldiers I once saw in the streets of Dresden in the once-upon-a-time when Wilhelm of the withered arm and the protestant moustache was Emperor of all the Germanies; Dresden one of the art capitals of Europe.

Which brings me down thirty-four years to a corridor and staircase in the Strasbourg Opera House. A stone corridor and a stone staircase still echoing to German jackboots, still crowded with dark-blue German uniforms. I was a delegate to the Council of Europe, and that night in my hotel I had a pre-recording of the next day's proceedings. The man in the bedroom next door, was Robert Boothby, Conservative M.P. for Aberdeen; the bedroom walls were thin; Boothby (now Lord Boothby) in full spate, rehearsing his speech for next day in the assembly.

It was a very good speech; next day, as I expected after hearing it the night before, it not only brought down the house but flattened his enemies in the Council of Europe. It consisted in stating that he, Boothby, had driven all the way from the English Channel to Strasbourg; that on the way he had passed cemetery after cemetery crammed with British dead, the flower of a British generation. If he had added small plantations crammed with Irish dead, the flower of an Irish generation, he would have set the record straight with Europe.

As it was, it floored the assembly, left behind it the same sensation as that August night outside Armentières, when in the silence that followed the applause for 'O pure and tender star of eve,' we all leaned against our parapets wondering what we were supposed to do next behind our lines of sandbags, our aprons of barbed wire, our machine-gun nests, our *minenwerfer* emplacements, our occasional, very occasional, corpses—all, including the corpses, illuminated like a stage-set by the light of an enormous harvest moon over Lille.

Postscript for Aristotle of Stagyra

We came down through the defile to the sea and bivouacked where we fell, on the beach, to the sound of Aegean breakers breaking with clockwork regularity. Late spring or early summer. Stavros. At least that's what it said on the maps. We stayed there a couple of days, resting men, horses, mules, bathing in the 'many-laughing' waters; clear Aegean green; the Strymonic gulf beyond which we had heard the guns at Gallipoli.

Then north beside the glassy-sounding breakers, making for the mouth of the Struma that was once the Strymon. Behind us, from the peak of Athos, violent thunderstorms, sudden violet spears stabbing the gulf. News trickled through from Salonika, by horse, mule, ammunition cart—a naval battle in the North Sea, artillery fire in the heart of Dublin. But it was all Greek to us. We simply marched, slept, bathed in clear green surf. History was what happened somewhere else.

Behind us was Stavros, but nobody knew what Stavros was, except that it was a map reference, the first place we hit the sea. Now, fifty-four years on, reading a life of Alexander, I realise it was Stagyra, the birthplace of Aristotle—all that history now just sand and glassy-sounding breakers. But now I know the light on his gulf, the crashing of Aegean breakers on his beach, the sound of thunder from Athos, the stabbing of violet spears in the Aegean.

We marched on northwards, to the tawny hills at the mouth of the Struma, where the man from Stagyra cropped up again. Or would have cropped up if in the evenings, in candle-lit bivouacks, we had been studying Greek and Macedonian history instead of back numbers of *La vie Parisienne*. This time instead of being connected with Alexander the Great he was connected with our latrines in the environs of Amphipolis, the city where Thucydides got the sack for failure with Brasidas—a failure which, in the tradition of disgruntled brass-hats writing their memoirs, set him writing his *History of the Peloponnesian War*—still in the libraries whereas Amphipolis is just sand and malarial mosquitoes beside the Struma.

Thucydides and his *Peloponnesian War* were, in fact, down at the bottom of our latrines. When the malefactors from our make-shift orderly-room were set to dig latrines, they brought up history by the spadeful, busty young women, emperors, kings—all on coins, no actual corpses. I have

164

some still, stored in a drawer; the most significant stamped with the head of Alexander the Great. Along with his father, Philip II of Macedon (382—336 BC). Also a figure from the Byzantine empire (1081—1118 AD); the explanation being that our latrines stood on or near the remains of the Via Egnatia, the road that ran from Rome to Byzantium—a thought that never occurred to us when *in situ* on the latrines, *La vie Parisienne* being in the ascendant, *Venus à sa proie attachée*. In addition I have a Roman coin of the first century BC, showing a head of Jason, with a beautifully-executed quadriga on the reverse. I had at any rate the wit to note in my field notebook something about Amphipolis having a rich subsoil of cultures, one piled on top of the other, with our latrines on top of the heap. The coins were collected by my Cockney servant, who proclaimed them a lot of old trash.

Trudging through, or seated above, the ruins of Greece and Rome, unable to see them for the illustrations in *La vie Parisienne* (*Venus à sa proie*)—that's how we were occupied about the time the guns of *Helga* boomed from the Liffey; English Lancers lay dead alongside their horses in Sackville Street; and, only a fortnight later, German star-shells glittered over the North Sea in the bloody aftermath to Jutland. Aristotle of Stagyra may have read those thunderstorms from Athos, those violet spears plunging in the green Strymonic gulf, simply as excess of the energy that now tingles in my electric shaver. Looking back to Sackville Street, Jutland, and that vanished fleet at Lough Swilly, I see them as anger of the gods.

My Father Encountered King Edward

Back at the beginning of the century when 'Lily' Langtry was a reigning beauty in London my father encountered King Edward on the shore of Strangford Lough. He was cycling through the tunnel of Mountstewart woods, when, striding towards him through the green twilight under the trees, he was astonished to see the globular, tweed-clad figure of Edward VII, looking, as we say in Belfast, 'very like himself,' early 20th-century plus-fours, deerstalker hat, and all—as if got up for the grouse moors.

My father, as a good Victorian, pince-nez, cycling knickerbockers, and all, not so much dismounted from, as promptly fell off, his bicycle, snatched off whatever was considered fashionable sports headgear amongst Belfast linen merchants, and said, 'God bless your Majesty!'

What King Edward said is not recorded. Nevertheless, I like that story. Every time I rehearse it for my wife, with, at her request, suitable gestures and noises-off representing King Edward—which is every time we motor through the green tunnel of Mountstewart woods—there rises before us, along with the portly ghosts of his Majesty and his loyal subject, the sixty-four thousand dollar question of the whole affair—namely, *where were the detectives*? In all the family saga of my father encountering King Edward, not so much dismounting from as falling off his bicycle, and snatching off his Edwardian cycling headgear, whatever it may have been—maybe another deerstalker?—there is, unlike *Emil and the Detectives*, no mention of detectives. How come the Fenians weren't lurking behind the Mountstewart trees, hiding in the green tunnel, looking 'very like themselves;' that is, very unlike Fenians in early volumes of *Punch*?

The answer is probably that, paraphrasing a Victorian Poet Laureate, 'along the wire no electric message came,' or if it did, his Majesty's Post Office suppressed it somewhere about Newry and the Gap of the North. Second that, disguised in Sherlock Holmes capes, though possibly omitting pipes and magnifying glasses, there *were* detectives lurking in the Mountstewart undergrowth, whole squads of them. My father, taken up with the problem of dismounting and at the same time displaying loyalty to the Throne, probably never noticed them—regular stage armies of them, all too conscious, what with midges and damp county Down ferns, of just why the Emerald Isle remained so uncompromisingly emerald, not to mention Fenian.

Be that as it may, I like, in retrospect, to enlarge that scene in the green tunnel of the Mountstewart woods; to construct what my Presbyterian ancestors (my father had unfortunate leanings towards the Church of Ireland!) would have called a 'concordance.' Down in Dublin, while Lily Langtry was queening it in London and my father was cycling, knickerbockers and all, along the shores of Strangford Lough, James Joyce was assembling fragments for *Ulysses*, including that suggested list of portraits for his Majesty's study ('No doubt reasons of space prevented his Majesty'—or words to that effect, with Gaiety girls substituted for his Majesty's racehorses). In Belfast Martin Harvey (no relation to the footballer) was reducing us all to tears in *The Only Way* ('It is a far, far better thing I do than I have ever done; it is a far, far better rest I go to than I have ever known.') As the *Belfast Telegraph* succinctly remarked, 'Not a dry eye in the house.' Other theatrical offerings (to coin a phrase) were *The Face at the Window* and *A Royal Divorce* ('Not to-night, Josephine!').

Which, by association of ideas, reminds me not so much of what the butler saw at Mountstewart as what the butler (or major domo) probably did at Mountstewart; that is, continued an old royal custom by placing a cold capon accompanied by a bottle of claret by his Majesty's bedside for fear his Majesty would feel faint in the night. Anyhow, outside the royal windows would be the sound of the lough—the lough my wife and I were watching the other night from Mountstewart bay at brimming full tide on a calm June evening when Scrabo was a blue-grey shadow in the direction of Belfast and squads of Yeatsian swans were up-ending themselves on the mirror-like surface near the shore.

At this point the Mountstewart woods crowd close to the water's edge, woods of which that literary crowd in Dublin, back in the early 1900s, were making Deirdre cry out:

> Woods of Cuan, O woods of Cuan
> In which are the cold waters . . .

a nice Yeatsian picture. But the night my wife and I were watching, over beyond the Yeatsian swans and the sheltering bulk of Scrabo, the angry red-brick city of Belfast was reflecting back into Europe nothing but television images of hate, fire, and destruction, blotting the Ulster copybook. What my father and his friends of the Reform Club (including Fred 'Load of Rifles' Crawford) had forgotten was that when Edward VII went walking in the woods of Mountstewart he was also walking in the woods of Cuan. It is a point the planters never appreciated; and the bill for their insensitivity keeps dropping through our northern Irish letter-box, account repeatedly rendered but not yet paid.

Hengist-and-Horsa's Other Island

In the year 1904, when my father was cycling along the shore of Strangford Lough, and that provincial Jesus, Leopold Bloom, on the verge of encountering Gerty MacDowell, *Home Chat* drawers and all, was putting down saucers of milk for the cat, *John Bull's Other Island* was gossip-column news at the Court Theatre, London. Picture the audience dispersing in a jingle of hansom cabs under the shade-trees and gas-lamps of Sloane Square, taking with it the assurance that God was in His heaven and King Edward (who broke a chair in the theatre laughing) on his throne.

Or maybe it was the other way round, the English are never very sure. Anyhow, Ireland was comfortably lost in the mists of the Atlantic and that fellow Shaw a bit of a bounder, but clever, mind you, damned clever. Out there in the mists of the Atlantic, with the rain falling on them, the Irish, unlike Gaul, were divided into two parts, the Anglo-Irish and the others. The others, according to bounder Shaw, were never likely to get anywhere —always dreaming in the mist that does be on the bog, always plotting in the shebeen. The fact that teetotaller Shaw had never been in a shebeen and wouldn't have understood a word if he had, slightly distracted from the message, but didn't worry big fat Edwardianised John Bull, who just hoisted himself (or was propelled from behind) into his hansom cab and was driven away from the Court Theatre, first giving (see the works of another Irish bounder called Wilde) an address on the fashionable side of whatever was the fashionable square in Belgravia. According to the bounder Shaw, the island in the mists was still the property of a somewhat Forsyte-ish John Bull, God was (or shortly would be) in a Socialist heaven; and the Irish, as distinct from the Anglo-Irish, were still arguing in the shebeen.

Thirty years on, the scene, according to bounder Shaw's successor, looks different, but is at heart the same. The scene is Dublin, there is now a native government, the rain is still falling, and it's all the same stewed cup of tea. True, of course, that in the interval John Bull's intelligence system in Ireland has been paralysed by the same half-witted plotters who, according to bounder Shaw, not to forget that literary shadow of an

'Ulster' gunman, St. John Ervine, were always dreaming in the mist that does be on the bog and not fit to run a cockle stall. But forget that, it must have been an accident, says the next Anglo-Irish dramatist lined up after Shaw—Denis Johnston, and you couldn't call him a bounder for his father was a judge and he'd been to an English university—and here he was, thirty years on, saying the same thing as Shaw, only worse, in a play called *The Moon That Does Be In the Yellow River*—I beg your pardon, *The Moon in the Yellow River*—very profound, slightly unintelligible (the Expressionists done him wrong)—and him with his I.R.A. Willie Reilly that was a scream and had your actual Anglo-Irish roaring their heads off in the Gate Theatre, the cocktail-lounge of the Shelbourne, the *Irish Times*, the Kildare Street Club—anywhere your actual Anglo-Irish, plus the shoneens attached to them, did be roaring their Anglo-Irish heads off.

Which was fun for the Anglo-Irish, but not much illumination for Hengist-and-Horsa. Or so it seemed to my wife and myself, emerging last night from the Lyric Theatre, Belfast, after watching *John Bull's Other Island* sixty-seven years on and slightly dented. The moon did be in the Orange and Green Lagan below, and, judging by the explosions and the sound of machine-gun fire on the Falls, the half-witted Willy Reilly seemed to be doing rightly, even if his mother didn't know he was out.

But then maybe Hengist-and-Horsa doesn't *need* to know about the other island; he knows all about it already. One swift look through the wrong end of a telescope from the neighbourhood of the Fastnet rock (rocks are coming up in his horoscope!), and Bob's (Lord Robert's) your uncle. If you're rude enough, and show them your big Saxon teeth, the Irish will just lie down or go away or something, leaving you, with the assistance of 'Unionist' *agents provocateurs* at Westminster, to steer the good ship Britannia (with Britannia conveniently waiving the constitutional rules) straight for the Common Market; that is, if there's any Common Market left now that the curtain has risen on the cardinals of the New Unholy Roman Empire squabbling behind the scenes in Brussels about who's to be Pope of the new Unholy Empire.

It may be, of course, that in the intervals of trimming his sails to the Financial Establishment Hengist-and-Horsa never took time off to see *John Bull's Other Island*. Or if he did, he probably didn't realise, any more than last night's audience at the Lyric Theatre overlooking the Lagan, that the gelignite packed in *John Bull's Other Island* is in the preface, not the play, in that landmine for the opening of Belfast's mock Parliament in 1921:

> 'When the Orangeman sacrifices his nationality to his hatred of the priest, and fights against his own country for its conqueror, he is doing something for which, no matter now bravely he fights, history and humanity will never forgive him—English history and humanity, to their credit be it said, least of all.'

The finest journalism since Swift, and, incidentally, what King George should have said fifty years ago in Belfast's Edwardian City Hall the day

168

my father turned out in his top hat and frockcoat, with that Edwardian strip of white piqué buttoned inside the opening of his waistcoat. He may have set down Shaw as a bit of a *farceur* but in the end the *farceur* had the last word.

Thirteen Dead in Derry

With the blood hardly dry on the streets of Derry, a commando fires tracer bullets into a burning farmhouse. Beyond where television cameras show the commando firing into the burning farmhouse, down where the Narrow Water joins Carlingford Lough, at the foot of the mountains where afforestation starts to climb like a steep green stair carpet, stands a lough-side hotel. In the lounge of that hotel, thirty-four years ago, we sat listening to a wireless-set. The sounds we were expecting would announce whether our world would continue in the shape it had, with minor alterations, maintained since the Congress of Vienna. It was like waiting for the Last Trump. While the tension mounted I was taking notes:

> 'Nobody moves or speaks. Beyond the windows, the snot-green, mirror-like lough, the green-reflected mountainsides steeped in golden sunlight, the spinach slabs of forestry, the rock bastions of Mourne, loom more unreal than ever, like a stage-set in *Swan Lake*, waiting for the entrance of the evil magician unfolding stagey black-out wings. Silence. An interval before the clock strikes. Then after preliminary whirrings of weights and chains, an unctuous B.B.C. voice announces that the Munich conference has ended in agreement, that life in the Bavarian Alps is once more *couleur de rose*.'

Thirty-four years later, the clock strikes again. Paratroopers notch up thirteen; a commando fires trace bullets into an already blazing farmhouse; in Downing Street the big Saxon teeth are presented, a spectacle greeted with nauseating applause at Stormont, and, in all probability, renewed study of North Atlantic charts in Leningrad.

It seems a curious curtain-raiser for the great Transformation Scene and Grand Parade into Europe. But the Great Illusionist stage-managed it himself, walking backwards into the 18th century, his face towards those favourite implements of Anglo-Irish persuasion, the thumb-screw and the pitch-cap, now modernised to the noise-machine and the blow behind the knee with a truncheon. The fact that they haven't worked in 800 years doesn't deter the belated Peel in Downing street. The Great Anachronism with the flat-backed head, looking like a cartoon in *Simplicissimus*, is not evil, merely insensitive, too insensitive to see that blood on the streets of Derry might some day endanger the north-west approaches, now that a new, totalitarian navy patrols the north Atlantic. I remember that empty arc of sometimes blue-grey, sometimes slate-green ocean stretching up from fleet-harbouring Swilly towards Iceland, and the old man on the Inishowen mountain road staring rheumily at the spot where *Audacious* sank in October 1914. Before oil-tankers explode again, or submarines start nosing southwards past Inishtrahull, the Great Illusionist would be wise to settle something on account against the pitch-cap, the starvation, the coffin ships, the exodus of millions to the grave or America. Every ruined Irish cottage with rafters stark against the sky is a reminder of the debt.

Hooded Man Found Shot

In the townland of Ballynahatty. Looking down from Terrace Hill on the serpentine reaches of the Lagan above Shaw's Bridge. Below, hidden in thick woods, beyond more bends in the Lagan, Edenderry House, Georgian red brick fronting an ancient rath and a grove of beech-trees, with attendant whitewashed linen mill, foundation for the fortune of the red-brick mansion, murmuring beyond the beech grove. In the reign of Victoria my father and mother, not long married, drove six miles from a red-brick terrace in the political jungle of Belfast to attend a ball in Edenderry House, down there beyond the plantation, at the bend of the river. They drove in a four-wheeler, through the freezing winter night, my father clutching his white gloves for the Sir Roger de Coverley and the schottische, his feet buried in the straw on the floor. It was the golden era of the Irish linen trade that followed the American Civil War and the blockade of American cotton. Nursing his white gloves, feet buried in odoriferous straw, he was on his way to become manufacturer as well as merchant, to own a small factory in the county Armagh and hand out yarn to farmer-weavers working hand-looms in whitewashed cottages.

Yet something escaped the double-entry, the day-books recording how much yarn had been handed out to which hand-loom weaver. Yesterday, looking down from Terrace Hill at the red-brick mansion and the grove of beech-trees, I evoked Victorian ghosts dancing to 19th-century dance music; to-day, in bomb-blasted Belfast that looks like Ypres in the 1914-18 war, I found a *memento mori* for their way of lfe. It was a desolation, a vast open space, a wasteland littered with half-bricks: the site, and nothing but the site, of the towering warehouse and offices that were the pride and property of the family with the whitewashed linen mill beyond the rath and the plantation of beeches at the thickly-wooded bend of the Lagan.

The genteel, polka-prancing ghosts in the red-brick mansion must have been astonished; theirs was not an occupation in which they listened for the ticking of time-bombs. Even with the 18th-century-façaded White Linen Hall still occupying the site for the new Portland-stone, Edwardian-domed City Hall that was to witness the conversion of horse-trams to electricity—even back in the days of horse-trams clattering over square-setts in Donegall Place and Dickens readings in the Ulster Hall, the main factors of their trade diverted their attention. Then as now raw material

170

was largely imported from abroad; finished products exported to Britain, America, Australia, with steamship lines, railway companies, luxury hotels the principal targets for hard-faced salesmen from Belfast dispensing brandies and sodas—with behind them the tribal gods of the Belfast scene, the Victorian Economic Men, soon to be frockcoated in stone outside the new Edwardian-domed City Hall. This was business as understood under the corresponding smoke clouds of Bradford, Leeds, Manchester—our factory chimneys smoke, therefore we belong in the New Jerusalem—and the less it had to do with Ireland (except to use harps, wolfhounds, and colleens as advertisements), the better.

So what had my father, driving in his four-wheeler to the Christmas ball at Edenderry, to do with the buried civilisation left after Kinsale, its remnants not far to the north of him in Inishowen? Nursing his white gloves for the schottische and the polka, he would probably have denied that any such civilisation, buried or unburied, ever existed. Deafened by Handel's *Messiah* and other Teutonic elaborations of the obvious, he might even have denied there was music of any sort behind names like Raftery, hidden or otherwise. Still more likely, he might never have heard of Raftery in the first place.

Yet only the day before yesterday, forty years after his funeral procession, the buried civilisation smashed the windows of his first warehouse behind the City Hall; blasted out of existence the towering warehouse and offices of his principal competitors, his hosts on the night of the ball. And driving to the ball through the murk of that Victorian Christmas, he would have been scandalised to look out of the windows of his four-wheeler to see the hooded body of a man shot through the head lying on the green grassy bank of the lane leading to Edenderry House. Yet according to the police, the hooded body of a man shot through the head was lying there last night, at 6.30 p.m., in broad June daylight. One factor the Belfast Victorians had omitted from their double-entry book-keeping was the title-deeds of the field in which they were so confidently building.

A Bomb at the Belfast Boat Club

In the shadow of the trees at the far side of the tennis courts, ghosts, including the shade of Forrest Reid, Belfast's exotic novelist, who held up his late-Victorian tennis trousers with a faded Oxbridge tie, played a fiery game in spite of literary pince-nez, and to the background music of Elgar's Enigma Variations was a friend of E. M. Forster.

Victorians all, right down to yesterday's 50 lb bomb that wrecked the clubhouse, including the new bar and lounge. In good King Edward's golden days we had no bar; just made do, in the company of what were then known as 'nice girls,' with tepid tea from a Victorian urn. After that, except for tepid tea to tepid gin and tonic, no change right down to the day of the explosion; sailing directions remained unaltered, inculcated by the brazen statue of Sir Edward, shaking his brazen fist above there on the green grassy slopes of Stormont beside the mothball Parliament that looks like a left-over from the British Empire Exhibition at Wembley, concrete pediments, and all.

Not that, at the edge of the grass courts, under the shade-trees, lulled by the sound of the Lagan falling over the weir, we didn't have our intimations of political mortality. As I wrote in the year 1935 in my journal, published the following year as *From the Irish Shore*:

'A suburban tennis club. In the distance, *popping* sounds, like the distant drawing of corks. No-one takes any notice; the white-clad figures weave and rearrange, as if in a combined maze; water continues to fall with a subdued roaring over the weir.

The *poppings* begin again, this time in a kind of pattern. Somebody says something about a machine-gun. The tea interval arrives, and we drift over to the pavilion. The *poppings* continue. But nobody discusses them. They are *vieux jeu*, and the conversation is all about the latest scores from Wimbledon.'

A few days later, down in the hot, dusty city, I noted:

'An hotel lounge. In the street outside the aftermath of riot in the form of smashed windows and knots of police stationed at corners with rifles. A green-uniformed inspector of constabulary snores exhausted in an armchair; another, too strung-up to sleep, drinks a whiskey-and-soda with the rapid jerky motions of a marionette.'

But nobody took any notice of exhausted policemen, shots, and smashed windows. The political stations of the Cross continued; the rocks showed up more plainly on the lee shore. Until yesterday, when the bomb blew up the Boat Club and the Lagan continued its requiem beside the ruins, flowing uneasily down past Edenderry and the Georgian mansion where my father danced the schottische and sampled his linen trade competitors' Christmas jellies, down past the gas-works exalted by John Betjeman to the status of a Victorian sheet-iron cathedral, down to the Gaelic-named ford at the sandbank of Bealfeirste, where the whole business—including my father's shattered warehouse in Linenhall Street and Forrest Reid's tennis trousers as worn by curates in *Punch*—began.

Which brings me back to 1915, the snow-topped mountains of Serbia, and what I called 'the stop-press dissolution of empires.'

'First the Austro-Hungarian
Embalmed in its glass coffin
'Up there beyond Macedonian mountains
Illuminated by gilt flambeaux
And historical chandeliers
Sheltered by illusory curtains . . .'

To which, remembering that scene outside Salonika when we were

172

searching for a missing tin of plum-and-apple jam and at the same time watching Austrian aeroplanes disappear towards Vienna, I added:

> 'Up there in Zurich
> With a bottle of wine on the table
> Faintly in the aura of Mozart and Haydn
> James Joyce assembling jig-saw fragments
> Of masterpieces to come
> The complete grammar of chaos
> While the propped-up scenery of Europe
> Fell down round his restaurant table.'

Part of the propped-up scenery of Europe being the Belfast Boat Club. Except that, with the usual Irish time-lag, the explosion came later, having first travelled round via Irish history and the battle of Kinsale.

Journey into the Protestant Mind

At the top of the white-painted gate was a small cross, also painted white. We discussed that. It hadn't been there in the old days, fifty years back, when the W's lived in the big house half-hidden beyond a turn in the wooded drive. In the field to the left of the drive stood white-painted posts, goal-posts for Gaelic football. The goal-posts, the small white cross convinced us. The house was now a Roman Catholic school; the wooded lands surrounding it—where the young lord and master once wandered with dog and gun—for the recreation of Catholic schoolboys.

A man came down the road, past the gate with the white cross. We conversed. He was old enough to remember our friends of the big house, legends for the whole townland. Yes, the place was now a school. And what was that church away over there on the hill, dominating the quiet county Down landscape of green rounded hills and dark patches of plantation? Ballycranbeg. Thank you. With references to the absence of traffic on these quiet by-roads, we parted. The countryman went his way; vanished, as if by magic, into the landscape. Ballycranbeg church still dominated the green rounded hills on the skyline.

Peaceful. Deep green solitude. Yet I kept returning in my mind to that white cross on the gate, that wooded drive leading to white goal-posts, those green mushroom-bearing fields where the young lord and master once wandered with his dog and his gun. A school, yes. The man on the road agreed. But nobody said, 'A Catholic school.' The man on the road hadn't said it, and we, as visitors, returning to 'banquet halls' long deserted, never asked. In north-east Ulster you didn't ask. The mere mention of the word 'Catholic' would have switched on floodlights, lit up the landscape all round us. So nobody touched the switch, and the countryman went on down the by-road and into the landscape without anybody being the wiser. It was a typical 'Ulster' conversation, with gaps and deliberate omissions reaching right back to the Boyne and the Penal laws. Better keep your mouth shut and no harm done.

Then there was that church dominating the green hills to the south. Ballycranbeg. Neither of us said to the man on the road, 'What does that mean in English?' For one thing, he might not have known, and we would only have been showing our ignorance. Yet as we drove on across the peninsula, away from the Irish Sea, I kept wondering. I wondered if the young master with the gun knew the meaning of Ballycranbeg. Probably not. Fifty years ago in our north-east corner, wealthy, influential Protestants did not translate Irish place names. Or even look them up in Joyce. Their world was a succession of closed doors; doors they preferred to keep locked for fear something would jump out at them. They were doing very nicely, thank you, just being wealthy and Protestant.

Over on the other side of the Ards, in a Presbyterian church overlooking Strangford Lough, doors were still locked. 'They,' said the church officer, 'are creeping in.' He said this gloomily, like a military commander who finds his troops surrounded. What he meant was that the Catholic population was increasing in the Ards. Shutting the gates had worked in 1688, shutting the Protestant mind might work in 1972. But he didn't seem too sure about it. 17th century ghosts had been exorcised by Orange drums only to be replaced by 20th century ghosts, with white-painted Gaelic goal-posts sprouting in what had been, at any rate for a century, Protestant fields.

We stood looking out through the plain glass of Presbyterian theology at the brimming tide of Strangford Lough. What the decent man besides me was thinking, I don't know. But in all probability he was thinking negative thoughts—still turning keys, still slamming gates, still exorcising 17th century ghosts. Just as British policy on Ireland was find out what the Irish are up to and stop them, so Protestant policy in the north-east was find out what the Catholics are up to and circumvent them. It never seems to have occurred to my co-religionists to stop closing and defending gates; to go over to the Irish offensive by, for example, learning enough Irish to turn up the lights on their Irish surroundings. Above all, as Protestants to start protesting in terms of the 20th, not the 17th century. For example, by protesting against the gradual exorcism of individual rights (not to mention small shops and businesses) by gigantic corporations, with ranged behind them again, financial powers and principalities. It might be a secular protest, but this is a secular century.

Now, as we stood looking out at Strangford Lough's not-so-soundless tide brimming round the Ards peninsula, an area of reefs and raging surf surrounded 'Ulster.' For the inept navigation that stranded it there, I blamed, not the decent gate-slamming Presbyterian beside me, but my one-time establishment friends from the big house where white-painted Gaelic goal-posts sprouted beside the wooded drive. They had been God-fearing, church-attending, Bible-reading, but when the Bible was closed, they and their wealthy, influential friends sat back in their wealthy, influential enclosures while little minds conspired, not only to leave 'Ulster' stranded on a lee shore, but to shatter the Protestant heritage. The policy of 'Better keep your mouth shut and no harm done' was a sorry downfall

174

for men whose forefathers had, in the words of Shaw about the siege of Derry, 'put up one of the famous fights of history.' Now from the recesses of the once brilliant Ulster Protestant mind nothing emerges but an empty clanging of gates against ghosts that no longer exist. The Ulster Protestant power to floodlight a political scene by clarity of thought—the power that helped to found those United States of America—has now been paralysed by sheer negation, by a refusal to face the founding of the united states of Ireland.

Notes Set Down to a Sound of Shots

I

I was standing on the outskirts of a political meeting in Dublin, talking to John Betjeman. Ferocious sounds were coming from the platform. I said:
  'When they get into this tribal mood, they terrify me.'
  John Betjeman said: 'Me too.'
  The shots came thirty years later, in Derry and Belfast. But then neither the Poet Laureate nor myself had ever been starving.
  Or homeless. Except in so far as I once lived through a Macedonian winter in a hole in the ground. The hole in the ground was in the shadow of Kotos, just north of where mountain lions ate the baggage animals of Xerxes' army marching against Athens.

II

  Yesterday we had an interval of comparative peace. Except for a minor garden tragedy, the death of a young collar-dove. I wrote a poem about it:

> Pursued by some fury, or reflection of fury,
> It crashed into our kitchen window pane.
> When I picked it up, the little grey head
> With its first sketch for a black collar
> Fell forward with a terrible acquiescence
> And the milk-blue veils of the eyes said,
> I accept, I accept . . .

t day, as I finished digging its grave behind the hydrangea, there was
burst of machine-gun fire from the Falls. Then the thud of a nail-
there on the Black Mountain, in the stone forest where my
forefathers are sleeping, even the grave-diggers are in danger,
led down by rifle-fire.
brick city I see from my study window (a French journalist
une ville sanglante) other footnotes include the sniper behind
tain, the masked assassin at the front door, the tortured
t-out, hijacked car. As Goya wrote on one of his Cap-
l sueno de la razon produce monstruos—'the sleep of
monsters.'